CAMBRIDGE STUDIES IN MUSIC

GENERAL EDITORS: JOHN STEVENS AND PETER LE HURAY

The musical language of Berlioz

CAMBRIDGE STUDIES IN MUSIC

GENERAL EDITORS: JOHN STEVENS AND PETER LE HURAY

Volumes in the series include:

The musical language of Berlioz

JULIAN RUSHTON

CAMBRIDGE UNIVERSITY PRESS

CAMBRIDGE

LONDON   NEW YORK   NEW ROCHELLE

MELBOURNE   SYDNEY

Published by the Press Syndicate of the University of Cambridge
The Pitt Building, Trumpington Street, Cambridge CB2 1RP
32 East 57th Street, New York, NY 10022, USA
296 Beaconsfield Parade, Middle Park, Melbourne 3206, Australia

First published 1983

Printed in Great Britain at the University Press, Cambridge

Library of Congress catalogue card number: 82–19829

British Library Cataloguing in Publication Data
Rushton, Julian
The musical language of Berlioz.
—(Cambridge studies in music)
1. Berlioz, Hector
I. Title
780′.92′4   ML410.B5
ISBN 0 521 24279 7

'Stendhal's prose bears a marked resemblance to eighteenth-century prose, but this resemblance is deceptive. It was certainly founded on the classic syntax, but though the structure of his sentences is often similar, the movement of his paragraphs is sometimes quite different. The difference has been well expressed by M. Gide. "With Stendhal", he writes, "one sentence never calls the next into being, nor is it born of the one that went before. Each of them stands perpendicularly to the fact or idea." [*Journal des faux-monnayeurs*, Paris, 1927, pp. 28–9] His prose does not move steadily forward from one fixed point to another. It has greater density and greater range. Each sentence or each clause in a sentence corresponds to what the French call a *fait psychique*, and their relation to one another forms the pattern of his style.'

M. Turnell (*The Novel in France*)

Contents

vii

Acknowledgments

It was the interest shown by Alan Frank which started me on this project, and although the book has gone to the Press of the other place, I am grateful to him and Anthony Mulgan for initial encouragement. I am profoundly grateful to Peter le Huray and Rosemary Dooley, whose support at a critical stage prevented the work from foundering, and to Judith Nagley and others at Cambridge University Press. I also wish to thank the anonymous readers of my typescript, who were full of helpful suggestions, not always followed up; Hugh Macdonald, for years of friendly support; and other scholars on whose shoulders I totter, particularly David Cairns and D. Kern Holoman. I also gladly acknowledge the encouraging interest of many friends including Ian Kemp, Eric Gräbner, David Charlton, Barry Gibson, Arnold Whittall, Robert Pascall, Roger Nichols, and others whom I will not list for fear of invidious omissions. My beloved family has upheld a fine academic tradition by hindering progress until the result had the chance of being matured by experience. Much of the writing has been done on sabbatical leave from the University of Cambridge. I am grateful to the New Berlioz Edition for financial assistance towards travelling, directed towards editorial work which I have found enlightening in many ways; and also, for further financial support, to Cambridge University, to King's College, Cambridge, and to the British Academy.

Julian Rushton
Leeds 1982

ix

Note on abbreviations

Sources: RISM library sigla are used for manuscripts (MS); the only unusual one is F-CSA (Musée Berlioz, La Côte-Saint-André).

Bibliographical abbreviations used for reference within the text are detailed in the Bibliography on pp. 293–6.

Musical terms: Keys and chords are normally spelled out (e.g. C major, the dominant), but occasionally 'C' is used for C major, 'c' for c minor, 'V' for the dominant, etc. Roman numerals (mainly in music examples and tables) are to be interpreted similarly: 'III' is a major chord on the mediant, 'iii' a minor chord, regardless of signature (but of course in C major 'III' is E major, in C minor it is E♭ major, etc.; E♭ in C major is '♭III'). Actual pitches are generally referred to by capital letters; where it has seemed necessary I have used the convention C (8 foot), c (4 foot), c¹ (middle C), c², etc. Figured-bass symbols include 'X' for a diminished 7th (FriRH, 286) and 'Y' for an augmented 6th. Conventions of graphic analysis are employed in no unusual way unless an explanation is given.

References to Berlioz's works are given in the forms indicated in the selective catalogue on pp. 279–92; it includes short references (e.g. *Harold* IV) and movement titles, both of which are used in the text, and a catalogue reference for each movement.

Introduction

Berlioz has generally and rightly been regarded as an eccentric among major composers. The intensity of his musical communication seldom fails to make its mark, but reactions to it cover the widest possible spectrum between irrational hostility and equally irrational adulation. The critical heritage has much to say about his inspired handling of the orchestra, by turns brilliant, grotesque, and tender; his polyphony, lean and exposed over a simple chordal basis, in an era of harmonic sumptuousness; his long, irregularly constructed melodies; and his forms, especially those which mix apparently incompatible genres – symphonic, programmatic, operatic.

Recognition, however, does not imply acceptance. The increase in performances and particularly recordings has not silenced dissent, and by no means all attacks on Berlioz, in his own day or in ours, proceed from negligible sources. One of the most absurd, and the most evidently informed by ignorance and prejudice, acquires authority by its inclusion in the fifth edition of *Grove*. The sober and accurate article in *The New Grove* cannot obliterate it. These critical onslaughts are more numerous, and if true would be more devastating, than those suffered by any other composer of comparable stature. Berlioz's aesthetics, and much else about him, may be problematic; but the main cause of dispute is, quite simply, his musical *competence*. We may well consider ridiculous the frequent assertion that he lacked invention, particularly in melody and rhythm, and no-one now doubts his ability to make the most of his material by beguiling instrumentation, although his scoring is often of disarming simplicity. But this leaves his polyphony, his power to combine a melody with a secure bass and other parts whether conceived in lines or derived from chords. The subject of whether his music makes sense, as it were 'in black and white', will not be closed until criticisms are not merely denied, but refuted. Simply to dismiss a body of critical response which receives support from such outstanding musical brains as Tovey and Schenker, and from certain major composers, is an unpardonable evasion.

This book is itself an act of criticism, not the history of a critical heritage: criticism in the sense claimed by Leonard B. Meyer, which 'seeks to explain how the structure and process of a particular composition are related to the

I

competent listener's comprehension of it'. Meyer observes that the literary critic does not have to point out that *King Lear* is a great work, for that is implicit in his analysis even where he seems to be considering its defects.[1] If I draw attention to Berlioz's peculiarities, it is because I can see no point in veiling the fundamental differences between him and other composers of his time; a criticism which does not relish his heterodoxy does him no more justice than one which denounces it to the academic inquisition. One of my main purposes is to study how in essence this music departs from conventions, norms, and expectations; and to explore the reasons, which may be historical, in so far as they concern Berlioz's musical training and the formation of his habits, or expressive, in so far as unorthodoxies have a direct effect on musical communication. Such considerations are necessarily intertwined, and may have to be artificially disentangled in discussions of characteristic elements of his musical language; it is hoped that some of the threads of the argument will be drawn together in analyses of works or sections in their entirety.

I shall not, however, attempt discussion of Berlioz's major works as wholes. An entire book would not exhaust the historical interest, nor the musical and dramatic significance, of some of them; at least three already exist on *La damnation de Faust* alone. Admirable studies of groups of works or aspects of them date back to those of Berlioz's friends, such as Pohl and Ernst (both 1884). Apart from biographical studies, major scholarly and critical investigations were stimulated by the centenary of the composer's birth; for all its defects, the first complete edition (OBE) was a massive undertaking, and studies by critics such as Prod'homme, Tiersot, Wotton, and Newman appeared between 1903 and the 1939 war. Since then the volume of work bears comparison with other major figures of the nineteenth century, although it has scarcely developed into an industry like Beethoven, Schubert, Wagner, or Verdi studies. The centenary of Berlioz's death saw the launching of the central project, the establishment of a really complete, accurate, and fully researched edition of his music, the New Berlioz Edition (NBE). Its general editor, Hugh Macdonald, and D. Kern Holoman have made major contributions to the study of Berlioz's working methods and the chronology of his music, to which I am frankly indebted (MacNG, HolCP, and elsewhere). Specialized biographical studies have been stimulated by the appearance, also in 1969, of two editions of Berlioz's *Mémoires*, in French (edited by Pierre Citron) and English (edited by David Cairns). Closer to the substance of the present study come analytical commentaries, a comparatively recent phenomenon, notably those of Friedheim, Primmer, Gräbner, and Bockholdt – even if their value is sometimes to the better articulation of disagreement. That different listeners should have different priorities in their analyses of a major composer is to be expected, and desired. I hope to have sufficiently acknowledged prior work in the field, whether or not it has influenced my thinking (it quite often happens that one finds one's already formed ideas corroborated by someone else – usually Cone – and to anyone who feels inadequately acknowledged I offer my apologies).

I conclude these introductory remarks with a *credo* and a *caveat*. I believe Berlioz to be a major figure, and not just of nineteenth-century music. He stands with Rameau and Debussy, preeminent among French composers of modern times (I exclude the living). In his own time he stands among the greatest of any nation, and his work embodies a significant complexity which is totally different from, but which stands comparison with, the work of his contemporaries, among them Alkan, Verdi, Liszt, the earlier Wagner. I warn the reader, however, that some of what I shall have to say might seem to be detrimental to Berlioz. If so, it would be a misunderstanding arising from comparisons with other music and implied or written 'corrections' to Berlioz's own, whereas in fact the intention is only to define and explore its uniqueness. Nothing in what follows is intended to condemn, unless it does so explicitly. I do not think that every bar of Berlioz works, although I think most of them do, very well; but then my high estimation, or better, my love of his music, is the *raison d'être* of the whole undertaking.

PART I

1   Background and education (1)

> 'In the whole history of music there is no other example of a composer who to his nineteenth year knew and heard so little music as Berlioz; he had scarcely any idea of what musicians call music.'
>
> Ferdinand Hiller (1880, p. 101)

In analysing Berlioz's musical language, we are confronted with the consequences of a temperament and upbringing unique among major composers. This is neither a biographical nor a psychological study; but a glance at the composer's life and character is necessarily its context, and the following pages intend some definition of the 'paradoxe fait homme', as Saint-Saëns called him, in terms useful for the description of his music.

In Berlioz, the ardour of romanticism was tempered by classical reserve, the eager iconoclasm of a revolutionary by veneration for masters of the recent past. His life, wonderfully interesting to the lover of his works, was comparatively uneventful; there is little political in it, no exile, as with Hugo or Wagner, no perilous flirtations with bankruptcy, as in the wild schemes of Balzac which so amused the composer. Viewed beside such larger-than-life figures, Berlioz – the psychopathic dreamer of the *Symphonie fantastique*, the demonic composer of 'La course à l'abîme', hobnobber with brigands, lover of Harriet and Estelle – seems almost prosaic in his constant concern with making a meagre living and with the practical elements of his craft. Only rarely did he cultivate an exacerbated sensibility, never the fashionable self-pity. Often severely ill, harassed by debts he wished to repay, and conscious of being widely misunderstood to the extent of being admired more as a journalist than as a musician, he preserved a sense of humour which he often directed against himself. His loneliness and sufferings were certainly acute. The 'mal d'isolement' and the drug-taking of the *Fantastique* are drawn from his own experience, despite the literary echoes (NBE 16, pp. 191–3). They are observed with the clinical objectivity of the *bachelier de sciences physiques*, but are no less deep for that, and probably transmuted all the better into art.

The *Fantastique*, still by far his most successful work in terms of performance, does not consist only of torment and *diablerie*; the tender, restrained, and exalted music rings just as truly, a fact which should not be overlooked in his most autobiographical and romantic work just because it appeared as if preordained in 1830, the year of Hugo's *Hernani* and the July revolution. Berlioz was never wholly in tune with his fellow artists of Gautier's trinity of French romanticism: Hugo, Delacroix, Berlioz. Delacroix could not stomach Berlioz, failing to perceive the classical restraint he so loved in Mozart and Chopin; Berlioz showed little interest in painting. With Hugo there was a measure of artistic collaboration, but Berlioz was equivocal about *Hernani* itself even as he brought to music those new modes of beauty, the sublime embracing the grotesque, that were proclaimed by Hugo in his preface to *Cromwell*. Berlioz included several literary men among his friends, but in his correspondence he seems closer to the less glamorous who, like himself, were practical working musicians. Balzac's dedication to Berlioz of *Ferragus* reflects no obvious artistic kinship, and Berlioz had still less in common with the spirit of decadence, the misery of the white-faced Pierrot, Deburau, the putrid beauty of Baudelaire. Berlioz was indeed a conservative in that his literary and musical tastes were founded in the classics he encountered early – Virgil, Gluck – and in heroic figures of the 1820s – Shakespeare, Beethoven – rather than in rejection of either the distant or the immediate past or in a developing awareness of his own contemporaries.

Berlioz was only 45 when he began his memoirs, a valedictory act undertaken in a spirit of alienation from the 1848 revolution. He was to write much more fine music, but mostly in fulfilment of earlier projects and in a style which represents refinement rather than advance. Wagner, in contrast, was ten years younger, and 1848–9 was his revolution, as 1830 was Berlioz's. At 45 Wagner was immersed in his most revolutionary undertaking, *Tristan*. I am making no value-judgment here; but it is sad to compare Lesueur's reaction to Beethoven's Fifth Symphony, as reported by Berlioz – astounding, but such things *ought not to be written* (Mem20) – with Berlioz's equally negative reaction to *Tristan* (AT, 310/G, 327). In his last critical article, Berlioz acclaimed the young Bizet, but as a prophetic gesture it hardly compares with Schumann's last essay, on Brahms.

It is more easy than useful to compare Berlioz with Wagner, and it is a common critical fallacy to treat them as contemporaries. Berlioz's contemporaries include Berwald (b. 1796), Schubert and Donizetti (1797), Bellini (1801), Glinka (1804), and Mendelssohn (1809), plus a host of minor figures from these years (Halévy, Niedermeyer, Adam, Monpou, Clapisson, in France; Lortzing, J. Strauss the elder, Balfe). Berlioz outlived Chopin, Schumann, and Nicolai, but was markedly their senior, as he was to Félicien David; all these were born in 1810. Berlioz's most brilliant and fertile decade was the 1830s; Wagner's was the 1850s. One can hardly call Berlioz an early developer, certainly not beside Mendelssohn, but the eighteen years between the revolutions in which he and Wagner took part, or between *Roméo* and *Tristan*, better represent the difference than the ten years which separate them in age. In musical language, Berlioz has more in common with Schubert, who died when Wagner was fifteen; it is with him, or Bellini, or Mendelssohn, as well as with his most significant models – Gluck, Spontini, and Beethoven – that it is most worth comparing Berlioz in order to isolate what is so special about his style.

Much of Berlioz's undoubted oddity must be attributed to the circumstances of his early life. This matters far more than his unwilling pursuit of medicine, a profession he never wanted to enter (study of another subject, usually law, is common among musicians who do not come from families practising music as a craft, like the Bachs). What matters is that most composers grow up in homes where music is cultivated to a reasonable standard, or in a city where good music, professionally performed, can be regularly experienced. These conditions favoured the development of Schubert, Schumann, Mendelssohn, and Wagner, but were totally lacking at La Côte-Saint-André in the early nineteenth century. Not only is it a small town itself; its larger neighbours such as Grenoble could boast little serious musical culture. Even Lyon, whose culture in the eighteenth century was as rich as that of any French city after Paris, had gone through a lean period as a result of the Revolution. Berlioz seems not to have gone to a theatre, nor heard an orchestra, until he reached Paris in 1821, when he was nearly eighteen.

At La Côte, neither the music he heard nor its performance can have been of a very high standard. The local quartet played the estimable but unimaginative Pleyel; Berlioz said he learned harmony by listening. The players could not cope with his most ambitious attempt at chamber music (Mem4). The music-making of the town also included the band of the National Guard, from whom there may have been some intimation of broader musical effects, as well as of popular idioms such as the march, which Berlioz was occasionally to deploy. There was also the folk music of the region, orally transmitted; a repertory still rich when Tiersot was collecting.[2] The music in church included a sort of plainchant, often adapted from secular models. Berlioz used a specimen in 'La course à l'abîme', and quoted it to illustrate the 'bad prosody customary in France' (Mem43). He also disclosed that his 'first musical impression' was at his first communion; Boschot dates this 1816, and it can hardly have been earlier, since Nanci Berlioz (b. 1806) took hers at the same time. The musical image, of fresh young voices in unison, remained with Berlioz – in *Prière du matin* and on an enlarged scale (and further inspired by the singing of the Charity Children in St Paul's: SO, 21) in the *Te Deum* and 'Apothéose' of *La damnation* – even when he knew that the communion music was adapted from an opera by Dalayrac. The 'impression' was perhaps also a foreknowledge of his vocation. There does not appear to be any very striking influence from these early musical impressions upon Berlioz's style, although both folk and church music may have sown the seeds of his interest in scales other than major and minor (see Chapters 4 and 10).[3]

It may well have been before his 'first musical impression' that Berlioz performed his first musical feat, picking out 'Marlborough' on the flageolet, for he was learning this instrument by 1816 (CG 1, p. 29). The chronology of his memoirs is understandably vague at this point (while in what matters, the truth of his feelings, the book is not to be doubted). Berlioz refers to attempts at composition in his thirteenth year (1816), including in-strumental works which it seems likely were in fact written later. Surely by this age he cannot have struggled through Rameau's harmony treatise (simplified by d'Alembert), and Catel's shorter treatise (see Chapter 5)? Moreover the ensemble which played the chamber works included Berlioz's first professional teacher, Imbert, who began work at La Côte only in May 1817; Berlioz was thus probably nearer fourteen before he composed his lost quintets and *Potpourri*. Imbert was a violinist at the Théâtre des Célestins at Lyon, and also played the clarinet; he seems to have taught Berlioz singing (and thus implicitly reading and ear-training), and the flute, which Berlioz had started under his father, using Devienne's *Nouvelle méthode* (1794; the music in this, with Pleyel's, is another source of respectable classical mediocrity).

In July 1819 Imbert was succeeded by another teacher, Dorant. Already proficient on the flute, Berlioz soon learned to play the guitar as well as his teacher. It was apparently under Dorant's guidance that Berlioz first arranged popular items from the romance repertory for voice and guitar, presumably from a piano original (there is said to have been no piano at La Côte). At all events, an accompaniment to Pollet's *Fleuve du Tage* (H 5) is ascribed to Berlioz, but it is probably in Dorant's hand. Melodies such as Martini's *Plaisir d'amour*, which Berlioz arranged not for guitar but for orchestra in 1859, are not the least of influences on his melodic idiom.

As early as March 1819, Berlioz had offered his *Potpourri* and unspecified romances for voice and piano to a Parisian publisher, and one song, *Le dépit de la bergère* (Cat. 1A), may even have been published that year (CG 1, pp. 30–33). The *Recueil de romances* (Cat. 2A) includes another setting of *Fleuve du Tage*, and the survival of a few autographs of romances (Cat. 1C, 1F) at La Côte suggests that they originated some time before publication in 1822–3. If *Le dépit* is indeed as early as 1819, it shows a certain precocious originality (see Chapter 5), and one early romance, *Toi qui l'aimas* (Cat. 1G), has a truly Berliozian poignancy.

These works show that, through no fault of his own, Berlioz was certainly backward in technique. Wagner, on the other hand, at the age of nineteen wrote a symphony in C with no Wagnerian character but with ample technical solidity; his later development towards full originality was as consistent as Berlioz's was explosive. The most stimulating and valuable experiences of these years for Berlioz were probably the mountains of Dauphiné, Estelle (his *stella montis*), Virgil, books of travel, musical biographies, and the sight of blank music-paper with many staves. When he went to Paris in October 1821, major formative influences still awaited him.[4]

Berlioz took his *baccalauréat* in 1824, by which time he had published a number of romance-type compositions and begun private tuition with Lesueur. He did not officially enter the Conservatoire for another two years, when he was nearly twenty-three. By the time he began systematic instruction in counterpoint from Reicha, therefore, he was already rich in musical experience and, although weak in traditional skills, had completed several large-scale works: a Mass (see Cat. 3), some cantata-type compositions now lost with the exception of the *Scène héroïque* (Cat. 4), and most of an opera, *Les francs-juges* (Cat. 6).

The nature of that experience is important, for it did not include the most advanced and significant developments of musical language, which happened to be taking place at this time in Germany and Austria. Beethoven's successor, as Paganini was to proclaim him, did not become fully aware of the stature of the greatest composer working during his youth until he was in his twenty-fourth year and Beethoven was dead. Apart from Weber, the music he knew before this encounter was either fairly old, like Gluck, or not very good, the product of the French establishment and the Opéra in a silver age. Berlioz showed sound critical judgment in recognizing the real value of the best of this, except that his personal antipathy to Cherubini probably prevented him giving his work its due until later. Lesueur had been a rebel in his youth, a reformer of church music along expressive lines which must have appealed to his most famous pupil, and an innovator in stage music. But by now Lesueur's rebellious days were over. He remained an example of adherence to principle, and had won through to eminence after neglect and hostility; Berlioz's career, although less successful, has something of the same qualities.

In 1826 Berlioz entered the competition for the Prix de Rome, falling at the first hurdle, strict counterpoint and fugue (see Chapter 8). The purpose of his enrolment at the Conservatoire was purely mechanical; he had to leap that hurdle in order to compete in the part of the competition involving real music, the cantata. It is unfortunate, in view of the problems of his musical language, that we know so little about the formal instruction Berlioz received. Certain ideas which he is likely to have come across, in treatises or by example, will be mentioned below, as will the possible influence of the fact that he learned the guitar to an advanced standard, but not the piano (see Chapter 5).

Berlioz's principal formative influences were musical and dramatic, not pedagogical, and the most significant are mentioned in the memoirs: above all, Gluck and Beethoven, Virgil and Shakespeare; then Weber, Spontini, Goethe, and so on. Berlioz also speaks with some warmth of Lesueur and Méhul. Many aspects of the French school of the early nineteenth century anticipate the kind of sonority and disposition of ideas that we associate with Berlioz, as Dent, for one, has observed.[5] It would be a lengthy, and in my view not a very profitable, study to determine whence Berlioz might, consciously or otherwise, have borrowed this idea or that. If we find a precedent for something eminently Berliozian, we learn only what has always been known of, say, Mozart; that he did what any sensible composer does when an idea appeals to him – adapt it to his own ends. There seems to be no question with Berlioz of the technique of composition by conscious imitation, for he had the high regard of the romantic for originality.[6] Occasional ideas, like the alternation of dynamic extremes, the combination of metres, the spatial disposition of forces, find their way into his music from Grétry, Lesueur, Gluck; one cannot really determine which source is of paramount importance. We may also see what Berlioz admired, and why, from the copious examples in his treatise on orchestration. Often, however, the correlation with his own work is inexact, the source quite possibly unknown. Such details are in any case biographical, not analytical, nor, except in certain major instances, necessarily of concern to the critic.

2 Concerning method and style

> 'it sometimes happened that Berlioz would improvise a tune by whistling it and, not writing it down, merely content himself with using it to teach some Conservatoire student to take down music from dictation. The pupil would then take down the fleeting melody, harmonize it in his own hasty fashion and hand his master the results of this unequally inspired collaboration; and Berlioz would erect his ingenious orchestral edifices on such composite raw material.'
>
> Léon Vallas (ValG5, 664)

A discussion of Berlioz's style is hampered by the extreme degree to which his work resists categorization. We cannot order our ideas under headings of genre, or 'style periods', or of the chronological development of a particular musical element. His genres are mixed, with song and drama deeply ingrained in symphony; symphony, song, and architectural manner in opera. He explored musical resources continually; yet he might have agreed that he scarcely developed the essentials of his language at all. Any change of manner resulted from the choice of subject: 'I would have written *L'enfance du Christ* in the same way twenty years ago' (MemPS). His *Huit scènes de Faust*, refined but not substantially altered or developed, remain perfectly congruous with the style of *La damnation* into which they were incorporated after seventeen years (see Cat. 32). Gaps between Berlioz's major works are not followed, as with Wagner or Schumann, by significant changes in orientation.

This constancy does not, however, preclude extreme variety; Berlioz practically never repeated himself. Some of his most striking harmonic inventions occur only once, or, if twice, in contexts remote in date, mood, or texture. All his large forms are as individual, when reduced to a scheme, as the melodies which are their main material. His minor works, the pieces for harmonium, the romances, small choruses, and albumleaves, are seldom as good as passages of similar scale and mood in the full-length works where he is inspired by a great subject, but they could never be misattributed. Berlioz's hackwork is all journalism; he never became a creature of musical habit, repeating tricks as easily as a Rossini or an Auber.

11

This paradox, of an unchanging but non-repeating idiom, has probably contributed as much as anything to the extraordinary degree of misunderstanding or misinformation in the critical literature. Ferdinand Hiller, who was very close to Berlioz around 1829–30, later observed that his friend composed only with difficulty, and wondered whether he wrote real music.[7] Yet the evidence, of Berlioz's letters, the memoirs, and, above all, of his manuscripts, is clear; he composed spontaneously and at speed. He may have conceived works years before their composition, and delayed years more before publication, during which time he engaged in revisions until he could find no further improvements to make (Mem49, on *Roméo*). But the period of realization of the project is short. With the *Requiem* he speaks of ideas coming with such pressure that a special shorthand was needed (Mem46); these notations are unfortunately lost. *Roméo*, a large score, was mainly set down in nine months; scarcely more time sufficed for *La damnation*; and the huge *Les troyens* took only two years.

Berlioz's revisions tell us that he was a perfectionist, and that his works initially suffered from too much facility, for he much more often cut than expanded them. He also occasionally failed in the initial effort to realize an idea, although not always, curiously enough, with ideas that are particularly original. Hiller's question must apply more forcibly to style than to speed of composition. It is a fact that in rehearsal and performance Berlioz responded immediately to longueurs or miscalculations of balance by making appropriate alterations. This habit suited his reluctance to let his works go forth in published form until he had introduced them to audiences himself. Fifteen years between composition and publication is not uncommon: as late as 1844 revisions were made when the *Fantastique* was in proof, and in 1846, two years before publication, revisions to *Harold* were made on the backs of sketches for *La damnation* (HolCP; Macdonald, 1968; Rushton, 1975).

Another reason for questioning Berlioz's facility might be his extensive self-borrowing. Berlioz worked best on large projects; when he could see no future for them he preferred not to compose. He repressed the idea for a symphony, and even considered abandoning composition altogether before *Les troyens* (Mem59). His best ideas are of such striking individuality that if they were first used in a comparatively minor project, he was prepared to jettison it in order to give the idea a worthier setting. At the same time he seldom left any idea unaltered in its new context, but revised it in detail to fit its more mature musical and dramatic position. Thus a modest *chansonnette* and a romance become the serenade and Harlequin's 'song' in *Benvenuto* (see Cat. 23); the former remained unpublished, the latter, which had appeared in a periodical, was not included in later collections of songs. The central episode of an overture yields the main theme of a symphony; because of *Harold*, therefore, *Rob Roy* was suppressed and survives by accident. This recognition of the unique qualities of an idea, and determination to use it to best advantage, recalls Gluck's practice, of which Berlioz was aware (SO, 23; AT, 148/G, 168), rather than Handel's or Bach's, whose re-use of pieces resulted from pressure to provide more music than 'inspiration' allowed. Berlioz's ideas were, with the exception of the *Huit scènes*, necessarily assimilated to different dramatic or programmatic ideas, but this really raises no very serious aesthetic issues. Self-borrowing, of course, is no contradiction of Berlioz's tendency not to repeat himself. On the contrary, it is because he could not cut a similar idea out of a pattern-book that he had to employ the *same* idea and suppress its original context (on self-borrowing, see MacBS).

The most grotesque of all libels on Berlioz's musicianship is surely that of Léon Vallas (see epigraph). Yet in one important respect he is right: Berlioz did improvise. At home, travelling, out for a walk, he noted down ideas which served for compositions then germinating. He was not at this stage a calculating composer; he depended on the moment of impact of an idea which we may as well call 'improvisation' as the more usual 'inspiration'. A work would be conceived as a dramatic entity; ideas would then be allowed to come, and notated lest they be forgotten (see Mem54, *La damnation*; Mem45, *Harold*; MemPF, *Béatrice*; and CG 2, p. 203, where he declares himself unable to compose a simple romance, as 'such things should so to speak be improvised, and if one does not succeed at the first attempt, my belief is that it is better to give up'). Unfortunately most of Berlioz's sketches have not survived. What must have been one of many sketchbooks has recently been rediscovered (H 62; see additional note, p. 278). Extended sketches survive for parts of *Les troyens* (Macdonald, 1968), revealing another paradox; Berlioz remarked of the love-duet in Act IV that the music 'settled on this scene like a bird on ripe fruit' (NBE 2c, p. 755), yet it took him sixteen pages of sketches to get it right. If it seemed easy in retrospect it must have been because he enjoyed every moment of rigorous self-criticism.

As is natural for a lyrical composer, Berlioz's first ideas were generally melodic. Thus far, too, Vallas was right. In contrast to Beethoven's, his first notations contain much of the musical value of the final version (but Beethoven was wrestling with symphonic problems, motives, bridges, and harmonic proportions, of a kind which Berlioz either evaded or used in a way which can already be implied by a first notation). Next came the bass (Mem39, on *La captive*). Need it be said that Berlioz never had a Conservatoire class and that no Conservatoire pupil would have written anything so unconventional as the kind of bass which appears even in his earliest works? Having got down this framework, he would then complete the accompaniment, or draft a complete harmonic filling and flesh out the result by orchestration. This rather obvious procedure has no possible causal relationship to the oddity of the results. Numerous commentators have found fault with his basses (see Chapter 7), and some, following

Schumann, with his inner parts (ConFS, 242). But the alleged deficiencies do not derive from methods of composition. Berlioz himself acknowledged his 'heterodoxy in matters of harmonic and rhythmic theory' (MemPS), and cited with approval the lofty attitude of Gluck and Beethoven towards academic rules (MemPS; AT, 158/G, 178). Sketches, revisions, and the fascinating layers of work in the autograph full scores which form the bulk of his manuscript legacy show that Berlioz thought freshly about every passage, and confirm what most people hear with varying degrees of delight or discomfort, that even in such normally routine situations as cadences he failed to develop automatic responses. But this refusal to learn habits is a matter of temperament, not of working methods (in which he is typical of the fluent type of composer, like Schubert).

STYLE: THE 'CHANSON DE BRIGANDS'

As consideration of Berlioz's methods of composition provides no evidence of anything extraordinary, it remains to establish what in the music itself is so out of step with conventional expectations. Before attempting to determine some of the causes of Berlioz's idiosyncrasy, or to dissect elements of music to describe his language more exactly, I shall examine a single composition, the 'Chanson de brigands' from *Lélio* (Cat. 17/III), in order to show some of the things which so outraged contemporary criticism. The choice of a rather coarse, not to say inebriated, composition is deliberate, for it presents concisely characteristics which elsewhere are separated or disguised by refinement: simple chord-structures whose freshness results from unusual juxtapositions, wiry orchestration, with no feather-bedding, energetic and irregular rhythmic propulsion, highly strung melodic shapes, elliptical forms, and a general absence both of routine and self-indulgence. The 'Chanson de brigands' is certainly the sort of thing which gave Berlioz the reputation of an extravagant *poseur*; but the pose would have been more evidently a pose had the music been more ordinary, less personal. The result is quite unlike the routine piratical and brigandish choruses, ripe for Sullivan's satire, which Berlioz mocked so entertainingly in his review of Auber's *Les diamants de la couronne* (MM, 43); and unlike Auber, Berlioz remains worthy of our serious attention.

Berlioz, or Lélio, talks in the third monologue of the fate of genius at the hands of 'sad occupants of the temple of routine', and inveighs against correctors of masterpieces: pigeons soiling public statues. He contemplates escape from the stifling atmosphere of bourgeois pedantry by joining the brigands of the Calabria for 'a concert of screams of horror accompanied by an orchestra of carbines, sabres and daggers, blood and lachryma-christi, a bed of lava lulled by earthquakes'. The music reflects this fantasy by a series of shocks both motivic and harmonic, within a headlong movement in F major (Ex. 1: bars 10–16 are omitted; they may be supplied by proceeding from the second beat of bar 1 (as the first of 10) to the first of bar 8).

Ex. 1

Ex. 1 (contd)

Section A: bars 1–17

The rhythm begins regularly, unless we count the slight ambiguity, significant later on, as to which of the first two bars is metrically stronger: the dissonant *sforzando* of bar 2 rivals the *fortissimo* tonic of bar 1. The first real upset is harmonic. Bar 3 lurches to ♭VI, to which an augmented 6th is added (see analytical line). The normal resolution would be to a dominant of F; it is replaced by the tonic, the bass D♭–A♮ being wilfully angular. The relatively unstable $\frac{6}{3}$, so oddly approached, is quitted simply by moving to root position; it is thus a thing-in-itself, not the result of organic or linear processes. In the consequent phrase (bars 5–8), the ♭VI receives more orderly treatment, coming sooner, with the first of four *sforzando* markings, and more smoothly through the intervention of the tonic minor, to which it is diatonically a simple relation. The harmonic rate of change is faster; nevertheless this phrase is asymmetrically expanded to four and a half bars by dwelling on the dominant chord. This chord is *minor*: the anticipated degree of the scale but the wrong mode, contradicting its function. With an insouciance more grisly than the modulation itself, Berlioz repeats the first phrase in F major as if he had used a normal dominant. The eight and a half bars are repeated in a metrical displacement; accordingly at bar 17 the C minor arrives on the strong beat, righting the balance – but only for the moment, as similar displacements in the verse finally require the insertion of a 3/8 bar (see Ex. 2 below).

Section B: bars 18–35

The key of bars 18–27 is the subdominant of F *minor*, a step down from C minor and singularly unrelated to it. After three bars an A major chord is inserted; in the full score the bass C♯ is notated enharmonically as D♭. Again the chords are unrelated, but they share the mediant note (D♭/C♯); this double meaning produces a chord-progression much favoured by Berlioz (see Chapter 4). From bar 18 the two four-bar phrases are harmonically static, since the A major simply switches back to B♭ minor, and is thus heard as a colouration of it; bars 25–6 lunge down to a B♭ minor cadence. For the first time two phrases overlap, on the first beat of bar 26. The music proceeds in an irregular ascent and harmonic acceleration towards its goal, a V–I cadence (35–6). Yet tonal return is suggested well before the full dominant chord (35) and climactic tonic (36), by the $^6_3$ of bar 32; linear and harmonic patterns seem to be out of phase.

Section C: bars 36–40

Bar 36 begins a refrain which precedes all four verses. Even here, in unequivocal F major, there is no relaxation. The sequence seems regular; but the chordal underpinning is strange, E minor (bar 37) being more foreign to F major than the D♭ of bar 3 (which is demonstrably borrowed from F minor). To rationalize it as mediant of V, or dominant of iii, would be absurd in this context; it is the thickening of a unison, the root-position chords enhancing the broad *melodic* steps. Functionally related chords would actually detract from this effect (see analytical line). Berlioz's procedure is as characteristic as it is unorthodox.

Section D: bars 40–50

The verse (Ex. 2) is more complex and uses elements – notably melody – virtually absent from the introduction. It makes much play with the metrical ambiguity already mentioned, and also between the two beats of the 6/8 bar. Bar 40 is the last accent of the introduction, bar 41 the first of the verse, which is borne out by the weakness of bar 42 and the strength (high C) of 43 (see accents above staff). The sudden harmonic incursion of bar 44, the diminished 7th, brings the accent forward; the harmony is unchanged in 45 and the melodic rise of the chorus does not effect a significant accent in the long term, because of the repetition in 46. The Captain, a virtuoso of rhythm as of the sabre and bottle (or Byronic skull), plays with the alternative half-bar accents for the rest of the verse. He enters syncopated (46), implying chord-change on the third quaver. As the orchestra is not syncopated, the result is an accent on the half-bars of 46 and 47, for the negative accent of the

Ex. 2

Ex. 2 (contd)

syncope overrides the rather ordinary harmonic change on the first beats of 47 and 48. Even if it did not, the issue is clarified by the undoubted melodic accents on 'pape' and 'adore', on half-bars and, successively, on the highest notes of the verse. The harmony, however, tries to maintain regularity; it resolves a cadence in B♭ on the first beat of bar 50, reinforced by the semiquaver flourish.

Section E: bars 51–64

There follows the fullest justification for Berlioz's extraordinary employment, in an F major which goes so firmly to B♭, of natural trumpets and horns in E. With chromatic cornets (in B♭) and a pair of C horns, Berlioz had enough force for the shock which breaks the easy flow of rhythm and harmony in bar 44. The instruments in E were used in bar 21 for the strident A major chord and the E minor chord of the refrain (37), a striking instance of orchestration underlining the non-functional aspects of a piece. Now the natural instruments in bar 52 establish the shocking E♮ which appears in bar 50 (the timpani add to the outrage by playing A♭ (G♯) and B♮; hitherto they have played only the normal F and C, being silent in bar 44).

Orchestration cannot, of course, justify the tritone progression B♭–E, keys generally and rightly regarded as virtually unconnectable. 'Franchissons rochers et torrents!': Berlioz leaps the barricades of civilized logic. To escape from E major is easy; it becomes V of A minor, which is so close to F that the return (bar 59) is unremarkable, even casual – a fact no less characteristic than the preceding shock. The diminished 7th leading to G minor (60–62) is a normal enough preparation for an F major cadence (ii–V–I); but this cadence only comes in the fourth verse, when the texture is filled out by string chords. The first three verses end with a plagal cadence and further rhythmic dislocation. Berlioz acknowledges the final F major chord as a strong beat by inserting the 3/8 bar, so that the emphatic downbeat of the refrain (bar 65, identical to 36) falls two beats after the last note of the verse.

This rhythm may be understood in different ways. In the voice the accents form 9/8 bars, but the harmony reaches the tonic under 'leurs' (bar 63), producing a simple 6/8 from bar 59, and making 63–4 into a 9/8 (table 1). Again, the elements are out of phase. There may be other interpretations, but this suffices to explain the 3/8 bar; it clearly implies Berlioz's understanding of the previous ambiguities. The deletion of the 3/8 bar from verse 4 seems to reinforce the upper-line interpretation of table 1, making 6/8 plausible throughout in retrospect; in its place comes the first bar of Ex. 1, a repeat of the introduction as coda. I merely wish to raise such problems, however, not solve them; the ambiguity is part of the music's character.

The verse has fallen into halves separated by the chasm – it is no modulation – between B♭ and E. The progression B♭–E–A minor is quite ordinary, with B♭ as 'Neapolitan' in the supertonic–dominant–tonic (♭II–V–i); but it is not articulated like that and no amount of explication is going to prevent it sounding abrupt. At least, we must hope not, for the

Table 1

composer certainly intended it to offend the bourgeois sensibilities of his audience.[8]

Berlioz's own analytical approach, in particular to Gluck and Beethoven, provides the justification for thus considering the minutiae of his style in relation to effect. He attributes the ferocity of the assassins' music in Act V of *Les Huguenots* ('Abjurez, Huguenots, le ciel l'ordonne') to

> the alteration of the sixth note of the minor mode. The brutal phrase into which this note is flung is in A minor, and the F (6th degree), which ought to be natural, is continually sharpened. The truly horrific effect which results is a new example of the pronounced character of combinations to which this degree, with or without alteration, can give rise. Gluck had already made good use of it on several occasions, in his own way; I will confine myself to citing the famous bass of the air in Act III of *Iphigénie en Tauride*, at the words 'Ah! ce n'est plus qu'aux sombres bords'. The air is in G minor, and as the bass works by step towards the E♮ (sharp 6th) at this point, the unexpected note immediately colours the harmony with a lugubrious blackness, which produces the *frisson*. In *Les Huguenots*, on the other hand, it shines forth like a naked sword (MM, 104–5).

The Gluck example clearly belongs to the category of *frissons* brought about by judicious deployment of counterpoint, since the rising line goes through

the 6th and F♯ to the tonic (Ex. 3A). Meyerbeer, on the other hand, uses the sharp 6th as a deliberate oddity, countering any suggestions of modality, however, by the modulation to C and the diminished chords (Ex. 3B).

I do not wish to imply that any outlandish musical syntax can be justified by the effect if the musical result is actually incoherent, especially if the motivation is so trivial as the exaggerated depiction of an outlaw, or the purpose merely *épater le bourgeois*. There are other factors in Berlioz's 'Chanson de brigands' which make it cohere. One is obvious; the verse comes four times. The oddest happenings may seem to have been explained, when they have merely become familiar, and by verses 3 and 4 the harmonic chasm has become an expectation, duly fulfilled, the strongest possible aid to coherence. Yet it does not lose its breezy insouciance. Berlioz prepared for bar 50ff, without risk to its impact, not by obvious means such as motivic tritones, but by making it a synthesis of earlier unusual events. These include the curious harmony of bar 37: E follows F and B♭ is needed, in bar 38, to redress the balance (this explains the break in the sequence of 4ths, bracketed in Ex. 1); bar 44, where the melody loses its too easy swing by going to B♮, a tritone from the tonic, with a chord sharing two notes with E major and, indeed, commonly substituted for it; and bars 21 and 37, the glare of the E trumpets. All of which may not convince the listener who is not already convinced by hearing. To me, however, what matters, and what has implications for the study of Berlioz's handling of pitch-elements in particular, is that the harmonic and rhythmic jolt at bar 51 sounds brutal *but right* even in the first verse.

3 Concerning pitch (1): chord and progression

'I saw that he had no taste for melody and but a feeble notion of rhythm;
that his harmony, composed by piling up tones into heaps that were often
monstrous, was nevertheless flat and monotonous.'

F. J. Fétis, in 1835 (ConFS, 217)

In his own most extended remarks about his style, Berlioz pays little
attention to pitch organization as such: 'Generally my style is very bold, but
it has not the slightest tendency to destroy what might be regarded as the
constituent elements of music. On the contrary, I seek to increase the
number of these elements ... The predominant qualities of my music
are passionate expression, inner ardour, rhythmic impetus, and
unexpectedness.'[9] The first two of these, scarcely technical considerations,
demand no shift in the relative importance of the constituent elements.
Rhythmic impetus is impotence if pitches do not actively support it;
unexpectedness is as much determined by pitches as by any other element.
Thus, although it is Berlioz I am discussing, I have no hesitation in treating
pitch elements first.

There has been a tendency in the twentieth century to increase emphasis
on non-pitch elements, to the point of granting them structural significance,
and Berlioz, in whom such elements acquire an importance perhaps
unparalleled in any European composer between the Renaissance and our
own time, is godfather to that tendency. Nevertheless one of the leading
composers of today roundly declares that 'Pitch and duration seem to me to
form the basis of a compositional dialectic, while intensity and timbre belong
to secondary characteristics.'[10] It follows that the vexed question of the
normality and coherence of Berlioz must begin with pitch, and indeed more
work has probably been done on this than any other element; as Friedheim
observes, 'the ultimate basis for the judgment of any composition ... must
rest in the notes themselves' (FriRH, 282). Other writers on harmony,
polyphony, and fugue implicitly take the same view (Collet, 1954; ChaBH;
ConSH; PriBS; Hirschberg, 1974; MacNG). It is true that pitch is nothing
without other elements; harmony, as a horizontal force, is inseparable from

23

duration; melody is a combination of pitch and rhythm, and although it is not, therefore, a primary element of musical discourse, it becomes in a lyrical composer like Berlioz a primary determinant of form. Nor do I pretend that timbre and intensity are dispensable; who, after all, now that Liszt is dead, wants to hear the *Fantastique* played on a piano?

Preliminary concentration on pitch should not be confused with applying the discredited 'black and white' test, a method of criticism whose exclusive concern with abstractions of pitch has led to many of the silliest misjudgments of Berlioz. But even without much consideration of secondary elements, we can get to the heart of the main question about Berlioz; whether he is some sort of freak, or whether the admitted differences between his and others' musical thought are a matter of degree or of kind. The most articulate supporter of the latter view is probably Rudolf Bockholdt, who strenuously disputes whether Berlioz's music should be analysed by traditional reductive methods at all; and since much of the present undertaking will involve reduction, and I have chosen to begin with pitch elements, his view requires brief exploration here (BocBS; BocMS).[11]

Bockholdt argues that Berlioz's music cannot be reduced to a black-and-white pitch-duration skeleton, a *Satz*. In contrast he cites a phrase of Mendelssohn which, although it benefits expressively from its orchestral dress (it is the 'Holyrood' opening of the 'Scotch' Symphony), exists as a perfectly intelligible and complete musical unit 'in black and white' (BocMS). He contends that such reduction will not work with Berlioz. On the face of it, his view is justifiable; it is certain that Berlioz's music loses far more in transcription for piano than, say, Mendelssohn's or Wagner's. Bockholdt cites the 'Hostias' and 'Agnus' of the *Requiem*, which could not be discussed in black and white without concluding that they are musically undernourished – although they have been used to illustrate certain of Berlioz's harmonic proclivities just because chordal juxtaposition *is* the musical content, apart from timbre (FriRH; DalIU). But in such passages the word 'instrumentation' is wrong; the colour, the very sound, the proper acoustical conditions, *are* the music, and Bockholdt is correct in saying that without the realized sound and space, the music does not exist as Mendelssohn's *Satz* exists.

It is easy to argue that Bockholdt's examples are either such extreme instances from acoustically conceived or 'architectural' works, or extremities of movements (the close of 'Scène aux champs', BocMS). But what he says has wider implications, also explored by Cone (1953; ConSH; 1980–81). Berlioz's whole manner of conceiving a work compels analytical consideration beyond the notes themselves. His originality in the symphonies consists less, for Bockholdt, in their programmes, than in the way they bring the theatre into the symphony – a view implicitly supported by Berlioz when he said that the *Fantastique* programme corresponded to linking dialogue in an opera (ConFS, 20), and in his detailed notes, amounting to stage-directions, in concert works such as *Roméo*, *L'enfance*, and *La damnation*. Such ideas are musically realized in combinations of themes and rhythms, and in spatial dispositions: players go 'off stage' in 'Scène aux champs' and 'Orgie de brigands', choruses are heard 'off' in *Roméo*, *L'enfance*, and *La damnation*. Bockholdt points to precedents for this type of musical effect in theatre music, including Lesueur.

Much of this is unexceptionable, and of vital importance in a full understanding of what Berlioz is about. But the argument cannot be upheld indiscriminately for all Berlioz's music. Berlioz's polyphony may be considered in terms of sonorities and 'the point of departure of sounds', which he himself lists among expressively valuable elements of music which are largely neglected (AT, 11/G, 29). But it is also a combination of pitches; and the problem remains, that it often sounds unsatisfactory to musical intelligences of good will and impeccable breeding. The appeal to the original sonority, to a polyphony of direction and colour, is of no avail when Berlioz writes for a homogeneous ensemble; questions are just as likely to be raised about the musical substance of pieces for chorus (especially when unaccompanied), for strings or a conventional orchestral layout, for harmonium, or for piano (song accompaniments, the majority of which Berlioz did not orchestrate). These pieces quite often flout the normal canons of polyphonic behaviour with no spatial or colouristic excuse.

Bockholdt's view is persuasively put; it is sympathetic and, in its positive aspect, important. But in its negative aspect, its virtual prohibition on analytical investigation of certain kinds (reductive and formal), it is obfuscatory and mystical. It cannot even be said that Berlioz needed spatial and colouristic polyphony to compose his best music. Part II and the final chorus of Part III of *L'enfance* are sufficient examples, the latter among the loveliest unaccompanied choral music of the nineteenth century and by no means dependent for most of its length on the unseen chorus of angels. Accordingly I do not think it improper to submit Berlioz's music to analytical reduction, to find the *Satz* and even, below it, the *Ursatz*. To do him justice we must recognize that he is just as inventive on this level as on any other, and just as markedly individual.

I now proceed to the discussion of certain pitch elements which, for all their bearing on issues of form and content, it seems possible to isolate. To some extent the discussion will focus on idiosyncrasy; and having determined what is typical of the composer, I can, in Chapter 5, give further consideration to the sources of idiosyncrasy. What follows is a series of discrete sections, rather than a continuous argument. This is in the nature of the material; but it is also because there already exist comparatively systematic discussions of Berlioz's pitch organization (FriRH, ConSH, PriBS). I intend not to duplicate these more than necessary, but, where my own analysis supports theirs, to take their conclusions as proven, and to proceed in various other directions, or towards other conclusions.

CONSONANCE AND DISSONANCE

'Harmony' is not usually understood today as merely the definition of verticals, a still picture of something properly experienced in motion. The most curious verticals in tonal music are passing effects of linear counterpoint, and there is little profit in the labour of cataloguing them. A composer's style may, however, be partly defined by his toleration of dissonance; thus it is obvious that, say, Monteverdi's tolerance is higher than Palestrina's, or Schumann's than Berlioz's. Bold clashes, however, are not *chords*, which are definable as units in the horizontal process of harmonic progression.

Even Berlioz's admirers have commented on the remarkable plainness of his chordal preferences. Tiersot calls Berlioz 'timorous', 'not going beyond Reicha and Lesueur'; Koechlin prefers to say 'not beyond Beethoven', which at once sounds less timorous.[12] Contemporary critics were more likely to regard him as barbarously dissonant. The idea of his plainness arises from a retrospective view, through the long-established association of Berlioz with 'music of the future' which began with his German admirers such as Pohl. Newman will serve as a classic statement of the Wagner fallacy in Berlioz criticism: 'Berlioz's harmony is always astonishingly simple and unadventurous; compared with Wagner's, it was quite "unmodern" even in his own day' (NewBR, 120). At least, however, we may reject the implied criticism by rejecting the explicit comparison. Curiously enough the comparison is there, but implicit, in 'the most remarkable fact about Berlioz's harmony . . . is the plain ordinariness of its vocabulary' (PriBS, 193), and in 'his harmonic vocabulary is not only standard but, for his day, somewhat limited' (ConSH, Part IV), although these come from authors fully aware of the range and freshness of Berlioz's harmonic relationships.

Berlioz's toleration of dissonance did not change much during his career; if anything, it lessened. But if Berlioz was backward in harmonic vocabulary, so were his contemporaries whose style was Italian-based; so were Mendelssohn and Gounod; while many of the most remarkable vertical complexes in Schubert or Schumann are in relatively early works. Berlioz refined his style and simplified his utterance, in a gradual move towards a form of neo-classicism which corresponds to such a move (evidently different in its musical consequences) in Schumann. Is it not Wagner who is unusual in so developing his toleration of dissonance over the years, and in developing a chromatic language of such range and complexity? Most masters of comparable longevity – besides Berlioz, Verdi, Brahms, Elgar – do not exhibit this tendency to anything like so marked a degree.

And what is Berlioz's 'time'? What is to be expected from a Frenchman born in 1803? Why go 'beyond' Reicha, Lesueur, or Beethoven, when different and effective uses can be found for the same resources? Compared to other composers active in Paris in his formative years, Berlioz's harmonic usage will not be found respectable or timid, but original, sensitive to nuance, and capable of very powerful development. Chailley remarks that Berlioz lacked 'esprit de suite', which might apply to other elements than harmony, for it is true that he was not interested in following up certain implications of his own earlier works. He preferred to approach each new project with a clean sheet. To criticize him on this score is to apply an anachronistic, Wagnerian or Schoenbergian, concept as to how a musician *ought* to develop. Chailley describes Berlioz's basic consonance ('consonance de base') as consisting of four notes, whereas Wagner's consists of five (ChaBH, 9). It is surely incorrect to suggest that the 7th, for Berlioz, or the 9th, for Wagner, is truly a consonance; but the comparison is right if one substitutes 'triad' for Berlioz, and '7th' for Wagner after about 1855.

Berlioz predominantly uses verticals of three pitch-classes, and diminished and dominant 7ths (although his dominants at cadences quite often lack the 7th). His 7ths are nearly always resolved functionally, and his 9ths, even at their boldest, are always related to a fundamental bass. In consequence his music is easy to analyse chord by chord. Structural analysis, however, is not made easier by these chordal preferences; on the contrary. When a chord is dissonant it contributes to musical motion through its need for resolution; the absence of dissonance makes the music more difficult to hear functionally. The more *outré* triadic relationships, of which Berlioz was fond, tend to blur the underlying harmonic functions in their brilliant interplay on the surface of his music.

These considerations must affect all my analyses throughout. Here I add a few examples of harmonic boldness, first in terms of verticals, then in terms of immediate, short-term progressions.

Despite his frequent assertion that music is free, Berlioz had strict ideas about the application of dissonance, and even Beethoven was not immune from criticism. Of the false horn entry in the 'Eroica' (I, 394): 'it is difficult to find a serious justification for this musical caprice' – which Wagner also disliked (AT, 24/G, 42).[13] Of the opening of the finale of the Ninth Symphony: 'the 6th degree of D minor grates horribly against the dominant and produces an excessively harsh effect'; and of the subsequent combination of seven pitches (bar 208): 'I have sought very hard to find the reason for this idea, and I am bound to admit that it eludes me' (AT, 57–9/G, 75–6). In 1861, discussing Wagner, Berlioz declared his opposition to wild literalism in programme music, a view which might have surprised his earlier critics (AT, 314ff/G, 330ff). In practice he was prepared to admit what may well be considered licences, but with a clear expressive cause.

The arpeggiated 4ths of the *Fantastique* (V, 11ff) and *Roméo* ('Roméo au tombeau', 168ff) are certainly a rarity before the twentieth century; but they are not compressed into chords as in early Schoenberg, and so create disturbance in the domain of pitch without actual dissonance. Berlioz was fond of having the flat 6th grate against the 5th, whether in dominant minor 9ths where the root is projected into the upper register which the 9th naturally inhabits, or, as in the Beethoven, with a tonic chord. *Elégie en prose* (Cat. 12J) has a fourth inversion of the minor 9th expressed as an auxiliary note in the bass with the root retained a 7th higher (Ex. 4A). In *Harold* IV (Ex. 4B, reduced score) the root D is retained over four octaves with the 9th in two of them. At the close of *Au cimetière* (Ex. 4C) the flat 6th grates gently against the dominant note of a major chord, a characteristic and fairly novel modal mixture which epitomizes the harmonic ambiguities of the song and its unresolved melancholy.

Ex. 4

The dominant minor 9th is Berlioz's harshest chord, and he was willing to attack it without preparation. One of the most extraordinary sounds in *Orphée* is an isolated minor 9th scored for brass, *fortissimo* with muted echo (Cat. 7/3); in *Herminie* a minor 9th begins an aria (Cat. 9/3) in violent disagreement of mood and tonality with what went before. (Theoretical backing for unprepared minor 9ths is given by Catel and Reicha: see Chapter 5; the former was a juror for the Prix de Rome competitions.) Other examples could be adduced. Berlioz gains a peculiar expressive force by juxtaposing major and minor 9ths (*Hamlet*, bars 11–13 and elsewhere; *Béatrice* No. 10, bars 91–4). He is generally partial to the flat 6th in dissonant combinations in the major. Ex. 5 shows two examples which have nothing in common otherwise: *Benvenuto* Act I, No. 3, soon after Cellini's entry, the hero sings with melting tenderness 'et calmez, O Teresa, votre frayeur' (note the prolonged Italianate appoggiatura) (Ex. 5A); *Les troyens* Act V, No. 39, Trojan chiefs rush on agitated by divine portents (the unclassifiable dissonance is caused by approaching the main chord chromatically from opposite auxiliaries, as in the famous example of an altered chord in Schoenberg's early song *Erwartung*, Op. 2) (Ex. 5B).

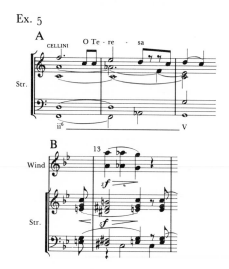

Ex. 5

Counterpoint leads to clashes such as the chain of $\begin{smallmatrix}6\\5\\3\end{smallmatrix}$ 'chords' in *Cléopâtre* (No. 3; also *Lélio* No. 2); they include every possibility: major with major 6th ('a'), minor with minor 6th ('b'), minor with major 6th ('c'), and the harshest, reserved for last, major with minor 6th ('d') (Ex. 6A). Counterpoint also lies behind the acute dissonances in the *Fantastique* (V, from 473), all within the ambiance of a prolonged dominant 7th (Ex. 6B).

Ex. 6

TONAL RESOURCES

The mixture of major and minor, for which Berlioz's proclivity has often been noticed, is fundamental to his pitch-vocabulary and tonal range. Nowhere is he more in conformity with the tendencies of the time. He is perhaps a little old-fashioned in his preference for major keys. In this he may have followed Gluck, who was a master of intensification through the introduction into the major of resources from the parallel minor (as at the climax of 'O malheureuse Iphigénie', whose powerful and unclassifiable dissonance is the subject of an anecdote in SO, 23). Berlioz also liked to destabilize the major by infiltration from the minor. This process allows a greater range than concentration on the inherently unstable minor alone. Thus while four songs in *Nuits d'été* are elegiac, only one (*Sur les lagunes*) is in the minor. Berlioz wrote few symphonic movements in the minor – the *Francs-juges* overture, the *Hamlet* march, at most five movements from the four symphonies – and most of them end in the major.

   That Berlioz was not out of tune with general harmonic tendencies may be judged from the following:

> An awareness of these three fundamental processes [mixture of major and minor, extension of Neapolitan relationships, frequent use of mediants, often borrowed from the opposite mode] gives an insight into the masterly way in which he handles his harmonic and tonal material. For with them, and with the added use of the standard diatonic progressions, the whole range of tonal colour in the chromatic scale was within his grasp, and he could pass freely between extreme keys, *without real abandonment of his tonic*.

This is M. J. E. Brown on Schubert;[14] but as much might be said of Berlioz, whose style was formed without any awareness that Schubert existed.

   Mixture will crop up again. Neapolitan relationships are less richly exploited by Berlioz, partly because he did not build them into the scheme of a symphonically conceived composition (as they are built into Schubert's C major quintet). Nevertheless they occur in unconventional ways in very early works, to excellent effect. A normal Neapolitan would relate Eb major to D minor; in *Orphée* Berlioz reverses this, passing from D major to Eb minor (see below, Ex. 38A; the chords are not related functionally by the normal dominant 7th/augmented 6th on Bb, a progression of which Berlioz was well aware, but by chromatic modification of one chord into the other). Berlioz also reversed the Neapolitan relationship by using the minor triad on the leading-note, which demands the sharpening of the 4th degree of the major scale. In *Harold* I the F♯ minor chord enhances the final cadence by its emphasis on the leading-note (Ex. 7A). The minor chord on the leading-note is actually the goal of the first cadence in the second movement (D♯ minor, bar 23), whence the music returns easily to the tonic. An earlier example, perhaps still more daring in its ambiguity of mode, is from *Irlande* (*Le coucher du soleil*), where the first cadence is in G (or g) from Ab, the tonic itself appearing as a conventional Neapolitan 6th (Ex. 7B).

Ex. 7

To exemplify Berlioz's fondness for mediants would be otiose; it is bound to appear in longer examples. This is something Berlioz shares with most nineteenth-century composers, such as Schubert, Brahms, and Fauré, and it has already been extensively examined (FriRH; PriBS). Whereas Schubert may have favoured submediants, especially the rich-sounding bVI (Ab from C), Berlioz had a predilection for mediants, especially when flattened (Eb from C major). Brown (see note 14) surmises that Schubert's attraction to bVI is partly due to his fondness for centring his melodies on the mediant; the mediant of bVI is the tonic note. Berlioz, who commented with some asperity on Bellini's excessive fondness for the mediant in his melodies (MM, 173), tends to centre his own on the dominant note (Schenkman,

1979); as this is the mediant of the mediant, a strong tonal connection is forged by melody.

Mediants are a potent source of major–minor mixture, and they enrich the possibilities available from another favourite device, linking remote chords by means of pedals (see also Chapter 8). The pedal may be concealed or open; the more open, the remoter the relationships that it can make intelligible. In Teresa's cavatina (Cat. 23C/2) the note F♯ is present in the texture for sixteen successive bars (counting as bar 1 the first of No. 2, 'Les belles fleurs': bars 57–72). The key is B; F♯ is the dominant note. At bar 57 it enters as mediant of D♯ minor. After a dominant chord it remains as mediant of D♮ major (59–61); bars 62–8 are dominant preparation, with F♯ an explicit pedal in 65–7; bars 69–72 begin the reprise (Ex. 8 shows the chord-structure).

Ex. 8

This concealed pedal binds, as it were by stealth, progressions not in themselves very startling. An overt pedal like the A♭ in the Largo of *Fantastique* I can hold together colourfully remote juxtapositions. The A♭ interrupts the dominant preparation for the Allegro, and might have been suggested by similar activity in Beethoven's overtures, *Leonora* Nos. 2 and 3 (Berlioz will have known No. 3). In No. 3 Beethoven interrupts a dominant (bar 9) by an A♭ which, however, pretends to be a key; significant material is introduced. Later A♭ is recovered (27) and resolved indirectly onto the dominant (a diminished 7th on A♮ intervenes). Berlioz's pedal-point is structurally analogous, but the music is marked by thematic amorphousness and the avoidance of key-sense through a kaleidoscopic juxtaposition of triads related by the common pitch A♭/G♯ (Ex. 9 is a reduction). As in the Beethoven the A♭ is clearly a parenthesis within a dominant; it resolves more obliquely however, treating the A♭ as a G♯ to lead functionally to A minor. Five of the six possible consonant triads are used in a consistent progression sharpwards, by means of enharmonic notation (in Ex. 9 parallel major and

Ex. 9

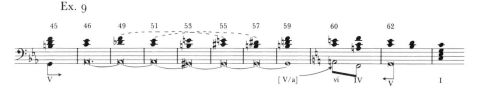

minor chords are joined by broken slurs). The passage seems so wayward and dreamlike that it is surprising to find only one true chromatic progression (A♭ to E; major to flattened submediant). The omitted triad is F minor, which with A♭ is the closest relation to the tonic. The whole passage effects a move from C minor to C major, each defined by its submediant: A♭, A minor. In such passages the solid underlying sense pointed out by reductive analysis evaporates in performance; the static pedal itself becomes an element of instability.

THE 'PUN'

It has not, I think, been noticed before that Berlioz was particularly attracted to the chord-relationship which arises when a major and minor chord share a mediant note (the minor is rooted a semitone higher; as in the A♭/a of Ex. 9). This pun, on the double meaning of a single note, might serve as an epitome of Berlioz's habits of chord and harmony, for it can arise out of pedals, concealed or overt (as in Ex. 8, d♯/D), can involve enharmony (in Ex. 38A the same chords are notated D/e♭), and intimately concerns mediants, not only because the note of double function is a mediant, but because the relationship most naturally arises when the two chords are the diatonic and altered mediant or submediant of the home key (as in Ex. 8, D♮/d♯ from B; in Ex. 9, the A♭/a from C).

The pun crops up all over Berlioz's music, in contexts at times almost casual (and thus, perhaps, the more revealing), but often in such a way as to derive the maximum force from the expressive potential of an unusual relationship. There are also longer-term uses, as when the mediant and flat mediant are used instead of dominant and subdominant to balance sharp and flat sides of a tonic. Clearly Berlioz regarded the alternative mediants as structurally equivalent, in the short and long term, as a few examples will show.

A change from C minor to C major in *Fantastique* V (cf. Ex. 9, from I) is effected by a mediant pun. The actual chords (E♭/e) are not used but they are outlined by the triadic theme of the 'Ronde du Sabbat', with brass emphasizing the prolonged dominant which governs bars 222–40 (Ex. 10). The composer here glories in the sound of the relationship. A similar tonal balance, bringing about a change from minor to major, occurs without direct juxtaposition near the end of the *Requiem*. The 'Agnus' is partly a reprise of

Ex. 10

the 'Hostias', which ends in B♭ minor, but it modifies a cadence to B♭ major, moving thence to the relative G minor and the end of the entire work in G major. The first, most crucial, change is accomplished by means of a submediant pun. The 'Hostias' has two balanced choral phrases, both ending in B♭ minor. In the 'Agnus' its first statement is followed by a reprise of the short introduction, starting on the pun partner of B♭ minor (A major, bar 40). The repeat of the second phrase is then modified (Ex. 11 juxtaposes a reduction of the two phrases). The top of the phrase is a submediant, but the expected G♭ (of bar 33) is replaced by G minor, the pitch G♭ appearing, as so often in such progressions, as an F♯, leading-note to G.

Structural equivalence is perhaps best shown by puns that do *not* occur in the final form of the music. In the 'Quaerens me' (*Requiem*, No. 5) Berlioz originally cadenced in both the mediant and flat mediant (iii, ♭III; from A, c♯/C). This apparent balance was, however, removed from the definitive version.[15] In the 'Concert de sylphes' (*Huit scènes*, Cat. 32A/3), Berlioz had a middle section in F major (♭III from D, from bar 92); in the revised form, in *La damnation* (Cat. 32B/7B), this music appears in F♯ minor (iii, from bar 61). Exactly the same tonal balance was retained, however, in *Le carnaval romain* (bars 112 and 202; the music is effectively a repeat but C♯ minor replaces C♮ major as mediant of A). Both keys frequently appear within a single movement. The interrupted cadence of Ex. 11 is paralleled by one in the 'Méditation' from *Cléopâtre*, where the enharmonic inflection of the 6th degree becomes a leading-note to an altered submediant (D minor from F minor: Ex. 12A). When Berlioz revised the music for *Lélio* No. 2 he used a diatonic cadence, D♭ replacing D minor (Ex. 12B). This is almost the only alteration Berlioz ever made to his music which weakens the effect. The juxtaposition of F and D minors coheres by virtue of the overall harmonic control – a move from D♭ to the dominant – and is splendidly blood-curdling; in the revision there is too much D♭.

Ex. II

Ex. 12

I have dwelt on the pun because while it does not solve any problems about Berlioz's harmonic thought, it illustrates perfectly the mixture of freedom and logic which imbues many of his most striking inventions in the domain of pitch. Moreover it embodies both immediate and more remote relationships, which in Berlioz are not always easy to disentangle because of his preference for unadulterated triads. Puns appear in every substantial work of Berlioz from the *Resurrexit* to *Béatrice*, and examples can be found involving every one of the twelve possible degrees of the scale (on the pattern I/bii, bII/ii; or C/c♯, Db/d, etc.); but I will spare the reader a catalogue. Berlioz did not invent the pun; it is to be found in all the Viennese classics (including Hummel), and with Berliozian ubiquity in Schubert. A fine example appears in one of Berlioz's favourite works, *La vestale* (Ex. 13A), and it is used by his unsympathetic contemporary, Adam, in *Giselle* (Ex. 13B; the sequence Db–Eb suggests that F will follow, but E minor is used). Adam relates the chords functionally by dominants, as Berlioz often does, and he is clearly affected by his dramatic context – the passage is followed by 'rire satanique des Wilis' – which must have suggested the grotesque, and therefore Berlioz. Noske remarks of Adolphe Vogel that he 'has a predilection for experiments in the harmonic domain. The way he juxtaposed chords a third apart . . . is quite audacious' (NosFS, 38). His

Ex. 13

example includes the progression B–d♯–B–D♮, the mediant pun. The piece dates from 1842, so it too could have been influenced by Berlioz; significantly, it is called *Satan* and subtitled 'Blasphème'. Berlioz's puns, however, are as likely to be witty as diabolical.

4 Concerning pitch (2): chromaticism, tonal relations, and modality

> 'It must also be admitted that Berlioz is by no means free of his own harmonic clichés. Certain chromatic progressions show up again and again in his music – especially what might be called the reversed resolution.'
>
> E. T. Cone (ConSH, Part IV)

It is perfectly true, as much of the previous chapter must imply, that Berlioz was capable of bringing any chord into some sort of relation to his tonic, and of making any modulation very rapidly. Primmer proposes a theoretical basis in an 'ambimodal and semichromatic scale' of eleven notes, on any of which major or minor chords might be used (PriBS, 45), but Berlioz is also likely to use the note Primmer omits, the tritone. For juxtaposition of chords a tritone apart, one need only recall the alternation of tonic (g) and D♭ chords in 'Marche au supplice' (bar 154ff), which was censured by Schenker and puzzled even Schumann.[16] Primmer himself discusses the polarity between keys a tritone apart in 'La course à l'abîme' (PriBS, 77), while Faust's air contains a cadence in B from a tonic F (see FriRH, and Chapter 14). Other similarly remote relationships suggest that Berlioz's chromatic range is potentially unlimited, despite his lack of interest in chromatically altered chords and his generally low toleration of dissonance. His preferences, of course, are relatively conventional, since he normally makes extended tonal relations only of keys a 3rd or 4th apart. No doubt he felt, as Tovey put it, that 'a modulation from C to F♯ is as easy as falling out of bed, but, however correct in grammar, it is not going to establish a key-relation'.[17] Berlioz's interest in such recondite progressions does nothing to invalidate this statement; it simply shows his awareness of the expressive value of lack of relationship.

Berlioz's flexible handling of movement between unrelated tonal areas can best be shown by another revision. In composing *La damnation* he first intended Margaret's ballad 'Le roi de Thulé' to remain in its original key of G (as in *Huit scènes*). He then decided to transpose it down to F, which necessitated altering the link from the preceding recitative. Margaret's account of her dream of a lover ends around B major (citing her 'Romance'); she murmurs 'Folie!', and the futility of dreams is embodied in the falling progression, B to D♯, both minor – remarkable enough for Wagner to use it a few years later as the *Leitmotiv* of the magical Tarnhelm (e – g♯). The link to the ballad in G was cancelled (Ex. 14A) and replaced by a link to F (Ex. 14B). It is perhaps possible to maintain that the first version is more natural (or less contrived) than the familiar one. Both depend on enharmony (D♯/E♭). The first adds a 7th and resolves it as an augmented 6th (D♭ as C♯), but still finds space for a bemusing diminished 7th before the dominant chord. The revision changes from d♯ to E♭ without the 7th, which seems more arbitrary, and more chords are needed: there are two diminished 7ths (X), resolved by side-slipping, not functionally as substitute-dominants; and one augmented 6th (Y) which resolves onto C minor, although the natural expectation from ♯6 on D♭, and the actual goal of the passage, are equally C *major*, V of F. Clearly Berlioz wrote the whole recitative with quite other considerations in mind than the key of the next aria, and he could no doubt have modulated anywhere else had it been necessary, in about this space of time.

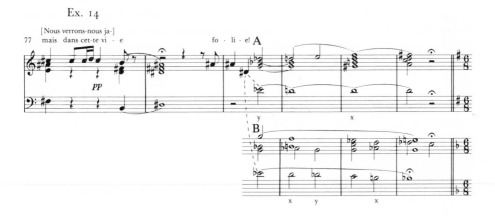

Ex. 14

Ex. 14 shows Berlioz's freedom of movement between keys – one can hardly call it key-relation – and the importance for him of the immediate impact of such passages, which behave more as expressive gestures than functional modulations. It also shows two further aspects of his chromatic practice.

One is his fondness for the diminished 7th as a passing sonority, multiplied so as to undermine the expectation of a functional resolution. An extreme instance is the slide over an octave of diminished 7ths in *Le spectre de la rose* (Cat. 27B; orchestral version, bars 37–40). The effect in such cases is the obliteration of the tonic; the new key is established by right of possession, not organically, and can sound remote even if it is not new at all (as in *Le spectre*, or 'Scène aux champs', bars 110–11). The technique is particularly useful to a composer who habitually does not remain for long periods out of touch with his tonic, for they regenerate its repeated appearances.

The second point shown by Ex. 14 is, if one may put it so, the perverse resolution of the augmented 6th. Berlioz makes frequent use of such resolution *à rebours*, of which the reversed resolution admirably described by Cone is a special case (see epigraph). Cone also attributes this habit particularly to Berlioz's middle years, but one of his examples from *La damnation* is the 'Romance', unaltered from its 1829 version (see Ex. 15B); it is surely the symptom of a lifelong preoccupation.

Ex. 15 shows three examples from two passages in the 'Romance'. Bars 2–3 (at X) are a fingerprint; the progression is so nearly normal. The bass C–B♮–B♭–A, harmonized as in Ex. 15C, is a commonplace. Instead Berlioz approaches B♮ directly from F, which would normally demand filling in the tritone gap by resolution to C. B♭ follows, however, bearing not the inversion of V⁷ in Ex. 15C but a parallel minor (supertonic) $^6_3$. The B♭ then awaits further directions from the upper parts before resolving. At this point (Y) the voice falls – without even an appoggiatura – from D to C♯, and this diminished 7th could be dominant in function to D minor. Its ambiguity is enhanced, in some statements of the melody, by a pause; then C♯ resolves backwards onto C♮. This is not a complex progression, and to notate C♯ as D♭ would make it look as simple as it sounds; but it points to events beyond the principal section. Later (Ex. 15B), Berlioz reaches an unequivocal dominant of D minor (bar 26), yet this too resolves backwards (Z), linked loosely by a semitone slip and a bass arpeggiation to the following F chord. Something rather similar happens in bars 66–7, with a diminished 7th

Ex. 15

coming after a D minor chord. Cone rightly remarks that this mannerism

> is less the result of a mere desire for novelty than the symptom of a pervasive
> attitude towards harmony. Berlioz, although working within the general
> outlines of classical tonality, never regards the functionality of a chord as
> sacrosanct . . . he frequently tends to emphasize certain chords as elements
> of colour – of immediate contrast – within a controlling functional
> progression (ConSH, part IV).

This attitude affects other elements than harmony, as will appear.

Cone's examples are of leading-notes that fall. The opposite also occurs: the flat 7th that rises. At the cadence of the Capulets' song (Cat. 25/III, 108), the double-basses fall from the leading-note to G♮ (Ex. 16) while the choral parts proceed in orthodox fashion, one bass-line having G♯–A, the other the roots, E–A. Berlioz has no intention of proceeding to the subdominant. The strings, however, are pursuing the mood of the introduction, before the choral entry, and the G♮ is a moment of vibrant mystery. Eventually it slides back to A. Identical in technique, but totally different in mood, is the end of Act III of *Les troyens* (No. 28, bar 369ff). A♮ breaks in on a choral cadence in B, but the expected gradual fall to the dominant never happens, and the sliding resolution up to B governs the whole coda. One might well call such events *faits psychiques*; Berlioz's musical syntax could then be compared to the prose of his fellow Dauphinois, Stendhal (see p. v).

Ex. 16

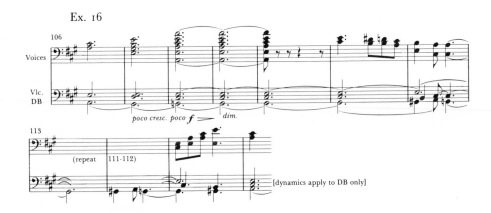

STRONG AND 'WEAK' DIATONIC PROGRESSIONS

Probably very few terms in Berlioz's vocabulary of single progressions cannot be paralleled in the works of masters of impeccable orthodoxy. What disconcerts some listeners even today is not the terms themselves, but their frequency of occurrence. Meyer discusses the opening of 'Un bal' in his chapter 'The Weakening of Shape'. 'Weakening' is descriptive, not pejorative; the evocative beauty of the passage depends on vagueness, the invisibility of its goal until the brilliant emergence of the A major $\substack{6 \\ 4}$ in bar 30. The first chord is tonic minor; the intermediate steps involve predominantly root movements by a 3rd, semitonal slides, and the sharpening of single notes, producing among other things two puns (F/f♯; b♭/A). As Meyer observes, 'The harmonic ambiguity of this passage is the product of minimal differentiation between successive vertical structures.'[18] Strongly directed functionality is almost absent.

Likewise seeking the elusive qualities of Berlioz's harmony, Friedheim (FriRH) discusses a fondness for so-called 'weak' progressions. Again, the term should not be understood pejoratively; Schoenberg's term 'descending' is to be preferred.[19] Some 'weak' progressions involve minimal differentia-tion; typically, the bass, or at least the root rises a 3rd, and the second chord contains only one note not in the first (as C–e): one-third new information to two-thirds repetition, with the root of the second chord anticipated in the first. Also classified as 'weak' is the descent of the bass or root by a step, although in terms of differentiation such a progression is identical to rising a step and thus, in Schoenberg's term, 'superstrong'; the second chord is entirely new information. Both the rising 3rd and falling tone are excluded by Reicha from the 'marche régulière' of harmony.[20]

Again, perhaps the terminology hardly matters; but the greater ambiguity of such progressions, and their relative frequency in Berlioz, does. Their effect is usually more piquant than weak. An example from Schubert may be set beside one from Berlioz to show how they differ when using similar progressions. In Schubert's *Im Frühling* the progression of bar 1 (Ex. 17A) is

Ex. 17

diatonic: the 'descending' I–iii is followed by the maximally differentiated iii–IV and the fall back to I. In bar 13, however (at B), the second chord is inflected, appearing as V[7] of D minor – although to analyse it as such, given the earlier statement as background, and to call the move to B♭ an interrupted cadence, would seem over-sophisticated. In Cellini's aria 'Sur les monts' (Cat. 23C/14), Berlioz uses similar chordal variation for his main material. Five statements are shown in Ex. 18. Ex. 18A goes unambiguously from tonic to dominant; then, with maximum differentiation, it falls back to the subdominant, also in root position (this V–IV progression occurs more normally when the IV is in first inversion, the bass rising as for an

Ex. 18

interrupted cadence; see below). Ex. 18B is a near-repeat, but varies the first two chords to bring in the relative minor; Ex. 18C has this as a $\frac{6}{3}$ followed by its dominant, which, however, leads to the subdominant expected at this point (cf. Ex. 17B). The subdominant is the only constant of the five versions. In Ex. 18D the rhythm is augmented, the progression being that of Ex. 17B; finally, in Ex. 18E, the simplest version appears, using A minor (cf. Ex. 17A), but passing from IV to ii to prepare a cadential $\frac{6}{4}$.

Obviously Berlioz liked these progressions; he did not blunder into them. The *Scène héroïque* (Cat. 4), written before he enrolled at the Conservatoire, contains a magnificent progression (Ex. 19: each bar represents two of the

Ex. 19

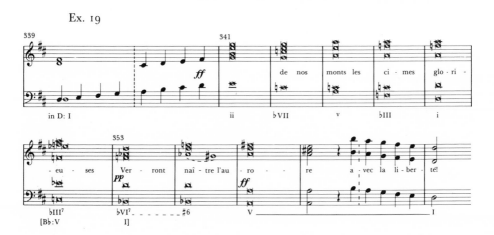

original) in which every step is 'strong' or regular (with one exception, a 'descending' i–bIII⁷; but the 7th counteracts the descending quality by its directional force towards the next chord). The exemplary augmented 6th provides an early example of simple enharmony (broken slur). Moreover, not every progression using rising steps and falling 3rds necessarily *sounds* strong, broad, or orthodox; they can acquire a wholly Berliozian flavour. In the 'Offertoire' (Ex. 20), the regular, 'ascending' march of rising tone and falling 3rd is governed by a descending progression by step (chords in semibreve notation); each descent is picked out by entries of the triadic fugue-subject on F, Eb, d, db, c, Bb. Even a chain of diminished 7ths could not give a more rootless feeling, a groping from one stable area (F, the mediant) to another, which happens to be the tonic. Another step or two, ending somewhere quite remote, could have been added without losing coherence. The main steps combine in every possible pattern of descents by step (major and minor, by tone or semitone), except minor descending to major by a semitone. The intervening chords (black noteheads) bear simple, but non-functional relationships to their neighbours (there are no applied dominants).

Ex. 20

Berlioz uses even bolder descending steps in his *Chant des chemins de fer* (Cat. 36/C), at the climactic cry of 'Peace! the King! the worker! the fatherland!'. Each exclamation is successively on root-position major chords of F♯, E, D, and C, overwhelming the simple modulation to bVI (from B to G). Berlioz's inspiration may have been the 'Eroica' (I, coda), where Beethoven opens new vistas after an apparently final cadence by the slowly descending progression Eb, Db, C, with each step picked out, as in Ex. 20, by the main arpeggiated motive (bars 554ff). The grandeur of such effects in Spontini also struck him:

> Some of Spontini's modulations are . . . flashes of genius. In the first rank among these I would put the abrupt move from the key of Eb to that of Db in the soldiers' chorus in *Cortez*: 'Quittons ces bords, l'Espagne nous rappelle'. At this unexpected tonal departure, the listener is suddenly struck so that his imagination leaps a vast distance in one bound; it flies, as it were, from one hemisphere to another, and forgetting Mexico, it follows the thoughts of the rebellious soldiers to Spain. Consider also . . . the astounding exclamation of the High Priest in *La vestale*, where the voice falls abruptly from the key of Db to that of C major at the line 'Vont-ils dans la chaos replonger l'univers?' (SO, 13).

Genius, we may feel, inheres for Berlioz as much in the effect as in the means used to produce it. Berlioz too can open new horizons by simple manoeuvres, down a tone from V to IV, or, on the same bass, a move from dominant to inverted supertonic (V–ii⁶), the latter normally the chord *before* the dominant. This move gives extraordinary breadth to the homophonic melody in the 'Offertoire' (Ex. 21A). More poignant, but no less expansive in

Ex. 21

its enlargement of a progression which seems to be tending towards the cadence, is the same progression in Margaret's 'Romance' (Ex. 21B); here there is a shuddering recognition of unutterable loss. Effectively a V–IV, although arguably a II–I in B, is the first 'Sanctus' of the *Te Deum* (No. 2; Ex. 22). Berlioz remarked of his architectural works, of which the *Te Deum* is the most mature, that they use 'progressions of formidable slowness, whose final goal cannot be predicted' (MemPS). A high level of ambiguity is to be expected in such cases (cf. Ex. 20). Simple as it may appear in reduction (in Ex. 22 one crochet unit represents a whole bar), the 'Sanctus' is a magnificently placed change of harmonic speed: the heavens seem to open.

Ex. 22

MAJOR, MINOR, AND MODAL SCALES

Despite the theoretical 'ambimodal' scale (see above, p. 38), Berlioz conceived nearly all his music within the major and minor modes, and blended them in ways perfectly familiar from most other nineteenth-century music. Mixture of parallel major and minor does not affect the overall tonality. Another ambiguity common at this period, however, is between a major tonic and its relative minor, or vice versa; Rosen remarks that for Chopin and Schumann they are virtually the same key.[21] The finale of Schumann's F♯ minor sonata is more in A than the tonic, and Chopin ends large pieces like the 'F minor' Fantasy and the 'B♭ minor' Scherzo in their relative majors, Ab and Db. Although examples of this in Berlioz are all parts of still larger works, he clearly shares the feeling of identification. Examples, totally different in mood and going in opposite directions, are the 'Choeur de buveurs' (Cat. 32B/6), from c to Eb, and 'Chanson d'Hylas' (Cat. 40A/38), from Bb to g. These are self-contained pieces. In the interests of continuity Berlioz ends the duet of sentinels (Cat. 40A/40) a tone lower than it began, without a final cadence.

An extension of possible ambiguity between relative keys is the practice of modality, in which Berlioz was presumably influenced by Lesueur. Berlioz's feeling for modality, however, is in reality less significant as an experiment in escaping from the major and minor scales than as an enrichment of the prevailing system. Thus for Berlioz the mediant chord of a minor key may be used (as Eb major in C minor), without itself becoming a centre of attraction, and, despite the flattening of the leading-note, without prejudice to the tonic. Some very beautiful passing moments are characterized by oscillation between a minor tonic and its mediant (Ex. 23). In the Act I Trio of *Benvenuto* (Cat. 23C/3), the music moves from C to cadence in A minor, oscillating between chords of C and a before moving back to F (Ex. 23A). In the

Ex. 23

transition before the scene on the banks of the Elbe in *La damnation* (Cat. 32B/end of 6C), Berlioz repeats a B major phrase in D, then revolves ambiguously between B minor and D before settling in the latter (Ex. 23B). In neither case does there seem to be any conscious question of modality; the oscillation is used both for its ambiguity and as an expressive tremor in its own right. The technique is, however, no different from that in an avowedly modal composition, the fugal overture to *La fuite en Egypte* (Cat. 38/8; Ex. 23C). It may be that Berlioz adopted modality for the last work because he liked the effect of such non-functional oscillation, rather than that the oscillation resulted from the choice of scale.

The importance of modality in Berlioz should not be over-rated; like other elements such as unusual metres, it stands out less by its frequent occurrence within his work than by its absence from that of his contemporaries (although Schubert, again, was fond of mediant oscillations; the 'Great' C major Symphony is full of them, and see also the wonderful *Totengräbers Heimweh*, D.842). Beethoven occasionally used modal scales, and Berlioz may well have been more impressed by the 'Et incarnatus' of the Mass in D than by anything of Lesueur's. But Berlioz's interest in modality was not dictated, as was Beethoven's, by the expression of reverence; the most reverent music he wrote, the closing chorus of *L'enfance*, is not modal at all, although it is in this work that modality is used most extensively. Berlioz was pleased by the *charm* of modal effects, and used them gladly for expressive ends, but his sources are as likely to be rustic as ecclesiastical, and he seldom employs them with devoted consistency.

An early instance of a modal inflection, and one certainly intended to be rustic, is in Margaret's 'chanson gothique', 'Le roi de Thulé'. The sharp 4th is, however, a leading-note to the dominant, balanced by the flat 6th and resolved by the full chromatic shape C–B♮–B♭ in the second whole bar (Ex. 24). In a letter of about six weeks after the composition of this ballad, Berlioz mentions a 'Walze au chalet' which he believed to be by Weber: 'the G♯ in the key of D and C♯ in the key of G are only there to give the tune some local colour; for you know that the instruments used by Swiss shepherds pitch the 4th of the scale too high. This Weber renders as a sharp, and one gets used to it in no time' (to his sister Nanci, November 1828; CG 1, p. 211, see also HolCP, 121). If not local colour, then charm rather than reverence,

Ex. 24

motivates the use of the Aeolian mode in the overture to *La fuite* (Berlioz noted in the score by the fugue-subject in f♯: 'E♮ not E♯'). The very idea of fugue at the 5th introduces elements foreign to the mode (which is not the case in the purer modality of Beethoven's 'Et incarnatus' or in Palestrina). Berlioz soon introduces tonal elements, an E♯ as early as bar 7 before the third entry of the subject, a B♯ in the bass beneath that entry, forming a diminished 5th (bar 9). The modulations for the counter-exposition in the woodwind and the homophonic theme at bar 84 are entirely tonal, as is the final cadence (see Ex. 23C). When the fugue-subject is used again to begin Part III (Cat. 38/10) it receives a tonal answer ('cellos, bar 11). Berlioz's most consistently modal piece is the 'Pas d'esclaves nubiennes' in *Les troyens* (No. 33C), where the motivation is pure exoticism, of a brilliance and charm unmatched by his contemporaries, even the oriental specialist David.

The expressive use of a modal inflection within a tonal piece preceded more self-consciously modal experiments – for example the cadence with minor dominant which ends Faust's 'Invocation' (see Chapter 14). This tendency is extended in *L'enfance*, so that the magnificent aria of Herod is avowedly modal but in fact chromatic, since it is not at all interested in modal consistency. In what is really G minor, Berlioz uses F♮ and F♯, A♭ and A♮, in mixtures of minor and Aeolian, or minor and Phrygian. At the opening, the sombre descending sequence avoids the tonal dominant, but it is chromatically inflected. It closes with a sort of Phrygian cadence (not to be confused with the Phrygian cadence in which the second chord, being major, may well sound like a dominant). Here the A♭ receives expressive weight precisely because A♮ is the norm of the preceding bars (Ex. 25A). Berlioz continues to play with this alternative 2nd degree; Herod's entry (bar 38) would be pure Phrygian but for the passing A♮ in the bassoon counterpoint. The frequent A♭s have a tonal consequence when, a few bars later (42), the music actually modulates to that key, strongly defined by its own subdominant, D♭. The music is never modal for more than a few notes; the section in D minor is full of C♯s, despite its modal cadence (bars 61–74). Every centre of attraction is clarified by a leading-note, then questioned by modal inflections. The effect is a human uncertainty, apt for the depiction of Herod's regal misery, where Beethoven's modality is ethereal; and a spontaneous expressive device, where Lesueur's modality is applied.

Berlioz was quite conscious of this: 'I have tried out some new inflections [*tournures*]: Herod's air of insomnia is written in G minor [sic] on this scale, classified by I know not what Greek name in plainchant [Ex. 25B follows]. This brings about very sombre harmonies, and cadences of a peculiar character which seemed to me to suit the situation.'[22] Writing of the overture to *La fuite* he publicly expressed his scepticism about the origin of the modes, and showed that for him their associations were not merely liturgical: 'this mode which is no longer *à la mode*, which resembles plainsong, and which the

Ex. 25

professors will tell you is derived from some Phrygian, or Dorian, or Lydian, mode of ancient Greece, which has nothing to do with the case; but it certainly retains something of the melancholy and rather naive character of old folk laments' (GM, 171/G, 187). This is evidence enough of the popular origin of Berlioz's modality.

In the period after *L'enfance*, during which he was chiefly occupied with *Les troyens*, Berlioz developed an interest in artificial scales. The chief practical result was the beautiful chorus of Trojan women, of which he wrote to Princess Wittgenstein:

> I think I can say to you that this score contains things worthy to be offered to you. There are even novelties. The second act contains a chorus of Trojan women in this vein, based on this strange scale [Ex. 26A follows]; and the accent of desolation which results from the continual predominance of G in relation to D♭ is something quite unusual. I feel I have sought out here the abandoned cries of Virgil's *feminae ululantes*.[23]

Yet the tritone Berlioz singles out, while it forms the main melodic basis of the composition (No. 14), is subject to tonal tensions which he does little to resist; it frequently and conclusively resolves onto A♭ and C. The piece is not in a queer mode on G, as Berlioz implied, but in A♭ (Exx. 26B, C).

Associated with the sketches for *Les troyens* are jottings of odd chord-sequences under scales, ambitiously headed 'Nouveau ton mineur'

Ex. 26

and, still more daringly, 'majeur'. I present a selection of these in simplified form (for a complete transcription in notation equivalent to Berlioz's, see HolCP, 127–8). Ex. 27A attempts to combine the virtues of the Phrygian flat supertonic with a true leading-note; 27A[1] flattens the latter and is simply Phrygian (cf. Herod's air), and not new at all. The mixture of Phrygian with major (Ex. 27B) inescapably sounds like a prolongation of the dominant of A minor. Probably Berlioz came to the same conclusion, for although these jottings have curiosity value as indicating the kind of flexibility of style towards which he was developing during work on *Les troyens*, they were soon consigned to oblivion, and his next and last work, *Béatrice*, has no more than a few expressive modal inflections and no sign of systematic reform of the basis of tonality. The absence of what Verdi might have called 'enigmatic

Ex. 27

scales' is natural in a neo-classical *opéra comique*, where such things would be quite out of place; with Berlioz the subject and its proper expression always dictate the means.

We may conclude these notes on Berlioz's original ideas in the domain of pitch with his use of a symmetrical mode, the whole-tone scale. It is perhaps curious that Berlioz's keen interest in the diminished 7th did not lead him to the eight-note scale of alternating tones and semitones, constructed of the notes of any two diminished 7ths, which Messiaen calls the 'second mode of limited transposition'.[24] But he did stumble across Messiaen's 'first mode', the whole-tone scale, and used it twice, in the overture *Les francs-juges* (1826; Ex. 28A) and 37 years later in the prelude to *Les troyens à Carthage* (Cat. 40B; Ex. 28B). In neither case was he probably aware of the scale as a scale, since

Ex. 28

both result from the contrary motion of diminished 7ths; if one direction proceeds by semitones, the reverse has to be by whole tones in order to correspond. *Les francs-juges*, therefore, does not deprive Glinka of the glory of being the first to expose the whole-tone scale, as a symbol of supernatural power. In his appreciative review of *Russlan and Ludmilla* Berlioz makes no mention of this passage, in which Glinka admittedly subjects the scale to a tonal harmonization.[25] With Schubert, Berlioz was among the first actually to write a whole-tone scale; and it seems fair to end, therefore, by remarking that however plain his basic vocabulary of chords may seem, we certainly should not consider him timorous in matters of pitch organization.

5 Education (2): concerning Catel, the guitar, and works of the 1820s

'On the other hand, as I have said, there are awkward harmonies in Berlioz that make one scream; it is easy to see that he picked out his chords on the guitar and could hear almost nothing. It is all very well to claim that Berlioz's unusual chordal placing is a sign of his "genius": I think rather that it was clumsiness.'

Pierre Boulez (*Conversations with Célestin Deliège*, London, 1976, p. 20)

Even in the simpler levels of pitch organization, Berlioz's predilections reveal his peculiarity and originality as clearly as any other aspect of his music. The present chapter pursues a few lines of thought about the possible origins of these predilections and about their early manifestations during the crucial and frustrating 1820s – nominally the period of his official education but more importantly the period of supreme musical and dramatic experiences which, together with the emotional traumas associated with Harriet Smithson, were to combine in the production of his first truly outstanding work, the *Symphonie fantastique*, in 1830.

The paucity of serious musical experience in Berlioz's earliest years has already been mentioned. Even at La Côte, however, he had access to a couple of textbooks. Rameau's harmonic theory understandably perplexed him, even when simplified by d'Alembert. Catel's short treatise, written as the official textbook for the Conservatoire, is at least practical, although totally without examples from real music.[26] Catel includes Rameau's theory of fundamental bass, which is also said to have been taught by Lesueur (WotHB, 52); but Catel's ideas are not exclusively based upon it, and he includes instruction in the practice of figured bass, a technique later used by Berlioz as a musical shorthand in sketches.

Above all, Catel is free of dogma. He refrains almost throughout from declaring any progression strong, weak, bad, or even good. Unlike Cherubini, he does not supply copious examples of what *not* to do.[27] He expresses mild preferences; but he makes no clear distinction between regular and unusual progressions, as does Reicha (see above, p. 42). For example, Catel imposes no restraint upon the use of progressions in which the root rises a 3rd; he merely gives fewer examples. The young Berlioz may well have found these pleasing, and been moved to explore them further, his mind uncorrupted by routine. He said that 'by listening to Pleyel's quartets . . . and thanks to Catel's harmony treatise . . . I at last, and in a sense abruptly, found my way into the mysteries of the formation and linking of chords' (Mem4). Neither Pleyel, whose quartets were presumably not available to Berlioz in score, nor Devienne, who included six sonatas and several other pieces in his flute tutor, were strong enough personalities to impose habits. It seems that Berlioz, who did not attend harmony classes at the Conservatoire, did not forget the early lessons which he learned from Catel. That they were not what Catel meant to teach may be true, but hardly pertinent.

Catel states in his preface: 'I have made it my object in this work to teach harmony by instilling the elements of counterpoint'. That part-writing comes before chords is a surprisingly modern, even Schenkerian, idea; perhaps it explains why Catel's treatise was superseded by the more conventional and restrictive work of Berton. Berlioz, however, did not master counterpoint from Catel; he needed Reicha's instruction to get him over the preliminary hurdle for the Prix de Rome. Nevertheless, whatever his contrapuntal technique, the idea of linear direction was to underlie many of Berlioz's most characteristic progressions (although, Berlioz being Berlioz, there are as many passages not explicable in this way; see Chapter 7). Catel has a simple harmonic theory: 'There is only one single chord, which contains all the others.' From that chord, the major triad, he derives 7ths and 9ths: 'These chords, and their inversions, are the only ones which can be given without preparation' (including the diminished 7th and the dominant minor 9th). Other, more complex combinations are declared to be the result of counterpoint, by suspension, passing-notes, or chromatic alteration. (Reicha, on the other hand, multiplies the fundamental chords to thirteen; but he derives the augmented triad, as does Catel, from a chromatic alteration, from which it follows that it should not be included with the fundamental chords.)

If Catel's restrictions are few, his demonstration of possibilities is generous. He forbids the fourth inversion of the 9th; Berlioz was to criticize its use in *Lohengrin* (AT, 310/G, 327), although he himself only narrowly avoided it on at least two occasions.[28] Catel also demonstrates the side-slipping of diminished 7ths, while remarking that the use of this chord in the major is a licence. He makes a common-sense exposition of enharmony, including unexpected resolutions of the diminished 7th, and gives no such austere warning about its possible abuse as appears in Reicha and Berton.[29] Catel illustrates postponement of cadences, including an interruption Berlioz liked, which replaces the tonic by a diminished 7th; another example involves modulation to bIII. He also provides a table of modulations which shows extensive reliance on major-minor mixture. His routes from a tonic to ♭II and to ♭ii are identical but for the mode of the last chord (Ex. 29). Reicha poured scorn on modulation tables, asserting not unreasonably that they might limit the student's apprehension of possible routes; certainly Catel's bear no relation to any compositional situation. If Berlioz's modulatory links by a few chords (as in Ex. 14) seem in some sense arbitrary, not organically derived from what went before, we might blame the *idea* of a modulation table, although Berlioz cannot be accused of stereotyped thinking. Modulation tables may have served to stretch his ear as he read them (or picked them out on the guitar?), and they will have provided an inkling of possibilities far wider than were suggested by any music he then knew.

Ex. 29

Catel is not the key to all of Berlioz's peculiarities (he says little of Neapolitans, which Berlioz put to good use). His surprising neglect to provide firm guidance on the handling of ⁶₄ chords may have licenced certain crudities in earlier Berlioz (see Chapter 7); Devienne's pieces for two flutes, because of the medium, are also occasionally licentious in this respect. Unquestionably, there are ways of reading Catel which, especially when we consider the isolation in which Berlioz studied, suggest predilections and attitudes inexplicable by reference to his other teachers or to musical models. Berlioz's only other harmony teacher was a student of Lesueur's, Hyacinthe-Christophe Gerono, a musician of modest attainments who joined Lesueur's class in 1823 after graduating in harmony and counterpoint. He doubtless reminded his sceptical contemporary of certain Rameau-based principles – musical manners, as it were – which would enable him to attend at Lesueur's table.

We really know very little about Berlioz's formal education. There are no grounds for Tovey's remark that 'He notoriously failed to learn anything that his masters tried to teach him; and . . . almost everything they tried to teach him was wrong' (TovEM 4, p. 75); nor even for Wotton's implication that his education was regular and thorough, and included ear-training at the piano (WotHB, 52ff). The facts appear to be that he attended Reicha's counterpoint class, from after his richly deserved failure in the preliminary round of the 1826 Prix de Rome competition until his report gave him 'Congé' in July 1828; he also attended Lesueur's composition class, but no others. The rules must have been stretched, thanks no doubt to Lesueur, since Berlioz was over-age at entry and should have graduated in harmony before doing counterpoint, and counterpoint before composition.[30] In 1828 he took second Prix de Rome, and competed twice more. We possess another fugue, passable this time, of 1829, and three complete cantatas, with fragments of the winning *Sardanapale* of 1830. We do not possess any classwork; there are no documents to testify to the nature and thoroughness of his studies such as have emerged for Mendelssohn and Wagner.

We can only deduce that Reicha must have taught the things covered by Cherubini's treatise: species counterpoint, invertible counterpoint, and fugue. Reicha himself does not cover all these points in his treatises, which tend more to be analytical and speculative than pedagogical. In his *Traité de haute composition*, of which the second volume appeared in the year Berlioz became his pupil, he unhelpfully informs us that 'the words counterpoint and harmony are synonymous'. He regarded counterpoint in exactly the opposite light from Catel, as the animation of harmony. Berlioz testifies, however, to the practical efficiency of his teaching – 'he taught me a lot in a few months and with few words' – and acknowledged that he tried to justify rules as far as possible (Mem13). Reicha should certainly be given some of the credit for the improvement in Berlioz's handling of conventional techniques without which, it must be admitted, the major works could not have been accomplished. There may be a more general influence, not from Reicha's often eccentric but rather feeble compositions, but from other aspects of his teaching. His harmony treatise broke new ground by including a short manual of instrumentation, and in the counterpoint sections of the composition treatise he discusses imitation and fugue in all kinds of composition, including symphony and opera, and distinguishes between 'rigorous' and 'free' styles, the latter regarded clearly as modern, and expressive. This might have appealed to Berlioz and provided an example; but there is no evidence, so far as I am aware, that he studied these interesting volumes, and we cannot know how much time was spared to discuss such matters in class.

Even less of a technical nature can be discovered about Lesueur's teaching. As his class was in composition it seems likely that his teaching took the form of advice on work submitted rather than the prescription of exercises. His compositions and aesthetic convictions, for example about the desirability of using modern expressive means in sacred music, certainly had some impact on Berlioz; but his greatest contribution to his pupil's development was probably his belief in Berlioz's genius, which he was the first to recognize and champion against his colleagues and the composer's family. Berlioz describes the end of the pupil–teacher relationship enigmatically, heading a chapter (Mem20) with 'Persistance de Lesueur dans son opinion systématique'. The word 'system' suggests harmonic theory; the context suggests an aesthetic difference of opinion, arising from

Lesueur's failure to accept the experience of Beethoven. A child of the eighteenth century, he objected to being so moved – ' "ému, troublé, bouleversée" ' – that ' "when leaving my box and wanting to put on my hat, I thought I couldn't find my head" ' (*ibid.*).

Berlioz probably learned most from Lesueur when he was a private pupil, in a period (1823–6) from which nearly all his compositions are lost (the published romances proudly headed 'Elève de M. Lesueur' were composed before their meeting). Official attendance at Lesueur's class thereafter probably amounted to little more than a continuing friendly relationship with some overtones of discipleship, and a sop to red tape. Already, in 1825–6, Berlioz had written the *Scène héroïque* and the first version of *Les francs-juges*, works which show that if his imagination outstripped his technique, it was not by very far. To all intents and purposes Berlioz was self-taught, or taught by Beethoven, Weber, Spontini, and Gluck; the influence of these masters and his own native wisdom and intuition were always more powerful than the personalities and pedagogical methods of his teachers. Apart from the mechanics of counterpoint, from which his musical technique unquestionably benefited, he had completed his education before entering the Conservatoire; what more could Lesueur teach the composer of *Les francs-juges*?

THE GUITAR

Disagreement continues about the role in the formation of Berlioz's language of the only polyphonic instrument which he played to any standard. The negative effect of Berlioz's not being a pianist is generally agreed; the difficulty is to define any positive effect of his playing the guitar. The two factors are not wholly unrelated. Whether or not he picked out chords on the guitar, as Boulez alleges (see epigraph), he certainly did not pick them out on the piano. He remarked himself, while admitting that piano technique would have been useful to him: 'When I consider the frightful number of platitudes which the piano brings forth every day . . . I cannot but thank the chance which made it necessary for me to find out how to compose in silence and freely, and so guaranteed me from the tyranny of finger-habits, so dangerous to thought' (Mem4). Hiller expresses the typical view of the nineteenth-century pianist in arguing that lack of knowledge of the piano could never be turned to profit; Berlioz 'made a virtue of necessity in clinging to this illusion'.[31]

Berlioz certainly composed on paper, in silence, and not 'at the guitar'. The question raised in the epigraph, however, remains; or rather, the two questions. The major one, perhaps, concerns the efficiency of Berlioz's inner ear, which Boulez is not the first to doubt, and to which in a sense this whole study is devoted. The immediate question is whether trying things out on the guitar – as there seems little reason to doubt that he did – assisted him in his formative years in developing predilections for sonorities and progressions, personal clichés different from those of the contemporary *lingua franca*.

Berlioz learned the guitar only from about his sixteenth year, but he continued to play it much later, and in the 1820s gave lessons. Most of what he composed for it is conventional, consisting of accompaniments to romances and original pieces which come into the category of theatrical effects – serenades or songs which would be sung in a play, such as the original form of Mephistopheles's serenade (Cat. 32A/8), and two numbers each in *Benvenuto* (Cat. 23C/1, 15) and *Béatrice* (Cat. 42/9, 12).[32] These pieces are expertly written, of course; but what matters is whether Berlioz's general style was affected by this expertise.

Tiersot considered the influence of the guitar to be evident, and deleterious, leading to harmonic habits which pianism would have eradicated; he speaks of bad habits 'contracted in childhood', like a disease.[33] Wotton is more specific, and does not condemn:

> his partiality for chords in root position [may have had] its origin in the greater resonance of the three lower strings of the guitar – in the first inversion of common chords, the third would be apt to be too prominent. That the thumb alone has to attend to these three lower strings may possibly account for a certain stiffness in his bass-line (WotHB, 59).

This is certainly evidence of a kind, although Berlioz uses inversions where roots are expected almost as often as the reverse; he may well have developed a liking for bass-heavy inversions precisely from the guitar's resonance.

The principal arguments for the guitar influence are given by Dallman (DalIU). Nevertheless some scholars take a contrary view. Macdonald considers the claim that Berlioz's harmonic idiom is founded in guitar practice 'has too weak a technical basis to be convincing' (MacNG, 599), while Holoman says: 'that Berlioz's vertical sonorities and voice-leading are rooted in the capabilities and limitations of the guitar is . . . far-fetched; that his harmonic practice was greatly affected by his early experience as a guitar player is unlikely' (1975b, pp. 44–5). No-one doubts, however, that the orchestral music of numerous composers is affected by their pianism, even if the results are as different as Schumann from Skryabin. There seems no inherent reason why a guitar-based training should not have an analogous effect. Since there is no question of the guitar, any more than Catel, being responsible for all Berlioz's divergences from the norm, the matter is scarcely capable of having a watertight 'technical basis'. It is a practical question open only to circumstantial demonstration – a network of instances, not proof.

In good guitar-writing the best sonority of the individual chord may be more important than the linear direction of the bass; hence sonority rather than line might dictate the choice of inversions or root positions in Berlioz's orchestral music. Berlioz's fondness for parallel motion in diminished 7ths and $\frac{6}{3}$ chords could reflect the ease of such procedures on the guitar, resulting from the sliding of a fixed finger-position or the use of the 'bar'. On the guitar it is easy and agreeable to relate major and minor chords rooted a semitone, tone, or minor 3rd apart (Ex. 30A), whereas a diatonic succession involves finger-changes (Ex. 30B, which is not difficult, but which would not arise from exploratory doodling). Exact parallelism is unnatural to the piano, for which the hand has to be continually adjusted for the black notes. The diminished 7th slides easily on the guitar (Ex. 30C) and resolves easily in different directions since the same fingering produces resolutions into a different key if the hand is moved up a minor 3rd (Ex. 30D indicates the necessary enharmony). The guitar is also more conducive than the piano to modal mixture, as it is easier to relate E major, for instance, to E minor, than to the relative C♯. The unexpected change of mode of one chord can produce an anti-tonal or modal effect. Dallman cites the opening of the 'Agnus' as an example both of guitaresque parallelism and mode-change, since the B♭ chord is identical in fingering to A major, and the unexpected A minor chord results from the lifting of a single finger (Ex. 30E; DalIU, 145–6).

Ex. 30

There is further evidence of this kind in DalIU. A few points may be added from pieces which use the guitar; they tend to bear out the idea that unusual basses may result from convenient fingerings. A chord-progression in

Mephistopheles's serenade in its guitar version (Ex. 31A) was altered when the piece was orchestrated (Cat. 32B/12C; Ex. 31B, transposed to E for comparison). The original uses an incorrectly resolved $^6_4$ and the bass lacks direction; passably sonorous on the guitar, the progression sounds disastrous 'in black and white'. The revision makes the bass linear, and replaces the simple subdominant with a supertonic 7th.

Ex. 31

The most original use of the guitar in Berlioz, because it owes nothing to the bucolic or convivial associations of the instrument, is the wedding hymn in *Béatrice* (No. 12). Dallman notes the use of diminished 7ths and parallel motion (DalIU, 82ff; see Ex. 32). Such things might come in any Berlioz piece, of course, but they work to perfection in this light ensemble, heard off-stage, using only higher voices. Also noteworthy is the relation between the guitar and the lowest voice (tenors). The guitar bass is sometimes in unison, sometimes an octave below, but in bar 6 ('x' in Ex. 32A) it forms a root position where the voices have a first inversion. A guitar G♯ would not be difficult to finger. Berlioz clearly wanted the open-string sonority of the E.

Ex. 32

Ex. 32 (contd)

(On the last beat the divergence must be simply to secure the progression without disturbing the smooth tenor line, as the guitar's root is not an open string.) In bar 20 the guitar projects its figuration into the lower octave, and in bar 22 it forms a root position below the tenors' 7th ('x' in Ex. 32B). Elsewhere the guitar skips a 7th instead of moving by step with the tenors, again securing an open string ('y' in Ex. 32A). The cause is ease of fingering and sonority; the result a divergence between the two lines bearing the bass which produces an ambiguity of function. Similar things are often encountered in Berlioz's orchestral music (see Chapter 6).

In bars 13–15 the top voice has an exact sequence, but the tenors, preserving their echo, begin from E instead of C♯ (Ex. 32C). Berlioz here desired the strength of the guitar's E string although it makes the chord into an inversion. At the end the gentle grating of the flat 6th (see above, p. 28) lies beautifully under the hand (Ex. 32D); who can say whether such an idea is dictated by the ear or the fingers? Since things natural to the guitar but not to nineteenth-century norms do appear in Berlioz's characteristic polyphony when he is not using the guitar, it seems fair to conclude that, for good or ill, the early study of the guitar was certainly productive of singularity of utterance and probably did have a permanent if limited effect on his musical thought.

CHARACTERISTICS OF EARLY BERLIOZ

The first works Berlioz made public were romances for voice and piano (Cat. 1). The romance must have formed a large part of his early musical diet, although the repertory known to him did not include what Noske (with apology for an apt pleonasm) calls 'the romantic Romance' (NosFS, 12ff), a development contemporaneous with Berlioz's own stretching of the form, in *Irlande* (Cat. 12), towards the 'mélodie' (*ibid.*, 93ff). It is a tribute to Berlioz's natural inventiveness that hints of such stretching occur in the earliest songs.

These survive by the curious accident of premature publication, whereas all larger works before the *Resurrexit* (Cat. 3) have been lost; and they survive in their original forms, whereas the *Resurrexit*, *Scène héroïque*, and *Orphée* exist only in manuscripts slightly later than composition and thus, possibly, representing revised versions. The most fruitful comparison across the decade is thus also the only possible comparison – between songs, in which Berlioz attained maturity (with the *Huit scènes* and *Irlande*) just ten years after we first hear of him trying to publish some.

My examples for comparison, probably written just ten years apart, have some similarity of character. Both are unpretentious pastorals, in compound time; and for all the necessary accidentals in the mature song, it is Berlioz's diatonic habits which they illustrate best. *Le dépit de la bergère* (Cat. 1A) may well be Berlioz's first published work. It shares with some of the other early songs the characteristic, which may be significant, that its piano accompaniment falls naturally under a guitarist's hand with slight modifications, whereas it sounds stiff on the piano. Ex. 33 shows a 'reconstruction' of a purely hypothetical original of *Le dépit*; it is not supposed that Berlioz ever wrote the piece down for guitar, but he might well have tried it over, and been influenced in his layout by the instrument to which he had access.[34]

This song has natural precocity, and is not bad for a boy of under eighteen with virtually no training. Its chief quality is an engaging melody, which Berlioz used again when possessed of a more assured technique, as a siciliano (Cat. 42/2bis). The harmony, however, would not do for the Berlioz of 1860, even if the guitar 'version' needs less touching up than the authentic setting

Ex. 33

for piano. In suggesting improvements I am mindful of Schumann's remark that to 'correct' Berlioz is to deprive his music of its character and produce a platitude (ConFS, 235). To put the blue pencil to *Le dépit*, however, is not to desecrate a monument, nor, I hope, to take the piece too seriously; and Berlioz himself made changes for his 'Sicilienne' which change the harmonic rhythm completely. In *Le dépit* itself he also provided an alternative harmonization for the opening of the melody, in the introduction which was probably added after composition of the verse (it is omitted from Ex. 33 because it is less evidently disguised guitar music). This introduction attempts a pianistic, linear bass – D–C♯–B for D–A–D – which is, however, bad because the C♯ doubles the melody and is approached by similar motion (Ex. 34, at 'x'). The best bass for both introduction and verse would surely be in contrary motion, as on the additional staff in Ex. 34; this shows what any student should write – a platitude, no doubt, but secure and pleasant to the ear (it requires adjustment to the lower notes in the right hand). It is also consistent with Berlioz in that it takes the quavers to be anticipations of the next harmony, and it restores the suspension of C♯ over G in bar 2 (the best feature of the verse – Ex. 33 bar 10 – inexplicably changed in the introduction).

The second phrase in the introduction appears unsure when to change chord. The supertonic appears on a half-bar (bar 5), and is held over to the next strong beat. Berlioz later exploited metrical ambiguities of this kind, but here the melody remains unperturbedly regular. The sudden drop to *pianissimo* makes no effect because there is no chord-change; and the treble and bass make poor counterpoint (doubling G in bar 5). The ⁶₄ on the

Ex. 34

second beat of bar 6 sounds clumsy and cannot be justified as an arpeggiation of the bass within a prolonged $^6_3$ on G. In the 'Sicilienne' Berlioz adopted a harmonic rhythm of one chord per bar. Ex. 35A shows how he harmonized the first phrase from *Le dépit* on its occurrence in the major, transposed from A for ease of comparison with Exx. 33–4. (The 'Sicilienne' is in F♯ minor: its opening phrase, incidentally, has the mediant in the bass on the second beat of the first bar – if Ex. 35A were in D minor,

Ex. 35

A

this would be an F♮ – to make an augmented 5th with the melody; experiment shows how much less pleasing the same thing would be in the major, with a perfect 5th.) The other phrase taken from *Le dépit* (Ex. 35B) uses an accented passing-note (bar 11; cf. Ex. 34, bar 5; Berlioz's is clearly a better 'correction' to *Le dépit* than mine in Ex. 34).

B

In the remainder of the verse of *Le dépit* (Ex. 33), the dominant arrives prematurely (bar 18) to be retained onto the strong beat; bar 18 would be better all tonic. By bar 22 we have had a surfeit of rootless 9ths, and a supertonic (bass G) on the second beat would better prepare the full dominant of the next bar. These last passages do not appear in the 'Sicilienne', but would doubtless have been altered if they had, with the mature technique which unerringly removes the unintentional idiosyncrasy, or simply the clumsiness, of youth.

La belle voyageuse (Moore's 'Rich and rare'; Cat. 12D) combines a similar rustic naivety with considerable sophistication. Hiller tells us that Berlioz said it was written over a fortnight, 'a couple of bars each morning, like a counterpoint exercise'.[35] After the gauche symmetries of *Le dépit* the rhythm is refreshingly elastic, but there is a measure of repetition to bind the verse, the second line repeating the rhythm of the first (table 2A). It would be more normal for the rhythm to run as in table 2B, which preserves Berlioz's 4 + 3 bar period, derived from the poem. But it is the fact that the girl travels alone – 'seulette' – that matters; and its lengthened syllable initiates a series of extensions and accelerations which work with the harmony into a more refined and delicate balance.

Table 2

The harmony also departs from the obvious (Ex. 36). The first line moves simply, if by no means normally to the subdominant. By a further subdominant plunge (D to G), the repetition is a tone lower, and ends in C♮ major, Berlioz's favourite ♭III. Berlioz gets there by an unusual route, but escapes by the easy one, taking ♭III as diatonic mediant of A minor. One might ask, however, whether the return to A major in three bars is not premature; the remotest point, C major, is only half-way through the verse.

Ex. 36

Ex. 36 (contd)

The direction of the third line is towards the dominant, a necessary corrective to the early flatward move and one which suggests a prolonged perfect cadence. Here Berlioz puts the backward progression V–IV to good use (see above, p. 45). There is no perfect cadence, only a long plagal fall. Precisely when the melody reaches its highest point, the harmony relaxes and broadens (bar 27); the orthodox cadence, charmingly handled, follows in the instrumental coda. The rhythmic diminution in the voice (bars 27–9; table 2A line 4 shows how 'efface' is hastened and the expected long note withheld for 'perle') brings it to an end on a half-bar. This combination of events is a wholly Berliozian piece of daring in which tension is maintained in an impossible situation (created by the early return of I and V) by causing the different elements to act out of phase.

One certainly cannot 'correct' *La belle voyageuse* as one can *Le dépit*, for a change in harmony requires a change in the melody, not just in an inner part. In this at least the elements are in phase; there is no escaping the move to ♭III without writing a different piece. Ex. 37 offers an attempt at normalizing the first line and the last two. In Ex. 37A the rhythm is that of table 2B, and the supertonic is prolonged by conventional chromaticism (bar 9). In Ex. 37B the root-position tonic is avoided (bar 24), at the cost of

Ex. 37

Ex. 37 (contd)

precipitous chord-change and a too jaunty melody (there is however a mildly Berliozian enharmony – broken slur). To avoid the V–IV would be to depart too far – and nothing even in theory can improve Berlioz's characteristic subdominant pedal (bars 26–8) – but the cadence can be normalized by cutting the value of 'perle' to squeeze in a V–I cadence.

But this time Schumann's caution is justified. If not platitudes – they are too near Berlioz for that – my versions lack 'rustic originality'[35] and their technical solidity is also predictability, even heaviness. Berlioz presents all the necessities of musical sense, but in a new balance. He uses a chain of 5ths, but not diatonically; each diatonic step bears a major triad, and is a perfect 5th, so from I he reaches ♭III. The tonic is restored with a $\substack{6 \\ 4}$ chord, duly resolved and followed by a root-position tonic; but this happens as early as the third line. He ends not IV–V–I but V–IV–I. Each oddity springs from the one before. A minor (bar 21) 'explains' C major, the emphatic dominant of line 3 counters the subdominant moves, the subdominant of line 4 prevents the tautology of another perfect cadence. As if to demonstrate both his independence and his acceptance of the norm, Berlioz rationalizes things in the coda, using a diatonic mediant (iii), repeating the appoggiatura of bar 8 in bar 37 as a perfect cadence, and reaching his close by a diatonic chain of 5ths from the sharp side: VI–ii–V–I (VI being a perfectly normal auxiliary dominant).

Evidently Berlioz had learned a lot since *Le dépit*. There is no doubt, also, that the more elaborate technique of the later song – the 'contrapuntal exercise' – is the product of more genuine feeling. The music adventures further, but makes no blunders such as misplaced $\substack{6 \\ 4}$ chords or inept basses (admittedly this is a very simple, even guitaresque, bass with most chords in root positions, a mobile drone). Harmonic change is nearly all on the strong beat, and against this firm background the melody can float with greater metric freedom, syncopating elegantly and disguising the still regular phrase-lengths.

No parallel picture of Berlioz's early development, of increasing security of technique coupled with greater originality of idea, can be made with larger works. The *Symphonie fantastique* did not, however, arise out of nothing. If the *Resurrexit* (Cat. 3) is crude, the more so when later uses of its ideas are more familiar, the *Scène héroïque* (Cat. 4) already marks an advance in the handling of large forces. It is a stiff and artificial conception, but there is real power in its choruses: in the first (No. 2), a grand crescendo and the climactic progression shown in Ex. 19; in the finale another crescendo using space, a combination of themes at bar 168ff, and an unprepared outburst of ♭III for coda (bar 219); between them, setting them off, a tender prayer making use of parallel motion in a Gluckian fashion, but anticipating the prayer of Trojan women, also in 6/8 and broadly lyrical in conception. Then came *Les francs-juges* (Cat. 6). It is unfortunately more than half lost, even given what can be detected as surviving in other works. In what survives complete, the music is fiercely original in bursts, but rather stodgy when it tries to expand. The influence of admired operatic models – Spontini, Weber – seems to have led to rather conscientious results (a less surprising access of operatic good manners later afflicted the surviving parts of *La nonne sanglante*, Cat. 29). The Hymn has a brutal force, but the solos are developed at excessive length. The most promising scene, the hero's dream, is dismembered beyond recall, but some of it (although the extent of any alterations, apart from instrumentation, is unclear) forms the central movement of the *Symphonie funèbre*. In this form it has a lugubrious eloquence which provides a good contrast to its grander neighbours, but it still sounds like juvenilia amid work of 1840, whereas music composed in 1829 – the *Huit scènes*, *Cléopâtre*, probably the 'Marche des gardes du Franc comte' which became 'Marche au supplice' – works well in maturer surroundings. Of the *Francs-juges* overture there will be more to say later.[36]

Even the Prix de Rome cantatas do not provide a consistent picture of development. In some ways the most interesting is the first, *La mort d'Orphée* (Cat. 7), for it is quite without inhibition. Its best dramatic idea, the echo of Orpheus's song at the end, is outstandingly original and far more apposite in this context than in *Lélio* (needless to say it was not asked for by the librettist). The harmonic range of *Orphée* greatly exceeds that of any previous work, both diatonically and chromatically. The song which forms the basis of *Lélio* IV (echoed in V) is characterized by diatonic chords in which a stepwise bass bears root-position or first-inversion chords in strange juxtapositions of almost modal quality. The dominant (Ex. 38A, bar 17) is followed by an inverted supertonic, and the move to the mediant, which one would expect to be major (with an A♯ referring back as auxiliary leading-note to the submediant B minor), is contradicted by the diatonic mediant minor (with A♮, although nothing would need to be altered to accommodate the A♯). As if in response to this ambiguity, Berlioz eliminated the submediant of bar 16 in *Lélio*, replacing it by a subdominant $^6_3$ (same melody and bass).

The very opening of *Orphée* (Ex. 38A, from bar 1) must have been sufficient to throw the pianist whose job it was to play the work to the judges (Mem 14). It is the sort of orchestral conception which defies reduction for two hands, a rapturous texture of ripplings and birdsong, anticipating the opening of *La damnation*. It begins, moreover, with the sort of harmonic adventure which is

Ex. 38

Ex. 38A (contd)

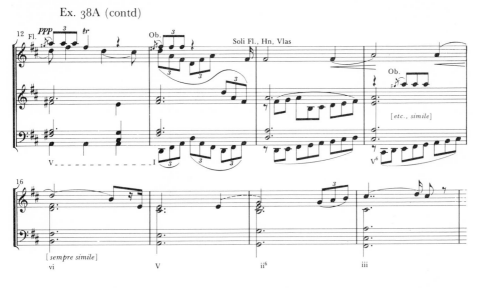

crippled when reduced to black and white, whereas orchestral performance does not so much disguise this discomfort but justifies the audacity by allowing it to bloom. (As the cantata is difficult to obtain I include a few bars of only slight reduction before resorting to a harmonic skeleton.) Berlioz first darkens the music by the tonic minor, then returns to a major 3rd with sharp 5th (or flat 6th) as a step towards the remote ♭ii of bar 6 (motivically balancing bar 3). This pun partner to the tonic is inflected to become V⁷ of A♭ (as easy as falling out of bed; see above, p. 38). The remote tritone is unsure of its position; the linear approach is to a $^6_3$ but it is adjusted to a root position by non-linear means (bar 9). A diminished 7th declares itself no less related to D minor than to A♭ (bars 10–11) and an augmented 6th precedes the cadence. The two-stage reduction in Ex. 38B shows a characteristic chromatic disposition of outer parts with a strongly directed move (bass, tonic by step to dominant; treble, mediant through chromatic steps to dominant) disguised by the intervention of the pun and the exchange of position of the A♭/G♯ in bars 9–11.

Ex. 38B

In *Herminie*, Berlioz remembered his manners, and despite several interesting features and fine ideas it is less novel than *Orphée*. *Cléopâtre* shows Berlioz's inventiveness still occasionally outstripping his powers of control, and although it is the best of these cantatas there are moments of stylistic uncertainty, as though the composer, confident of victory, began to let himself go but then thought better of it. An instance is the introduction to the first aria (Ex. 39). The straining violins are astonishing; the dissolution of

Ex. 39

their implied dominant prolongation (from bar 82) into a chromatically approached subdominant (88) is wonderfully expansive; bars 88–91 are a marvel, the first version of a phrase made famous only in its third use, in *Le carnaval romain*. And the reiterated cadence of bars 92–3, instead of binding these disparate ideas together, is a platitude. It may be an echo of Gluck (it is like bars 4–5 of Alceste's tremendous aria 'Ombre, larve' – in French 'Divinités du Styx'), but what is consistent with Gluck's idiom – and so, if a cliché, perfectly in place – is a sad let-down here.

The fourth cantata, *Sardanapale* (1830), is a fascinating fragment; in context, the final clarinet solo must have been superbly effective. But even before *Cléopâtre*, early in 1829, Berlioz had published what Ernest Newman was to call 'certainly the most astounding Opus One that the world of music had ever known' (NewBR, 187), the *Huit scènes de Faust*. The simpler pieces in this collection required little alteration for inclusion in *La damnation*; even the elaborate 'Romance' already approaches its final form, although here as elsewhere the instrumental enrichments are very telling in the revision. The bigger pieces show that, from the standpoint of 1846 at least, Berlioz's imagination still reached beyond his command of clear and effective progression and fully realized sonority. The 'Easter Hymn' and 'Chorus of Sylphs' were really recomposed, eliminating ineffective instrumental detail, abbreviating the latter, and in the former purging certain crude harmonies of the opening phrase (where the later, simpler version is immeasurably richer; Ex. 40A and B) and removing some clangorous consecutive 5ths (Ex. 40C

Ex. 40

Ex. 40 (contd)

and D). All this is accomplished without the slightest loss of originality or freshness. All these works richly reward study, and they set the pattern for Berlioz's later vocal music. But it is with the symphony and overture that he came into his own; with *Waverley*, technically his most secure work of the 1820s, with the *Symphonie fantastique*, and with *Le roi Lear*.

PART II

6 Concerning instrumentation

'R. C.: What is good instrumentation?
I. S.: When you are unaware that it *is* instrumentation. The word is a gloss. It pretends that one composes music and then orchestrates it . . . It is not, generally, a good sign when the first thing we remark about a work is its instrumentation; and the composers we remark it of – Berlioz, Rimsky-Korsakov, Ravel – are not the best composers . . . Berlioz's reputation as an orchestrator has always seemed highly suspect to me.'

Robert Craft and Igor Stravinsky (*Conversations with Igor Stravinsky*, London, 1959, pp. 28–9)

Berlioz's output was predominantly vocal. Nevertheless, as is suggested at the end of the previous chapter, his first strikingly original work, and his first technically assured one, were both orchestral overtures; originality and assurance come together in the *Symphonie fantastique*. The instrumental dimension is in any case vital to much of the vocal music. Moreover, Berlioz's reputation as a virtuoso of the orchestra, as my epigraph may suggest, has tended to obscure the constructive (dare one say purely compositional) aspects of his work. Clearly instrumentation is an integral part of his language; he did not 'compose music and then orchestrate it'. It seems right, therefore, to isolate this element before proceeding to other polyphonic considerations.

I have already mentioned Bockholdt's view that Berlioz's music does not comprise *Satz* and instrumentation, for its sound is inseparable from its sense (see above, p. 24f). Bockholdt quotes Hanslick: 'If there were such a thing as fine instrumentation on its own – whereas in fact we must always consider *what* is instrumented – then "Queen Mab" would be in the highest rank of compositions'; 'To be a specialist in one branch of musical technique is not to be a composer. There is no such thing as fine instrumentation *per se*; the first question remains: what was instrumented?'[37] Even *Mab* (Cat. 25/IV), however, does not depend entirely on instrumentation for its effect; the harmony is indispensable to its quicksilver movement, its uncanny intensity.

We may not conclude, therefore, that orchestration is a governing factor in the polyphonic texture and formal design of Berlioz's music. He did not, of course, write music for piano and then orchestrate it, like Brahms and Debussy on occasion; the nearest he got to tackling the problem of transcribing idiomatic piano music was with Schubert's *Erlkönig* (Cat. 45) and Weber's *Aufforderung zum Tanze* (Cat. 44). He was only secondarily a technician of the orchestra, author of a remarkable treatise; his primary reputation rests on his orchestral *conceptions*. Nevertheless, as we have seen, Berlioz in fact instrumented after fixing the outlines of his polyphony, his *Satz* (above, p. 13). Holoman observes that it is at a secondary stage, the 'pencil draft', that 'Berlioz's brilliant orchestral effects originated' (HolCP, 177), and he cites three separate remarks of Berlioz to the effect that a work was 'finished' before being fully scored (*ibid.*, 173). Obviously, orchestral detail, however integral to the musical idea, cannot be notated until the outlines of pitch and rhythm are decided; but with the exception of a few outstandingly coloured passages, it may safely be said that the substance of Berlioz's music is separable from its instrumentation.[38] Schumann's appreciation of the *Fantastique* from a piano reduction is evidence enough. The orchestration enhances polyphony by the sensitivity of its textures; it renders counterpoints of pitch and rhythm intelligible to the ear; but they remain the creation of the intellect. As Berlioz put it himself, the proper deployment of instrumental resources 'is exactly, in music, what colour is in painting' (AT, 11/G, 28). In what follows, I do not attempt to study all aspects of Berlioz's handling of the orchestra (another subject fit for an entire book), but aim to suggest certain ways in which the orchestral conception is an especially significant aspect of the whole.

Instrumental writing is often of primary importance to the sheer impact of the music. Sonorities of accompaniment are a case in point; the ball music in *Roméo* II is a good example because its harmony is so static (*Fantastique* II has similar qualities). Ex. 41 is an arrangement of the three statements of the principal melody and its accompaniment, showing numbered layers of musical texture and their rearrangement. The violins leave the tune and (B) introduce a counterpoint; their return to the tune (C) goes with the arrival of a second counterpoint (the slow melody, now in bars of 3/1; see below, Ex. 74B). In the accompaniment the strings (A) have a characteristic rhythm impelled by the triplet; the bassoons take the triplet as an arpeggio and so link the string idea to the other winds, whose arpeggio is in quavers. This arpeggio changes colour, becoming pizzicato (B), and ending with the harps (C). At first (A) the registers overlap, the tune in octaves descending below the top of the string accompaniment, and the wind arpeggios rocketing above both. The texture is thinned (B), then thickened to a uniform block of sound (C). The saturation of register here supports the harmonic stasis, and the hysterical activity of the surface is impotent in the face of this combination. The passage is labelled by Berlioz 'Réunion des deux thèmes',

Ex. 41

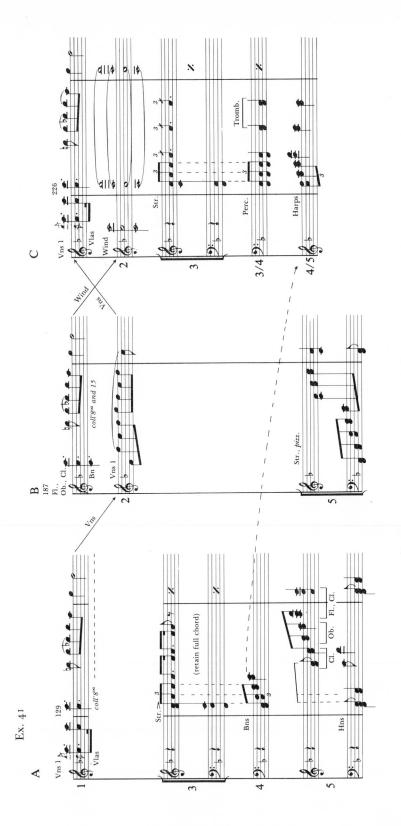

but is in fact a triple union, of two melodies and a thematic rhythm, reinforced by percussion (cf. the end of *Harold* III).

Ex. 41 shows how different strata of a composition, in one plane melody and accompaniment, in another timbre, may interlock and so articulate (not create) a formal pattern. The shifts in strata underline the shifting perspectives in the musical-dramatic conception (Cone, 1953). In only one composition does Berlioz actually separate musical ideas by timbre, so that the strata are rigidly distinct and interpenetrate only at the end; otherwise they collaborate in outlining similar (not necessarily identical) melodic and harmonic formations. This is in *Méditation religieuse* (Cat. 34A), which must have occupied a special place in Berlioz's affections, since he revised it for publication twenty-one years after its composition and partnered it with two superb newer pieces based on *Hamlet* (*Tristia*, Op. 18). At first sight (Ex. 42) the *Méditation* is a simple homophonic setting for chorus of Moore's poem(A), backed by wind; the strings provide a commentary. The strings are almost exclusively confined to a single motive, a falling semitone or tone (C), played twenty-two times in various octaves, and only once doubled in 3rds (bars 29–30). Very few additional notes are needed to define the harmonies (D). Although the wind announce the choral motive they also have their own material, punctuating and linking choral phrases, but largely independent in shape (B). At the end, the wind again become involved with the choral material, doubling and echoing. Otherwise the separation of groups is as near absolute as the language of the time allows.

Ex. 42

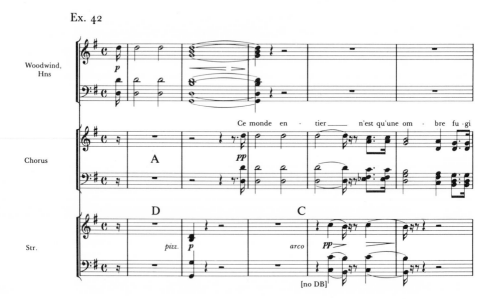

Ex. 42 (contd)

Table 3 shows the form of the whole piece in terms of stratification. Strand A is chorus, with some wind; strand B is woodwind and horns. Material which might be assigned to strand A, because it doubles the chorus, or to strand B, because played by the wind, is shown by broken lines; for instance, in bar 22 the wind enter doubling the chorus, although using the high register (defined in bars 11ff and 19–20 as the first flute's domain). At the chord-change the chorus stops on a quaver, the wind plays the dotted rhythm of its falling figure (Ex. 42, B), which is also used for repeated chords by the chorus (A).

Table 3

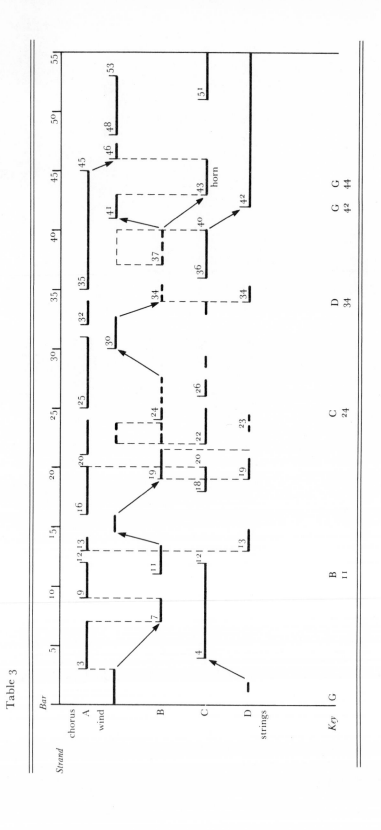

The string strand (C) is the most distinct. The fourth strand (D) consists of sustained notes, usually for double-basses, or other elements which serve to control progressions rather than function motivically. Thus in the coda (Ex. 43) strand D is the five-octave G (the upper parts bending to F♯ at the cadence). The choral material of bars 16 and 41 passes to the wind – note the low bassoons – and, the wind figure (Ex. 42, B) having disappeared, the string material passes to the horn. This magic is achieved more by shifting strata than by harmony, as luminously diatonic as anything in Berlioz. It is noteworthy that the strings take no part in the main cadences of the piece; they have a dominant in bar 39, then are silent until their octave Gs of bar 42.

It is unlikely that Berlioz set out to use distinct strata as a compositional principle, like Stravinsky.[39] Nevertheless he was alive to the effectiveness of separation of sonority and sound-source, and followed the idea up in several places, most obviously in the disposition of brass groups in the *Requiem* (Cat. 22) and 'Marche troyenne' (Cat. 40A/11). At the climax of the 'Tuba mirum' separate musical ideas are combined, although they are not exclusive to particular groups. The 'Lacrimosa' and 'Offertoire' are severely stratified compositions, but in the former the brass groups cooperate as one stratum, flinging notes or chords around the room rather in the manner of Stockhausen's *Gruppen*, while in the 'Offertoire' the separation is by techniques – fugue and pedal – as well as sonority. Few compositions contain elements of formal control by stratification.

Ex. 43

Ex. 43 (contd)

‘LA COURSE À L'ABÎME’

One that does, however, is 'La course à l'abîme' (Cat. 32B/18). Its musical material is so various, and it is so fluid in tonality and motivic shape, that its coherence is as much dependent on textures and submotivic phenomena as on key and shape. This is a claim which could reasonably be made of no more than a handful of nineteenth-century works.

The tonality of 'La course' appears to be C minor; but it is not only very restless from the start, it never returns beyond about half-way through. Parallel with this tonal dissolution, onto which no very cogent pattern can be imposed, is the dissolution of the opening texture and thematic structure. The formal elements of the opening play no part in the later stages. There is a clear phrase-articulation in the reprise (bar 54), and in the threefold choral chant (bars 20, 33, 47); but the third chant is incomplete, and the oboe, which managed to complete a C minor cadence to its first wandering phrase (bar 19), has no balancing pattern after the reprise. Tonal and phraseological description of the music is, therefore, of inordinate complexity; the music becomes rather a matter of illustration, an elaborate form of recitative. Yet it does not seem amorphous, mainly because of the ubiquitous rhythmic drive of the violins (hoofbeats).

Table 4 defines the various strands in terms of pitch, rhythmic characters, timbre, or another distinguishing element. Table 5 indicates the formal continuities and breaks down the movement in terms of these strands.

Table 4. *La course à l'abîme*

Strand	Bar of first use	Rhythmic or other characteristic	Instrumentation
A	1	♩ ♫	violins (later 'cellos)
B	1-2	♩ ♩ ♩ ♫	'cellos, basses, *pizz.*
C	2	melody, expressive	oboe
D	20	plainchant	chorus of women
E	61	low, sustained ⟨ ⟩	low brass, woodwind
F	67	triplets, repeated notes	strings, woodwind
G, G¹	72, 114	note-repetition (G¹ ♩ ♪♪ ♪♪)	high woodwind; G¹ woodwind, horns
H	97	oscillating, 3rds etc. ♩♩♩	low woodwind, basses
J	111/116	trill/roll	woodwind/percussion

Strand A persists throughout, although it loses some of its motivic, as opposed to rhythmic, definition. Strand B is purely a rhythmic-colouristic character. Both will fit practically any harmonic situation, but they are not dictated to by the oboe (strand C), whose cadence in bar 19 they interrupt, nor by the chorus (strand D), whose entries on the same pitch are differently harmonized. Harmonic progression is as much characterized by semitonal sliding as by functional relations: for instance, in bar 8 F minor moves to Gb (F♯) minor; a move from Gb (bar 10 of a C minor movement!) to its relative Eb minor is followed by a slide to E minor; and so on. Despite numerous dominants or near-dominants, no key shows signs of stability, and even in the opening oboe solo the phrase-structure is asymmetrical. A certain amount of interaction between oboe and chant defines the musical form until the brutal interruption of the latter at bar 52 ('Cri d'effroi').

The reprise from bar 54 is destroyed by strand E, the menace of sustained wind, at first isolated notes (trombone pedal), then a rudimentary polyphony in the lowest register. The triplets which enter among the strings from bar 67 (strand F) emerge forcefully in the wind as strand E reaches a climax (71). In a rare patch of harmonic stability from bar 73, the coarse cries of the woodwind, as of some monstrous bird, provide an idea of irregular reiteration which I have called strand G, resuming in different guise as G¹. (Such labels are scarcely definitive, however, as G¹ could be a new strand, and it certainly conforms with the triplets of strand F. The distinction is by timbre – string continuity for most of strand F, woodwind intervention for strand G/G¹.)

The form is governed by the increase of motivically amorphous elements, even as the tonality becomes so fluid as to defy attempts at reductive analysis (*pace* PriBS, 74–7). The passage around bars 70–85, where the horses slow down, is characterized by short bursts of alien strands; but at least it includes that sustained dominant of B minor. It *may* be significant that the goal of the movement is B major, the key of 'Pandaemonium', and that B major is the 'pun partner' of C minor. If so, however, Berlioz does his best to distract our ears from such connections. When the music resumes after the sound of the death-knell (bar 90), the oboe, which represents Margaret (the 'pauvre abandonnée'), tries again, in a foreign key (E♭ minor). Its final dissolution coincides with the entry of a new, motivically defined idea, strand H, which like strands A and B is capable of fitting any chord-progression. The last stages are characterized by the intervention of further elements, including the modification from pitched trill (the last note of strand H becoming strand J) to timpani roll, to the pitchless roar of rolled tamtam. These elements are simply superimposed; they no longer appear to react on each other, and the harmony leads a life of its own, remaining to the last as vagrant as possible.

ORCHESTRAL LAYOUT AND HARMONY

Several places in the *Méditation religieuse*, such as bars 6–9 and the coda (Exx. 42 and 43), and many in 'La course à l'abîme', notably the independent polyphony of strand D, seem to defy the classical norm of orchestration whereby each group of relatively homogeneous instruments (wind, brass) is polyphonically complete and conforms with the others in chord-structure, having the same bass. This practice is recommended by Reicha (*Cours complet*) and is normally followed by Berlioz in that his groups are independently complete. Berlioz was among the first to extend the principle to three groups, separating woodwind from brass, which he could do by extensive use of chromatic brass (trombones, piston cornets, ophicleide) and by scoring for four natural horns in up to four different keys (very occasionally he requires horns with pistons). In classical orchestration the groups will blend harmonically; the situation where natural brass, confined to the tonic area, break bounds and defy the prevailing tonality, is rare. A striking instance is in Beethoven's Ninth Symphony (I, bar 120ff); timpani and trumpets persist with A and D, mediants of dominant and tonic in the

Table 5

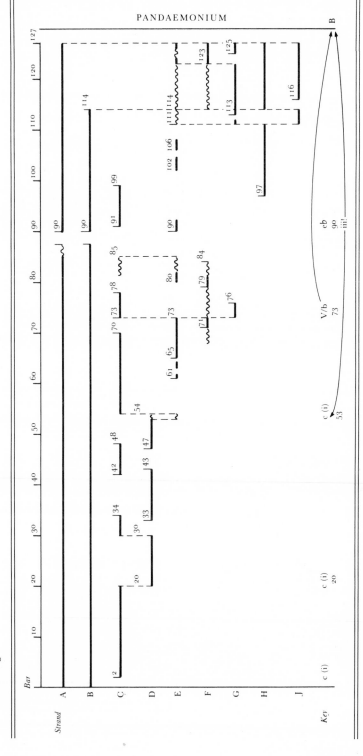

prevailing B♭. This effect is reversed by Berlioz with his intervention of trumpets in E in 'Chanson de brigands', see above, p. 20).

Berlioz usually had no need to break the blend, but he quite often chose to do so, using orchestration to distinguish strata of his polyphonic thought. In the *Méditation*, bars 6–9, the strings propose a low F♯ as fundamental; the chorus prefers the mediants, A♯ and A♮. In bars 23–4 Berlioz frankly disregards the usual principle: a stepwise, polyphonic bass (voices) reaches a cadence by G–A–B–C, while the string basses, in the same rhythm, propose a fundamental bass, C–F–G–C, with no kind of separation by other means. In 'La course' strand E acts independently of strands A, B, and F at the critical bar 67 where the oboe begins to fade; the strings have E major in root position, the brass in first inversion, the lowest note being the trombone pedal A♭. This effect, removing stability from the harmony and pointing up the conflict of strata, may in itself be deemed expressive. Nevertheless the reason for it is mechanical. Berlioz desired the colour of the trombone pedal; French orchestras used only tenor trombones, whose available pedal-notes are from G_1 to Bb_1; and thus the only pedal-note fitting the chord of E is G♯/A♭.[40] Strand E has its entire E major triad below the bass staff, the sort of gestural orchestration which in more normal contexts would simply sound bad. Again, in bar 71ff the acoustic bass and functional bass diverge; the larger context is the arrival on a dominant of B minor, expressed as a $^6_4$ resolved to a full dominant (which is however a 9th, bar 73). In bars 71–2 the sounding bass is first D, then F♯, making the B minor chord successively a $^6_3$, then a $^6_4$. The trombone pedal is indirectly responsible: the pedal G_1 cannot resolve onto $F\sharp_1$ and the trombone therefore ascends to G at the end of bar 70, leaving the bassoon and ophicleide below on D♭, then D♮.

Such nonconformity may well be associated with Berlioz's not being a pianist; he heard in polychrome, and was not disturbed by a conflict between such alternative basses. Nor is his music governed by a virtually autonomous harmonic direction, like Schumann's or Wagner's. If the harmony in 'La course' is independent, it is precisely because it lacks any overall sense of direction; continuity is assured by colour and, above all, by rhythm. In this manner of organizing musical forms by polyphonies of different kinds, rather than by a governing tonal direction, Berlioz seems to be the forerunner of Mahler and Stravinsky (both of whom, however, were fine pianists), and not typical of his own time. His threshold of dissonance is lower, but the principles behind Mahler's polyphonic thought and Stravinsky's more rigorous stratification are similar.

An expressive aim lies behind most of Berlioz's unorthodox orchestral dispositions. Sonorities with low mediants, whether in root-position or first-inversion chords, can sound particularly lugubrious, as at the opening of *Sur les lagunes* (Cat. 27C). The overall quality of a *tutti* is affected, since the low mediants set up resonances in conflict with the overtones of the fundamental.

Unexpected bass-notes have the effect of isolated gestures in contexts by no means emotionally extreme, seeming to provide a deeper perspective on the musical mood; for instance, at bar 159 of 'Scène aux champs', the double-basses conflict with the wind bass (second bassoon) (Ex. 44A). This is part of a tonic prolongation in the coda, so it is scarcely worth deciding which is the functional bass.

Ex. 44

Ex. 44 (contd)

More usually the brass section diverges, as in 'Songe d'une nuit de sabbat' at bars 467–72 (Ex. 44B). The chords are E minor, G⁷, and a diminished 7th. The strings and bassoon imply different chord-positions from the brass, and to confuse matters further the trombone goes below the brass bass (ophicleide) in the second chord. For this there is neither a contrapuntal nor a mechanical explanation. Normally, since he lacked a bass trombone, Berlioz could not adopt Schubert's practice of using one to double the bass-line extensively. In the richly expressive third statement of the lyrical melody in the slow section of *Lear*, Berlioz wished to withhold the ophicleide until the recovery of the tonic at bar 66; but the mediant harmonization (Ex. 44C) is brass-dominated. In bar 57 the movement of the string bass within the chord creates a slight ambiguity of position. In the next bar the trombone has a G because it cannot play the true bass, E♭; this discrepancy could only be resolved by creating another confusion, for to raise the third trombone to an octave above the bassoon would force a collision with the first, who is playing the melody.

A more complex case of orchestral strands producing an unexpected chord-position marks the climax of the introduction to *La damnation* (Cat. 32B/1) (Ex. 45). In the short term, an augmented 6th is to be resolved onto a

Ex. 45

dominant $^6_4$ at the recovery of the tonic, D. The larger context is the resolution of the structurally dissonant upper pedal B♭, in its turn a sequence of an upper pedal C♮ (bars 90 and 116ff; a fuller analysis of the movement is in RusBL, 60–64). The augmented 6th (second half of bar 134) is strangely positioned. The normal bass would be B♭ (Ex. 45B), which is ruled out by consecutive octaves with the resolving upper pedal. The best alternative, a bass G♯, is thwarted by the rising woodwind line, pushing chromatically through G♯ to A. Hence the main action of the augmented 6th resolving onto the dominant note is all in the treble register, in string and wind strata.

The remaining possible bass-note for bar 134 is thus D. Originally Berlioz retained this into bar 135, so that the augmented 6th resolved onto a $\frac{5}{3}$ (Ex. 45C: trombones and basses doubled the 'cellos in bar 135; this is the first reading of the autograph score and of the MS orchestral parts of 1846). Berlioz's revision, probably made after hearing the passage, produces a $\frac{6}{4}$ chord out of the blue. Clearly he felt the chord must be a $\frac{6}{4}$, but there was no contrapuntal approach possible. Berlioz seems to have recognized the anomaly, since he keeps the trombones on A and allows the basses to devise a reinforcement of the 'cello and bassoon descent through C♯; the basses touch A again at the end of the bar, then jump with the trombones to join the bass-line on C♮.

This works in performance because several factors overwhelm what might be considered a somewhat desperate remedy. The resolution of the B♭ onto A in the violins, helped by the wind G♯–A, unravels 45 bars of structural tension. The crescendo, the diminution of values in the upper pedal, the tremolo, the first trumpet entry of the work – all accentuate the heady, treble-dominated texture which the inverted pedal fosters. One's ear cannot be focussed on the bass-line. The tonal resolution is accomplished whatever position the chord is in; but the linearly approached $\frac{5}{3}$ would be too stable, and yet insufficiently like a real recovery, for which the $\frac{6}{4}$ is the expected sign (cf. Ex. 115 below). The accumulated dissonance requires more forceful resolution. Yet the $\frac{6}{4}$ is itself unstable because of the illogicality of the approach; and this serves Berlioz's larger purpose, which is to recover the tonic only to overthrow it by a still louder climax (adding a second trumpet, bar 138). Melodic and textural energies flow beyond the tonic, surging in stretto to a statement of the subject in G which is completed only after a truncated statement in C♮ (bar 141). There follows a short bridge to the dominant of E minor in preparation for the 'Ronde de paysans'. The critical $\frac{6}{4}$, then, is not only wrongly approached, it is scarcely resolved at all; the resolution of the dissonant 4th, C♯, is heard against a held D, and the true dominant chord never comes. The 'meaning' of the passage is given in Ex. 45D, but Berlioz elides the chord and its resolution within bar 135. How turgid would the more orthodox pedal have been, or some more respectable version of the underlying idea! The simultaneous recovery and overthrow of a tonic is the brilliant result of thinking in orchestral strata, free of the fetters of routine.

All this shows that Berlioz was no orchestrator. He was a thinker in orchestral terms. His music does not take the form of a homogeneous discourse on a single plane, but of a diversification, a polyphony of perspectives, which may find its expression in thematic and rhythmic combinations, in curious tonal connections, or in the separation of orchestral layers. Instrumental stratification is another strand in his polyphonic thought, now apparently conscious (as in the *Méditation*), now affecting only a passing moment (Ex. 44), now tending to the unorthodox and exhilarating climactic point ('La course' and Ex. 45).

'AUTHENTICITY'

I have referred to problems of the trombones usually available to Berlioz. He could certainly have written the affected passages otherwise; the limitations of the instrument do not hamper him but actually suggest solutions of particular expressive weight. It follows that in performance Berlioz's very detailed instrumental specifications should be borne in mind when deciding on the balance of orchestral forces and the choice of instruments.

When we listen to a Berlioz *tutti* today, we nearly always hear qualities of sound unknown to him. Particularly this must apply to the plangent voices of the brass. Both horns and trombones now have wider bores, and the former often use a different mouthpiece.[41] The sound is broader, somewhat coarser; this is the price we pay for avoiding cracked notes, for the modern forms of these intractable instruments are easier to play. Other, less fundamental, modifications affect the rest of the orchestra, including percussion.

It does not, perhaps, matter much if we do not hear the works as Berlioz did, nor even as he would have liked to, given the state of affairs in his time. What does matter is that we should hear them as Berlioz would have wanted them given the state of our modern orchestras. To do this it is essential to recognize the changes that have taken place; and to translate into present-day reality the practical directions he gave, for tempi, articulation, and numbers and disposition of performers. Much can be done to mitigate the effect of structural changes in the instruments, or of their obsolescence. The ophicleide is a noble instrument, but it would be foolish to take it into a modern orchestra with modern trombones; the blend, or lack of it, would be quite wrong. But there is no need to replace it with the huge BB♭ tuba, whose bore, weight, and timbre are post-Wagnerian. The tenor, or euphonium, just because it would not be using its ideal register, is a better modern approximation. The 'Dies irae' in the *Fantastique* V, a movement in which timbre is of especial importance, is usually very remote from the sounds Berlioz imagined. The bells, for which he required g and c' or *lower* (see his piano notation, bar 102ff, on G_1–G–g; see also NBE 16, p. xv), usually sound g' and c". The modern bass tuba replaces the ophicleide and turns a harsh parody into a Falstaffian romp.[42]

We may desire in vain the lovely sound of the true French horn; but at least the prevalent German or American type can observe with precision which notes Berlioz expected to be played stopped. The effect he intended cannot otherwise be obtained, at such crucial points as the opening of the 'Marche au supplice'; certainly not by mutes, for the piece mingles open and stopped notes. In the woodwind, clarinettists should use the C instrument where prescribed. Berlioz did not write for B♭ or C clarinets simply to conform with a key-signature. The *Fantastique* I is predominantly in C, yet he uses B♭ clarinets; conversely the 'Marche au supplice' is in G minor and B♭, but the more abrasive C instrument is prescribed and retained, with the small E♭, in the finale. As for bassoons, the modern instrument is again German, and was not known anywhere in Berlioz's time. The French bassoon, now seldom played, has a markedly different and more highly characterized tone-colour – drier, crisper, capable of great sweetness – and this is what the nineteenth century knew. The German instrument is easier to handle, but makes the wrong sound.[43]

But, it will be objected, Berlioz was enthusiastic for new developments in instrumental design. He was an expert, who acted as juror in the Great Exhibition; his treatise urges the application of the Boehm system to all the woodwind family. Appreciation of mechanical improvements, however, is not an open-ended commitment to 'progress'. He welcomed increased flexibility, the elimination of fingering impossibilities; he liked the increased security of intonation (the very first words of Devienne's flute tutor, which he used as a boy, concern intonation). He was happy to write, throughout his career, for new instruments; first the piston cornets and ophicleide, later valved horns, tuba, and occasionally saxhorns; the revived cor anglais; the bass clarinet. This does not entitle us to ignore the changes that new resources make in the sound and effect of music composed earlier. The *Traité* contains a clear warning to horn-players and conductors not to neglect, when valves are used, the composer's intentions when writing stopped notes, for this would actually constitute, in his view, a retrograde step, a diminishing of the instrument's powers of expression.

An 'authentic' performance of Berlioz is a complex conception. We do not always know which he would have preferred of the many alternatives encountered in a busy career. Doubtless he accepted the use of tubas and trumpets in German orchestras for his ophicleides and cornets; but did he prefer them? and exactly what were they, anyway? Such questions arise everywhere (but at least there seems no reason to doubt the accuracy of Berlioz's metronome). There are also problems with numbers. Berlioz's admirers are rightly at pains to point out that much of his best music, far from being grandiose, is quite intimate in scale. Nevertheless Berlioz shared with Mozart a taste for hearing his works given by large forces, even when immense volume is not required. He often specified numbers for strings and choirs as well as wind, in which we ought to observe at least his care for proportion. He expected more double-basses in relation to 'cellos than is now normal; his parts for them are remarkably independent and they sometimes provide a bass to quite large groups (see below, p. 107). Again, what he specified in certain circumstances, even in print, is not necessarily identical to what, in practice, won his approval. In *La damnation* he specified choral numbers very exactly: a minimum of sixty singers equally divided, ten to a part, with more men in 'Pandaemonium'. But this is only in the autograph. One number (Cat. 32A/3) was written in 1829 for six solo voices, and found ineffective in performance. In *La damnation* he contemplated a 'petit choeur' for this 'Choeur de sylphes' (Cat. 32B/7B), but may have allowed his sixty or so singers to do it, for in Mem26 he declares that he only realized its full effect when it was given by a choir of eighty. And in letters from Vienna in 1866 he declares his delight in hearing it sung by 250 voices (NBE 8b, Foreword). On this last occasion all forces were increased in proportion, with doubled woodwind.

The pursuit of archaeological exactitude in such matters is impractical, even if it is desirable. It is right to feel that what matters most is the spirit of the music; but it is only accessible through the letter, and distortion of that can distort meaning. Beecham's recording of *Lear*[44] doubles the string basses from bar 544 with the tuba, presumably because the bass theme did not sound powerful enough against the violent *tutti*. Certainly by comparison with bar 340ff, where violas, ophicleide, and woodwind are added, the later passage sounds weak indeed. It is also in slower values. It presumably did not occur to the conductor that Berlioz's bass theme is associated with the eponymous monarch, and that his growing weakness of mind and body is reflected in the change to his theme. Where such clear programmatic signposts are not available we should be all the more careful, for the letter and spirit of Berlioz's music are ultimately inseparable.

7   Concerning the bass

> 'for a few moments I try to concentrate upon the neuroticism, at once strident and flimsy, of Berlioz's music . . . Heavens! the bluster of noise the orchestra is making, and all about nothing, with no particular bass to be heard! It is like the gambollings of some monstrous, footloose creature – a drunken walrus, perhaps.'
>
>   Arnold Bax (*Farewell my Youth*, London, 1943, p. 84)

Berlioz's detractors, and even his admirers, if they deal with technique at all, infallibly seize on his basses as the subject for critical comment. The detractors are not all academics; to Bax and Boulez (composers as divergent in aim as possible: see epigraphs to Chapter 5 and this chapter) may be added Stravinsky: 'His basses are sometimes uncertain and the inner harmonic voices unclear'.[45] It cannot be assumed that these musical intelligences suffered an identical malfunction of the ear when confronted with Berlioz. There is no doubt that his choice of bass would often not have been made by anyone else.

It is not easy, however, to define where the differences arise. Macdonald has tried:

> Much has been said about Berlioz's 'false' basses and his love of root positions, both of which are clear misrepresentations. A root position is sometimes disturbing when it anticipates a cadence on to the same root, but Berlioz preferred a smooth, often stepwise, movement to the striding pattern of a functional bass. The bass line is in free counterpoint with the upper line, with harmonic filling. (MacNG, 599)

Most of this is unexceptionable; but it is only too easy to find exceptions to the 'smooth, often stepwise' pattern. I turn to a 'black and white' example, the lovely *Prière du matin* (Cat. 36D) – a mature piece, but deliberately simple, and scored for high voices with piano accompaniment (Ex. 46; the piano right hand, which largely doubles the voices, is omitted, and vocal rhythms are simplified to eliminate minor deviations between strophes). We cannot ascribe any curious features to irregular melodic phrases here, for every phrase lasts eight bars. The final cadence is very obviously *not* smooth or stepwise; nor is the bass of phrase A; yet B and C have a smooth, singing line.

Ex. 46

In phrase A, bars 7–9, the obvious linear bass to the top part (beneath the staff) inevitably doubles the leading-notes in the lower voice's imitation; the bass has to use the roots. The anticipated D (bars 9–10) is likewise inevitable; but the bass is still 'striding', 'functional'. In phrase B the stepwise movement attains its first goal, C, from A through B (broken slur). Simple minims (beneath staff) would define the harmonic direction better, and could be adapted to become the type of pliable, singing bass – at once a counterpoint and a harmonic controller – so expertly manipulated by Schumann. It is characteristic of Berlioz that the goal *is* reached, but without such evident purposefulness. Instead he has an ambiguous line that turns back through chromatic degrees to its point of departure, reaching the goal a bar later. Why? surely because this sinuous indirectness is itself expressive.

Berlioz twice uses an appoggiatura at cadences (bars 22, 30) but avoids one at bar 26 (the V could easily have come in bar 25; see below staff). The half-close in E minor at the end of phrase B is approached through the ambiguity of a passing $^6_4$ followed by a diminished chord, also in second inversion (bars 15–16); yet the opening of phrase C is, while chromatic, entirely orthodox in its combination of linear descent to the dominant and fundamental direction to the temporary repose on the subdominant (bar 22).

Phrase D, however, is undoubtedly odd. Another dividing subdominant (bar 30) is approached through a feint at the supertonic (A minor); bar 29 has a very fundamental bass in quavers, the first beat a D chord, the rest G. Melodic energy seems to overcome this apparent clumsiness, but the final cadence is less easy to explain, with its comprehensive use of root positions. Given that this time one could change the middle part (not imitative but 'harmonic filling'), four alternative basses present themselves, which could be multiplied by permutation (below staff). In Berlioz's setting the movement G–E–G (bar 31) seems particularly crude. One might argue, however, that it is not in fact a bass *voice*; it is distinct in timbre and its accompanimental function permits the use of fundamentals rather than a line. Berlioz would probably not have chosen these notes for a three-part vocal setting. Nevertheless the inconsistency remains; the bass changes its nature in the course of a short piece from fundamental, to linear, and back.

Any composer who worked as much as Berlioz did in fugal texture has to accustom himself to having a melodic line in the bass. Berlioz also does this in homophonic, monochromatic textures. My two examples are from the *Te Deum* (Cat. 33). In Ex. 47A from 'Tibi omnes', the half-close (bar 8) uses the inverted dominant, a curiosity arising from a change in the bass imitation of the treble: it starts a 5th down, reduced to a 4th (F♯–C♯ in bar 3 is compressed to B–G♯ in bar 7). This avoids further descent to subdominant regions at the cost of harmonic ambiguity, skilfully covered by continuous quaver counterpoint. Ex. 47B, from 'Te ergo quaesumus', is used by

Ex. 47

Friedheim to illustrate 'weak' progressions (FriRH, 284). The slurs and arrows show how most of the weak progressions are prolongations by oscillation, the stronger progressions being those which govern the phrase. Most of the chords are in root position, so this is a good example of a fundamental, as opposed to functional, bass with stepwise movement. A more ingenious harmonization might have detracted from the melodic aspect of the bass, whose individual notes Berlioz treats with equal intensity. Exx. 46 and 47 may suffice to show that generalization as to the vertical results of Berlioz's free counterpoint is almost impossible.

THE $^6_4$ CHORD

Berlioz's handling of the $^6_4$ deserves comment, for although he often uses it conventionally, he is also likely to omit it where it would be conventional. Ex. 46 (bar 31 or 32) is one case. At the end of the 'Marche hongroise' (Cat. 32B/3) the $^6_4$ appears a bar later than one might expect, deprived of its power to assert the tonality because in its conventional place stands a tonic chord in root position (Ex. 48). Berlioz may have wished to avoid duplicating bar 111, where the A major $^6_4$ is used to recover the tonic with garish irony (the reprise which follows being in the minor).

Occasionally such unusual handling amounts to more than a passing moment, and affects structure. The song *Elégie en prose* (Cat. 12J) is

Ex. 48

disturbing in more ways than one. Two nearly identical passages, perhaps the chief formal articulation of the song, differ mainly in their placement of the $^6_4$ (Ex. 49A, bars 24ff; Ex. 49B, bars 56ff). The stillness of the unison B, the vocal monotone, the gradual chromatic descent, are the same. At bar 30 the lowest pitches outline a tritone, F♮–B, on to a $^6_4$ which picks up the bass B of bar 24 and is therefore not so much a melodically descending tritone – we still hear F♮ moving to E – as the reopening of the low register. The whole passage is thus defined as a dominant prolongation, and it is secure, if not free from complacency. At bar 62, however, which is not far from the final cadence, the melodic aspect of the descent prevails; the lower register is opened with an E. Bars 56–62 thus no longer prolong the V but slide between dominant and tonic, yet the ear expects another V, as at bar 30. It is of little use to define the first resolution as harmonic, the second as contrapuntal; the anomaly remains. The very end (continuation of Ex. 49B) further delays the $^6_4$, which is to be expected in bar 65 after the supertonic inversion. Instead Berlioz reverts to E and winds chromatically up to the supertonic in root position before gaining the $^6_4$ in bar 67. To my ear there is a certain slackness here, which can only lead one to regret that the emotional associations of its composition prevented Berlioz from revising the song, or orchestrating the

Ex. 49

intransigent piano part, as he had intended (Mem18). As it is we are left, after some heart-rending declamation and magnificent harmonic invention, with one of the more uncomfortable results of his lack of cadential routine.

It is not only the $^6_4$ or the root position which at times occurs unexpectedly; it may also be the $^6_3$. At bar 44 of 'Scène aux champs' parallel octaves between treble and bass (Ex. 50: broken slurs) are mitigated by the arrival of a $^6_3$ instead of a root position. The bass A arrives from nowhere; it is not part of a line, for the next bass-register note is F (bar 46), and there is no linear progression to the next accented bass-note (B♭, bar 47), which is too remote from the A and in a higher octave. The lower bassoons adhere to F in bar 44, leaving the double-bass section divided between F and low A. The $^6_3$ chord appears to be pure colour, a *fait psychique*.

Ex. 50

In Ex. 50 we have left monochrome for the potentially stratified air of the orchestra. It is not possible, however, to explain every apparent anomaly or abnormality by orchestration. The third-inversion dominant 7th in *Absence* has aroused controversy by its failure to resolve onto a $^6_3$ (Ex. 51, at 'X'). It is certainly improved by orchestration and does not sound bad on the piano; but the 'defence' that the root is a reopening of the register of the first chord, which orchestration clarifies, will not altogether hold, since not only the horns (which could not sound A♯) but also the second violas proceed directly from B to low F♯.[46] Still less orthodox and more elegant is the resolution of the climactic $^6_4$ in this beautiful phrase (Ex. 51, bar 12). A root-position tonic intervenes before the dominant; and the $^6_4$ is not a passing chord since, for it to be understood that way, the bass would have to rise from the subsequent D♯ through to the tonic. Nothing prevents it, but the excess of dominant is better avoided, and the characteristic major-then-minor 3rd over G♯ is more subtly expressive. Berlioz here plays a small part in the emancipation of the $^6_4$ from its functional bondage. *Absence* is roughly contemporary with Gounod's *Le soir*, where the $^6_4$ appears at the opening as an unstable tonic, rather than a functional dominant; both, perhaps, point ahead to the lovely glow of the functionless second-inversion G major (VI) near the end of 'Celeste Aida'.

Ex. 51

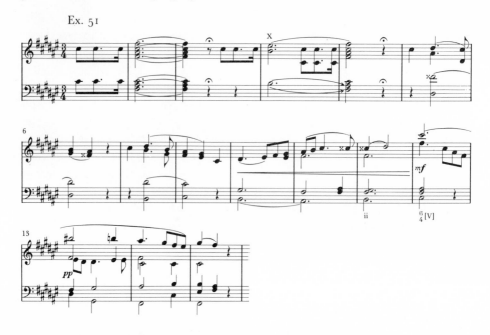

REHARMONIZATION

That Berlioz seldom repeated a melody without some kind of rearrangement of the harmony is a feature of his musical thought which has often been remarked upon (as in FriRH, 283ff; PriBS, 149ff). Occasionally, as in the eloquent 'Tibi omnes' (Cat. 33/2), the procedure deserves the term 'harmonic variation' (MacNG, 600) in that it amounts to a decorative enrichment of a repeated melody or *cantus*. Usually, however, there is no apparent structural reason; my examples therefore are mostly cases where reharmonization amounts to revision, and they include rejected workings, which may give some insight into the development of Berlioz's technique. Some alterations suggest greater technical command; others are occasioned by different rhythmic presentations of the same melody, a very characteristic procedure (see FriBR). Sometimes a single chord is changed for expressive enhancement, like the substitution of E♭ (♭VII) for the subdominant at bar 72 of Margaret's 'Romance' (Cat. 32B/15; originally 32A/7, bar 70). But Berlioz often seems to reharmonize gratuitously where repetition would be possible, even easy; such cases are the most revealing of an attitude to polyphony.

Chailley and Primmer have both suggested that Berlioz's whole approach to harmonization was unusual: his music depends on the melody as others' does on the bass, and he harmonized from the top downwards (ChaBH, 21; PriBS, 151). If this implies that most composers harmonize from the bass up, it is a grave oversimplification; and in Berlioz's case is is surely misleading. A melodic idea normally precedes its bass, and itself dictates the periodic structure upon which the harmonic pattern of a phrase depends, and which the bass articulates. In tonal music the harmonic framework is the sense of progression which the lines unfold contrapuntally. I cannot see that Berlioz's methods from this point of view are essentially different. The strangeness of his music results not from the sequence of his musical thought, but from its very nature. His melodies exist within a clear general harmonic framework; but it is not resolvable into symmetrical periods.

Because of Berlioz's asymmetries, his sprung rhythms, his musical prose, as it were, his melodies suggest no definitive, inalienable 'harmonization' from which the variations are evidently a departure. It is thus the rhythmic aspect of his style which precludes the composition of a single, periodically organized harmonization, a 'correct' bass. As Schumann observed: 'his melodies are distinguished by such intensity of almost every individual note that, like many old folksongs, they often defy ordinary harmonization and would lose sonority if subjected to it' (ConFS, 242–3). The choice of chord may well be determined, as I have already suggested in relation to Ex. 47B, by Berlioz's intuitive recognition of this situation; he therefore makes an empirical choice of chord to suit a particular context, on expressive rather than structural grounds. Consequently, as Schumann remarked, he may throw the melody into relief by using only 'a pedal or simple dominant and subdominant chords' (*ibid.*); or he may throw the apparently settled harmonic progression out with a strange chord, as in the 'Romance' cited above.

The 'idée fixe' of the *Fantastique* has been almost over-commented upon already, partly in relation to this question of reharmonization. It is easy to imagine a firm, linear bass to the opening phrase (Ex. 52, J); this, however, is the solution Berlioz never adopted. He may well have recognized that such solidity was at odds with the irregular phraseology of the melody. I confine myself to the antecedent of which no fewer than eight versions can be superimposed (Ex. 52, A–H): three from *Herminie* (A–C); a discarded version from *Fantastique* I (D; see NBE 16, p. 212/ConFS, 255); and four versions from the symphony, which I have reconciled as to key and metre.[47]

Most of these versions bear out Schumann's remark about pedal. But another characteristic of Berlioz – the avoidance of an expected appoggiatura or suspension, or their unexpected inclusion – plays its part in creating variation over the pedal as a result of movement in Berlioz's much-maligned inner parts. Points 'X', 'Y', and 'Z' in Ex. 52 require comment.

Point 'X'

There are two obvious harmonies for the F: a dominant 7th (figured $\frac{5}{4}$ with or without a 7; A, D, E); and a subdominant (B, C, F; in F the values are

Ex. 52

halved from the third bar and the full orchestra is deployed for the first time in the symphony, which probably explains the clarity of the chording). The two dance measures, 'Un bal' (G) and the 'air de danse ignoble, trivial et grotesque' of the finale (H), add the refinement of a ♭6; the former uses a different bass, producing a titillating minor 9th, and the latter has a diminished chord over the pedal. The conventional handling of this F would be contrapuntal – a suspension, which occurs only in *Herminie* (B), with doubled 3rds passing in the clarinets (in *Herminie* (A) a slight intensification is achieved by adding a B, the 7th, on the strong beat). Every other version returns to a tonic chord only with the melody's E, thus syncopating harmonically as well as melodically.

Point 'Y'

The E is repeated, not tied, but like the F it is an obvious candidate for a 7–6 suspension (as in my version J). The faster settings avoid this in the interests of clarity (F, H). Otherwise the suspension occurs over the pedal ($\frac{\leftarrow}{3-2}$), except in G where the bass moves to create the suspension (whereafter G = J). The inner parts produce variation between a 6th (implied supertonic: B, C, F, G) and a 5th (implied dominant: A, D, E, H). In bar 6 the D, wherever possible (i.e. not in G), is a 9–8 suspension; the exception is C where the bass treats itself as a dissonance on the weak part of bar 5 and resolves onto B, thus breaching two laws – that suspensions occur on strong beats, and that pedals are consonant at their beginning and end. Berlioz quite often uses such 'wrong' suspensions; if repeated they produce a metric displacement and thus legitimate themselves. This does not happen here (but *Herminie* still won second prize).

Point 'Z'

At the arrival of the dominant, the melodic C is suspended anyway, in a $^6_4$ or a $^5_4$. In B the dominant 7th prepares the interruption of the cadence by a bass G♯; in F the strong beat has no bass-note but $^5_4$ is clearly implied; in H, in the interests of vulgarity, Berlioz arpeggiates a tonic to reach V in the relatively weak bar 8.

This phrase is unharmonized at its first appearance in the symphony, except by a $^5_4$ in bar 78. The whole melody is seldom presented complete, and its high point (Ex. 53) is reached only five times. The melody attains the higher tonic note by sequence, then gradually falls. In *Herminie* (A), the climax is weakly placed over a tonic chord. The emphatic B of the second bar should then either be the resolution of a dissonant C, or be dissonant itself, but more expressively than this grating 7th; in fact Berlioz seems to intend a 4–3 over the subdominant, but weakens it with yet more pedal C, a conventional solution, used only in 'Un bal' (bar 3; cf. Ex. 52, G, also the most normal). The pedal in *Herminie* does not even have the strength of obstinacy; it begins only at this point (bar 110). In the later versions Berlioz uses a mediant, approached three different ways, all dominants (arrowed in Ex. 53). B and C have the same root-progression, iii–V–I; but in D the V is avoided, and in E nothing intervenes between iii and I (the rhythm is very compressed). In F I provide a conventional solution, but it requires a blander melodic rhythm; Berlioz's accompaniments derive, it may be said, from the rhythmical aspect of the melody.

Of particular interest is that the melody was demonstrably conceived with a different harmony from that which sounds so right in the symphony. In *Herminie* the preceding melodic sequence is the same – ♭6–♮6–♭7–8 – but

Ex. 53

instead of the harmonic sequence he was to use in the symphony (I–ii–iii–I, clearest from I, bar 418), Berlioz originally wrote I–vi–ii–I. In the symphony Berlioz eliminated both the lame subdominant of Ex. 52 (at 'X', except, with good reason, in F) and the weak tonic of Ex. 53, A. Thus he can be seen at work harmonizing a pre-existing melody, an exercise often given to students but not usually considered natural for composers. When he wrote *Herminie* he had finished his classwork at the Conservatoire. Nevertheless, he continued to refine his technique with experience, and by 1830 had already gone a long way.

Reharmonization is found everywhere in Berlioz. Sometimes it achieves astounding force; in Romeo's declaration of love, the music first heard darkly in C♯ minor ('Scène d'amour', Cat. 25/III, bar 146; Ex. 54A) is then given in the 'pun' partner key, C major (bar 172, Ex. 54B). But although the keys are the alternative mediants of the tonic, A, the melody reappears a 3rd higher, revolving round the 5th (of C) instead of the mediant (of C♯). On paper the harmonies appear only to substitute a pedal for an auxiliary bass-movement. In fact the intervening chord in Ex. 54A is quite unclassifiable, and Berlioz had to assure conductors that he meant it, by a note in the score. To its sombre expression succeeds the warmth of the C major version (Romeo now speaks loudly enough for Juliet to hear). The whole 'Scène d'amour' is enriched by harmonic variation of this material (e.g. cf. bars 274ff and 286ff).

Ex. 54

Elsewhere Berlioz's reharmonizations seem almost casual, as in several instances where instrumental ritornelli differ from the vocal statements which follow. This is a common source of divergence in rhythm (see FriBR) and harmony, as in Faust's air (see FriRH, 283; and below, Ex. 115). Another instance is Friar Lawrence's aria (Cat. 25/VII), in which the vocal melody appears to change as the result of reharmonization (Ex. 55). Although the chords in bars 2 and 6 both imply V of the supertonic, the expressive impact of the bass Db seems to draw the melody down in imitation; IV replaces ii in bar 7; and a striding bass becomes singing. In fact, of course, the curiously lame introduction would have been composed after the vocal version; it is the intensification in performance, however, which counts.

Ex. 55

I conclude with an example which shows no sign of structural or directly expressive intentions, although the reharmonization will be seen to affect mood. The romance *Je crois en vous* (Cat. 23A) was, like *Herminie*, superseded when its melody appeared in a major work. It appears in two widely separated contexts in *Benvenuto Cellini*: stated and somewhat developed in the overture, and used for the (instrumental) arietta of Harlequin in the Carnival scene.

Apart from its appealing melody, *Je crois en vous* is a tedious piece in six identical strophes, with a rather stolid piano accompaniment. It dates from 1834; the overture from early 1838. The order of composition, therefore, adopted in the layout of Ex. 56, is: *Je crois en vous* (transposed from D♭); arietta (in D); overture (transposed from G). The arietta resembles a

Ex. 56

Ex. 56 (contd)

romance in texture, cor anglais accompanied by harps; the bass is sustained by two solo 'cellos. Yet Berlioz altered both melody and harmony, the latter substantially. In the overture, after a false start in the dominant (bar 36), the melody is given to strings in octaves accompanied by wind arpeggios and pizzicato bass, a *tutti* without brass or percussion.

The melody falls into five sections (A–E). *Je crois en vous* is one bar shorter in A and D; A was thus expanded from three bars to four, a good instance of the squarer number producing the less constricted rhythm. In Ex. 56 the bass figuring is to be understood as applying to all the versions if it is not contradicted by another bass-note or figuring. Vertical lines mark where a chord is entirely the same; wavy lines indicate the same chord in a different inversion (where *Je crois en vous* and the overture coincide, but the arietta differs, the lines are necessarily curved). In the figuring 'X' signifies a diminished 7th. In the overture 'R' indicates chords in root position in this version only; 'TR' and 'DR' are respectively tonic and dominant root positions. Certain differences of detail I leave to be extracted from Ex. 56 without comment. Other differences worthy of note are summarized in table 6. The small notes referred to (overture) are of course an octave lower in bar 8 than they sound, but are at pitch in bars 10–12.

Table 6

Phrase (bar nos.)	Je crois en vous	Arietta	Overture
A (1–4)	3 bars only	4 bars, same harmonic outline	1–2 harmony simpler, 3–4 unchanged
B (5–8)	Square ties (Ex. 56): chord-change on weak beat, tied to strong	Eliminates this fault; harmony enriched	Chords of *Je crois en vous* restored, but on strong beats
(8–9)	Bass link to C	Same link	Link in melody also (Ex. 56, small notes)
C (9–14)	Steady chromatic ascent in bass	Crotchets; less chromatic but much the same	9–10 restores *Je crois en vous*: harmony richer in 10. Nearly every chord root position. New melodic detail in 10–12 (small notes)
D (14–17)	Two bars only. Unison accompaniment	Broader rhythm. Held G bass, otherwise unison	Harmonized: root bass-notes (double-bass); in-filling bass (bassoons)
E (17–23)		Minimal change	Little change. Arpeggio (18) from bass to flute (Ex. 56, small notes). From 18 horns added; double-bass *arco*; 19, 20, root positions

The arietta, written with the harp accompaniment which Berlioz certainly preferred to the piano, is an improvement on *Je crois en vous* – broadened, with richer harmonies, particularly in phrase B. Why, then, are features of *Je crois en vous* restored in the overture? The answer lies in the scale of the music. The ensemble is larger, the sound more lush (both melody and accompaniment are spread over two or more octaves). The melody is broadened by the simple crotchets in bar 11 and by the almost indissoluble linking of phrases B and C, where an ornamental addition draws the melody down (see small notes). Working on this less intimate scale, Berlioz preferred to remove intricacies of harmony which would have confused the gentle murmuring of his woodwind accompaniment by too frequent changes of chord. Moreover, his bass is not sustained, but plucked, by double-basses only, until the decisive $^6_4$ (bar 18). Plucking may have suggested guitaresque root positions, of which the overture has at least one more in every two bars than the arietta. In bar 11 Berlioz even avoids the obvious route from IV to V, which lies through G♯, a simpler chromatic move than one he used in bars 9–12 of *Je crois en vous*.

Yet the overture was not conceived for anything but orchestra. The harmonic choices are therefore the direct result of the orchestral layout, in which neither 'cellos nor bassoons are available to help the double-basses; the harmony must be defined by using the *basse fondamentale* as much as possible. If in performance, and on recordings (for which Berlioz is hardly to blame), the bass sounds weak, we should recall that Berlioz usually specifies a high proportion of double-basses to the other strings. But a little weakness, too, may be part of his intention. The harmony needs to be clear, but its rootedness should not be forced upon the listener. Moreover, when the string basses rest, the lowest note may well be the lower octave of the melody or, more often, the arpeggiating bassoons (not shown in Ex. 56). Thus in the overture the texture loses its incisive, classical edge; it becomes impressionistic, *flou*. Its solidity and sense may be inferred from a piano reduction, but the actual sound is more original and fascinating than a reduction would suggest. Berlioz was certainly not unaware of the uses of a linear bass, nor was he unable to write one, but he made another choice; the beauty of the result is his justification.

8 Concerning counterpoint, pedal, and fugue

'A similar weakness is observable in his counterpoint, except of course when he used it for purposes of burlesque. When he attempted it seriously, as in the first chorus of the *Te Deum*, he usually betrayed a want of mastery, which is intelligible enough if we realise the immense labour and concentration which the method demands and the antagonism which he felt for it throughout. On the other hand, the Amen chorus in *Faust* is an admirable travesty, and better still is the Wedding Cantata in *Béatrice et Bénédict*, with the unanswerable logic of its text and the angular trills and flourishes of its oboe obbligato.'

W. H. Hadow (HadSM 1, pp. 139–40)

Counterpoint is usually understood in the limited sense of imitative counterpoint. In its wider sense it has already been at issue in the study of Berlioz's basses, but even in the present chapter non-imitative forms of counterpoint will be considered. For a composer so resistant to academicism and archaicism, both widely spread infections of nineteenth-century music, Berlioz was surprisingly interested in imitation, as well as other contrapuntal devices such as the reunion of themes and rhythms.[48] Reunions are a familiar element in Berlioz's music, and properly belong to the consideration of form, although we may note that it takes a measure (if not, to be fair, a very large measure) of contrapuntal skill to set them up.

I begin by mentioning certain non-imitative textural devices, which are rightly included in counterpoint treatises: parallel motion and pedals. Parallelism, already mentioned in connection with guitar technique (see above, p. 58), may seem the antithesis of counterpoint; but it is, in free composition, a positive gesture on the contrapuntal level, and it occurs in numerous short passages, from the prayer in the *Scène héroïque* (Cat. 4/3, bar 72) to the prayer of Trojan women (Ex. 26C above). It usually involves $^6_3$ chords or diminished 7ths. The resulting inevitable weakness of function in the chords makes parallelism a useful method of undermining a tonal centre. A unison line can also serve this purpose, as in the brass recitative of *Roméo* (Cat. 25/I, from bar 78; see especially 110ff). For this process Chailley coined the phrase 'modulation par accrochage' (ChaBH, 23), implying modulation by arbitrary adherence to another centre at the end of a phrase. The dissolving diminished 7ths (see above, p. 39) can lead to equally inorganic key-changes.

Theory allowed parallel $^6_3$ chords and diminished 7ths, although Reicha calls the former, because of the consecutive 4ths, 'irregular . . . nevertheless agreeable to the ear' (1818, p. 25); Catel shows the possibilities without comment (1802, p. 41). Berlioz's parallel $^6_3$ chords often take on an archaic flavour, but there is no need to start the hare of mediaeval or renaissance influence.[49] The source is Gluck, whose 'Chaste fille de Latone' (*Iphigénie en Tauride*) has just this flavour (Ex. 57A); it is recaptured by Lesueur in the 'Introduction historique' of his oratorio *Debbora* (Ex. 57B). Besides the prayers mentioned above, 'Dans le ciel' (*La damnation*) is an example of simple piety (Ex. 57C); see also the parallelism in Berlioz's hymn-like works (e.g. Cat. 41A). Gluck uses wailing $^6_3$ chords in the storm from the same

opera (Ex. 58A); two storms of Berlioz, nearly thirty years apart, recall this image (*La tempête*, Cat. 17/VI, Ex. 58B; 'Chasse royale', Cat. 40A/29, Ex. 58C). Another form of parallelism is purely expressive, seeming to represent drooping spirits; its use by Spontini is uncannily Berliozian (*La vestale*, Act

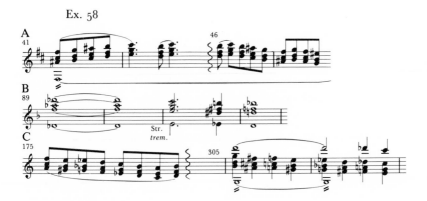

II; Ex. 59A), and Berlioz may have unconsciously remembered it at the end
of Cassandra's second air (Cat. 40A/10, Ex. 59B) and Beatrice's aria (Cat.
42/10) at 'tristesse alarmée' (Ex. 59C). The $^6_3$ progression can move more
slowly through the inclusion of chromatic degrees, often including the

Ex. 59

shared mediant 'pun', as in *Herminie* (Cat. 9/2, Ex. 60). This is in a way the
prototype for *Fantastique* I, bar 370ff, where the parallelism is also a
development of the 'idée fixe' and a counterpoint to the solo oboe.

Ex. 60

Such massive parallelisms are really thickened unisons, and it is not
surprising that a composer who liked to expose melodies without
accompaniment should resort to them at climaxes, like that of the
'Lacrimosa' (Cat. 22/6, 170). Only a little less overwhelming is the 'Marche
au supplice' (bar 114ff), where the trombones' parallel $^6_3$ chords are pitted
against a unison counterpoint in contrary motion. Besides the famous
chromatic scale in $^6_3$ chords (I, bar 198ff), Berlioz twice in the *Fantastique*
goes so far as to employ complete parallel triads including octaves on the
extremes of the texture: 'Scène aux champs', bars 148–9, and V, bar 408ff.
Most original in effect, if less strictly parallel, is the surge of the whole
orchestra in the first movement (115ff); only the basses resist the downward
rocketing of the rest, and from bar 143 the parallel ascent is almost uniform.

The whole polyphonic mass coalesces for a single, decisive gesture, at the moment of establishing a new key. Similar effects occur in the 'Chasse royale' (bars 96ff and 266ff); one might also mention the hilarious lifting of the whole mass from C to D in *Le corsaire* (bar 410) as a form of unison modulation, which Chailley compared to the 'granite modulations' of Ravel's *Boléro* (ChaBH, 17).

PEDALS

Berlioz was doubtless aware of the rules for pedals, formulated by Cherubini: they are on the tonic or dominant, and consonant at the beginning and end. Berlioz did not invent the pedal in the upper part, which is mentioned by Cherubini, Catel, and Reicha; he was probably not impressed by Gautier's pronouncement, that it 'can be treated like a bass pedal'.[50] However, he violates these very simple rules to excellent effect. Cherubini favoured the bass-pedal on the dominant; it is comparatively rare in Berlioz. I have already given two examples of extraordinary originality, beginning or ending on diminished 7ths – a bass-pedal on the flat 6th (Ex. 9) and upper pedals on the flat 7th and flat 6th (Ex. 45).

The traditional pedal is a stabilizing element, a massive braking which grips the most varied polyphony to the main key; it is thus best suited to codas. Berlioz's pedals are not hyper-excited, and their tension lies in their reinforcement of uncertainty. He seems reluctant to take advantage of the licence for dissonance, preferring a floating triadic and diminished 7th harmony which, being non-functional, causes tonal disorientation. I do not know any precedents for his discrete pedals, 'intermittent sounds' (see below, p. 138) which exert a large-scale rhythmic control and an intermittent control of pitch. These pedals are expressive and characteristic as well as structural. In *Harold* (Cat. 19/II) the ingeniously harmonized intervention of a low C♮ and high B ends each strophe and restores the tonic E major; it is also a bell effect. In the 'Offertoire' (Cat. 22/7) and 'Convoi funèbre' (Cat. 25/V) the pedal is a choral psalmody, transferred in the latter to the orchestra to become a funeral knell. In the 'Offertoire' and *Sur les lagunes* (Cat. 27/C) the intermittent pedal oscillates between the 5th and flat 6th (peculiarly poignant in the latter where the pedal fits with III and ♯iii chords: from F minor, A♭ and A minor, the pedal oscillating to the major 3rd, bar 15). In the septet of *Les troyens* (Cat. 40A/36) there is a continuous upper pedal on the dominant which occasionally oscillates to the flat 6th; this finally undermines the tonic when the flat 6th is taken as the new dominant (for No. 37, G♭ from F).

When Schumann remarked on Berlioz's tendency to fall back on pedals in harmonization, he was referring to a less constructive affair than in the above examples; rather, to a short-term pedal which exerts a temporary control, of

especial value when the melody does not fall into a clear periodic pattern
(ConFS, 243). The 'idée fixe' is an instance (see Exx. 52 and 53). In 'Scène
aux champs' (Cat. 13/III), bars 131–42, the combination of a version of the
main melody with a woodwind countermelody is set in relief by a pedal
which virtually abolishes harmonic movement (cf. also *Roméo*, Cat. 25/II, at
the 'Réunion des thèmes'; below, Ex. 74B). A good instance is in Beatrice's
'Il m'en souvient' (Cat. 42/10), where a pedal covers seven beats in the
middle of a phrase, providing what at such a point might seem a surplus of
tonic (Ex. 61). In fact it provides stability precisely where the melody is most
aimlessly chromatic, through immobility rather than functional harmonization. This enhances the move to the supertonic which follows (bar 61); the
tonic does not reappear in root position until the cadence of this twenty-bar
paragraph (bar 73).

Ex. 61

   Berlioz does not flout rules facetiously or wantonly, but for expression. He
was particularly fond of subdominant pedals, which have both a braking
effect and a residual ambiguity. Ex. 62 shows an intermittent subdominant
pedal in *Le corsaire*; it is dissonantly attacked (the favourite 4–3 appoggiatura
on the subdominant, bar 33). Its recurrence controls the whole four-phrase
melody, through its four different resolutions in various harmonic contexts
(see figures). Each pair of phrases is connected by an inner pedal E♭. The
first two, from the entry of the bass D♭, proceed from supertonic to
dominant; the second phrase (B) borrows from tonic minor (bars 38–40) to
effect an extension from four bars to six. The second pair of phrases repeats a
melody with the harmony altered at every point except the very end of the
pedal (a root-position IV – it is characteristic of Berlioz to keep the simplest
chord till last). The last two D♭ pedals are framed by the subdominant, but
in phrase C it is minor followed by (enharmonic) A major; in phrase D the
equivalent chord is the only acute dissonance over the pedal, and tonicizes
the supertonic (B♭ minor, pun partner to A).

Ex. 62

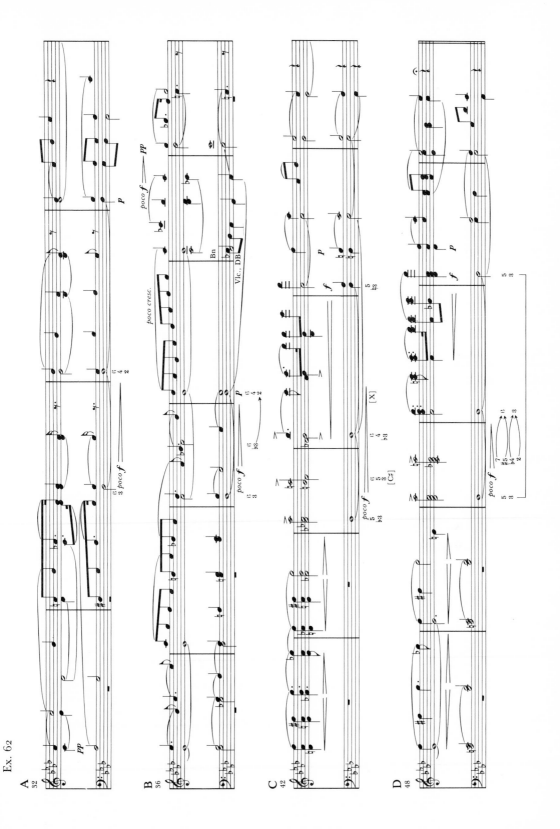

Ex. 62 is a good epitome of Berlioz's handling of free, harmonically colourful polyphony (e.g. the reharmonization of parallel diminished 7ths, bars 42 and 48). The pedal is a slightly asymmetrical element, distinct both instrumentally and dynamically (*poco forte, diminuendo*, against *piano* growing to *forte*). With Berlioz one always searches for the expressive reason, however difficult to pin down; here, perhaps the swell of the sea (cf. the septet in *Les troyens*, p. 138), in *Sur les lagunes* an anguished moan, in Ex. 61 the weight of memory, in Ex. 9 a timeless rêverie. Berlioz's pedals are the antithesis of the traditionally cumulative type, or of the dynamic repose of Bach's. Even when the pedal draws threads towards a cadence, like the beautiful subdominant pedal in 'Choeur de sylphes' (Cat. 32B/7B, 91–6), it is not so much constructive as an expressive addition to an idea that was conceived without it (Cat. 32A/3, 126ff). Pedals were actually added to music otherwise essentially unaltered in 'Chant de la fête de Pâques' (Cat. 32B/4B; see RusBL, 65). The 'Ballet de sylphes' (Cat. 32B/7C) is entirely over a tonic pedal, which defines the internal structure not at all, although it makes the whole movement a prolongation of the final tonic of 'Choeur de sylphes'. Berlioz does build on pedals, notably in the 'Dignare' (Cat. 33/3) with the ladder ascending and descending by 3rds; here, too, the traditional use is displaced by a structural device invented by the composer for the particular occasion.

FREE COUNTERPOINT, HETEROPHONY, AND CANON

Berlioz's originality in deploying assertively linear counterpoint appears equally in free and in imitative combinations. A notable example is the 'Dies irae' of the *Requiem* (Cat. 22/2), in which three ideas, one of them a magnificent invented plainchant, are introduced separately and then combined. The austerity of this counterpoint, which might (like the fugal 'Quaerens me') be interpreted as crudity, is an aspect of its expressiveness. Berlioz could invent orthodox counterpoint of splendid effectiveness, as in 'Marche au supplice' (Ex. 63). The theme is combined with its own inversion; the principal notes of the bassoon counterpoint (additional stems)

Ex. 63

Ex. 63 (contd)

skilfully avoid most of the pitches of the other parts, and when they do coincide (broken lines) the approach is firmly by contrary motion, except at the cadence. Less subversive pieces are actually less orthodox.

In symphonic movements Berlioz liked to intermingle elements of the main theme in the accompaniments to lyrical melodies; the *Béatrice* overture is a delectable example (bar 141ff). When preparing the *Fantastique* for publication, he introduced against the 'idée fixe' motives from the waltz-tune which imitate each other as it proceeds (bars 131–56).[51] More contrapuntal ingenuity is required to combine a melody with elements of itself, as in the delicate free imitation in the *Benvenuto* overture (Cat. 23D; Ex. 64).

Ex. 64

Berlioz's free counterpoints often incline to heterophony. Presumably Tovey condoned this when he remarked on the 'admirable florid counterpoint' in the Andante of *Lear* (TovEM 4, p. 85). The violin triplets often duplicate the melody (Ex. 65, connecting lines): in bars 74–9 the essential pitches are different, but in bar 50 there is a unison on the third beat, and the doubling is explicit in bars 51–2. Other examples include the delicate violin tracery, still more inconsistent in its mixture of counterpoint and doubling, in *Les troyens*: Choroebus's 'Mais le ciel et la terre' (No. 3, Andante) and the 'Marche sur le chant national' (No. 32). In 'Scène aux champs', from bar 131, the first violins' demisemiquaver figuration doubles

Ex. 65

the second violins' melody at the unison, octave, and 15th. To describe a counterpoint as essentially heterophonic, or to trace its inconsistency in application of a supposed principle, is not to condemn it; such filigree-work demands taste and skill.

Even in Berlioz's strictest imitative counterpoint the textural and expressive values still exceed in importance any question of rigour. Canon is potentially a determinant of form; perhaps for that reason Berlioz showed little interest in its consistent application. Apart from a few bars in 'Tibi omnes' (Cat. 33/2, bars 9–15), his only real canon is *Canon libre à la quinte*, published in 1823, a piece in the mood, though not the form, of a romance (Cat. 1D).[52] The canonic imitation is of variable quality, and very forced in places; the best moment, musically, is when it ceases in the coda. However, the experiment shows Berlioz already thinking more in terms of line than might have been expected so early.

Properly speaking, Berlioz wrote no other canons, but he often used canonic imitation for short sections, with no architectonic function. As in the case of pedals, a first version may exist with no canon. The ravishing setting for full orchestra of the 'idée fixe' in *Harold* (Cat. 19/I, bar 73ff) has a 'canon' between 'cello, harp, cornet, and bassoons (*dux*), and high wind with solo viola (*comes*). In the equivalent section of *Rob Roy* (Cat. 16, bar 301ff) all the harmonic and textural elements of the passage are present except the *comes*, which in *Harold* was superimposed onto something already complete. It is thus a decorative element, a textural enrichment more related to heterophony than to serious canon. The same may be said of the canon in the love-duet in *Benvenuto* (Cat. 23C/3), used in *Le carnaval romain* (Cat. 23E, bar 53ff); there is no tension in such close imitation over a tonic pedal, and after six bars it changes to a very beautiful free canon at the 4th, hardly more intellectually demanding than more informal imitation. The 'canon' in *Le corsaire* (Cat. 31, bar 106ff) is purely heterophonic.

FUGUE

Cherubini's witticism, that Berlioz disliked the fugue because the fugue didn't like him, was repeated against himself by Berlioz (MM, 39). It relates to a particular work – the 'Amen' from Beethoven's Mass in D. Berlioz had no objection either to the pedagogical study of fugue, although he liked rules to be justified; he objected only to the abuse of fugue, to its routine appearance at certain points in liturgical works where it seemed to counter the proper expression of the text.[53] Fugal texture had a positive attraction for Berlioz, and fugue or fugato appears in every major work except the anthologies.[54]

Berlioz would probably have accepted Reicha's categorization of fugues as strict (of which there are few examples in Berlioz) or informal. The latter are often in fugato, an exposition plus a few further entries; they are likely to occur in the middle of a piece and thus be developmental, rather than at the opening where fugal texture might imply a wholly contrapuntal continuation. Where fugato does open a movement, it is usually not the only thematic element, but alternates or is combined with other ideas. The 'Ronde du sabbat' (*Fantastique* V) falls between the categories; it is in the middle of the piece but seems to begin the movement proper. Schumann called it 'fugato . . . certainly not by Bach, but nevertheless clearly constructed according to the rules' (ConFS, 241); no doubt Hadow would have included it among the burlesques, for as with 'Amen' in *La damnation* its strictness is surely ironical.

We know more about Berlioz's training in fugue than in any other aspect of composition, for we have Reicha's and Cherubini's treatises and two surviving competition fugues. The requirements for the latter were: subject; correct answer; invertible countersubject (or second, and often third, subject); stretto; pedal; and a limited modulatory scheme. That only the first two are indispensable to Bach does not affect the value of academic fugue as training, and an improvement in Berlioz's counterpoint ran parallel with greater command of other musical materials.

Berlioz's first surviving fugue is that of 1826 (Cat. 5), and it is of some biographical interest to realize how well its failure was deserved. We also have the fugue by that year's winner, C. S. Paris.[55] It is as dull as Berlioz's, but technically far superior, as a comparison of the expositions makes clear (the examiners gave the first subject; in Ex. 66, A is by Berlioz, B by Paris). Berlioz had not yet entered Reicha's class, but he knew enough to place his entries and his (correct) answer where Paris has them. Paris's '2ᵐᵉ [sujet]' uses the same notes as Berlioz's, but is neater and livelier – how odd to find Berlioz defective in rhythm! – and his third propels the music forward by its upbeat structure. He avoids the unnecessary doubling of the D (bar 5, bass, alto) which leads Berlioz to a clumsy unison and crossing of parts in bar 10. It is fascinating to observe how Berlioz was lost when the rules did not tell

Ex. 66

him what to do. In bar 6 his fugue simply stops; nothing could be more obvious than Paris's linking bass, but it is at least efficient.

In the obligatory stretto (Ex. 67) Berlioz (A) begins after a *tonic* fermata, a poor springboard compared to Paris's dominant (B), and fumbles with superfluous bits of secondary counterpoint, while Paris builds a solid stretto on his first subject. Berlioz's statutory pedal shows that in this case he did not know the rules, and the results of ignorance are nasty and inept (the C begins on the weak minim of bar 72 with a 7th chord but the tied pedal is from bar 73, a $\frac{6}{4}$). Bars 73–4 are excruciating; the subject is seldom extended beyond four notes (or is vainly distorted: alto, 69–71). The tenor suspension (bar 78) is wrongly resolved, and its threefold A–G (79–81) is hardly an expressive oscillation; it resolves with consecutive octaves (alto, tenor, 81–2).

The second surviving fugue is of 1829 (Cat. 10A).[56] This one passed muster; it is poor music but mostly correct. The exposition (Ex. 68A) and second stretto (Ex. 68B) may serve as comparison with 1826. The mistakes are remedied; the second-subject quavers greatly enhance the flow, and the inane third subject is hidden by the cadence. The first stretto is on the model

Ex. 67

of Paris's (Ex. 67B); the second, with pedal, has far more drive and fewer crudities than Ex. 67A. (In the MS the examiners, presumably, have marked a few faulty suspensions in pencil, including bar 56, upper parts; the tenor is also prematurely resolved on the third beat. They did not remark a virtual unison between the upper parts in the episode from bar 17.)

Berlioz's continuing ability to learn is demonstrated by a much later fugue (Cat. 32B/6B) whose subject, Brander's song, dates from 1829 (Cat. 32A/4). Of course, the drunken mutterings of this burlesque 'Amen', its booming ophicleides, its howling tenors, are ridiculous, but its scholastic foundation is perfectly solid. It has been said that any student could have written it; would that were true today. Mephistopheles's ironic comment speaks for Berlioz:

Ex. 68

A

B

'On ne saurait exprimer mieux / Les sentiments pieux / Qu'en terminant ses
prières / L'Eglise en un seul mot résume'. The 'Amen' fugue is Berlioz's
satirical contribution to truth of expression; the final 'Amen' of the *Requiem*
(Cat. 22), and the 'Quam olim Abrahae', set with devotional tenderness
instead of the customary hearty fugue, are his positive contributions. There
is a noteworthy caution on the *Requiem*'s 'Hosanna': 'Chantez sans violence,
en tenant bien les notes au lieu de les accentuer isolément', which suggests
that fugues in sacred works may indeed habitually have been sung in the
manner of tipsy students.

The 'Hosanna' is probably nobody's favourite part of the *Requiem*; it
suffers by juxtaposition with the ethereal 'Sanctus' and by its repetition,
which, however, is varied not only by the normally inaudible continuation of
the high violins of the 'Sanctus' but by an eighteen-bar extension with a new,
unison climax. As an example of idiosyncratic application of severe
counterpoint, the 'Te Deum laudamus' is in another class. Its form, of
course, cannot be defined purely in fugal terms, but it is severe in its
deployment of strict exposition, stretto, and combination of the main subject

with the grand plainchant-like theme, equivalent to Bach's use of chorale tunes (Berlioz had heard the *St Matthew Passion* in Berlin in 1843; Mem51, 9th letter). In variety of technique a better comparison is Handel, for the sturdy counterpoint is regenerated by passages of awestruck homophony, and the form is further defined by the gradual accretion of orchestral colour into a fundamentally vocal conception. The final modulation catches the breath. Few nineteenth-century composers manage so convincingly to combine formal fugue with so little archaicism of technique.

Fugal texture is not usually maintained by Berlioz throughout a movement. His attraction to instrumental fugato probably derives from Beethoven's symphonies, for example the slow movements of Nos. 3 and 7, the imitation and combination of themes in the finale of No. 5, or the double fugue in the finale of No. 9 which, however (and perhaps significantly), Berlioz describes as a reunion of themes without mentioning fugue (AT, 60/G, 77). Beethoven may also be the source of certain liberties in fugato. The 'Sanctus' of the Mass in D superimposes entries each a 5th higher, a device Berlioz adopts in Balducci's fugato (*Benvenuto*, Cat. 23C/1, middle entries from bar 43 in c, g, d, a) and in the overture to *La fuite* (Cat. 38/7, bar 68ff, middle entries in A, E, b, f♯). Conceivably Berlioz knew the weird fugues of Reicha, in one of which the entries come in 3rds, using flattened degrees: in A major, A, C♮, E, G♮.[57] Berlioz never adopted quite so bizarre a scheme, preferring in *La damnation* (Cat. 32B/1, 'Introduction') to ascend by diatonic 3rds: D, f♯, A, and an incomplete entry in c♯.

Another freedom in fugato is to answer at the 5th, but not tonally. Ex. 69 shows the subjects of (A) *Harold* I, 321; (B) *Roméo* V; (C) *La damnation*, 'Introduction'. To each is added (1) a correct tonal answer, tonic answering dominant; (2) Berlioz's exact answer. Since he elsewhere uses a tonal answer when it suits him, his exact answers are no liberty but the result of an insistence, proper in such cases, on the melodic integrity of the subject. Also, because his fugati use melodies of marked expressive character, ill-fitted for combination with equally distinct countersubjects, Berlioz adapts fugal procedures to a variety of wholly original forms, and tailors his counterpoint to the expressive demands of each section. The counterpoint to the 'Ronde du sabbat' consists mainly of doubling in 3rds and 6ths, fragmented to create rhythmic counterpoint (Ex. 70). Berlioz is perfectly capable of producing a polyphonic flow in two parts, complementary in pitch and rhythm, as he does in the 'Introduction' to *La damnation* (Ex. 71; subject begins as in Ex. 69C).

I conclude by looking at a piece which for much of its length appears truly fugal, the 'Offertoire' (Cat. 22/7). The whole form, however, demands other terminologies; and even the fugal sections themselves, closely studied, show counterpoint yielding to a larger structural pattern. The more parts there are, the more neutral their melodic shape. Their function is increasingly to

Ex. 69

Ex. 70

Ex. 71

define, fill out, and enrich the harmony, rather than to provide independent interest, possibly at the expense of the eloquent subject. Directed by successive entries of this melody, the musical unfolding is experienced as strophic as well as fugal.

Ex. 72 indicates the beginnings of each part, and gives the three-part texture from bar 27, omitting the choral entries (which also control the musical flow, falling irregularly as a discrete pedal against the thirteen-bar periodicity of the fugue). From bar 14 the violins have a true countersubject, taken over by the violas at bar 27 (the slight alterations appear in small notes below the staff, transposed: the first two are occasioned by choral entries, the last by the modulation). The third part (violins from 27) is a new counterpoint chiefly defined by rhythm. Its melodic shape can be accommodated to any harmony, but it is surprising how often it actually adds no new pitch to the complete, spare two-part counterpoint (violas, bass), with its 3rds, 6ths, and contrary-motion octaves. With the fourth entry (bar 40) the rhythm of the third part passes, not, as logic would suggest, to the violas, but to the bass; its linear interest is dropped in favour of a pedal, and to metrical stability is added stability of pitch. Nevertheless there is a complete four-part texture, with three new parts. The original countersubject is lost, to return only fleetingly (bars 102–5). Instead the first violins set up a new rhythm with a diminished retrograde of the subject's main motive (square brackets) and pursue a rhythm complementary to the violas', so that there is continual semiquaver movement (cf. Ex. 71, from bar 16). The violas also provide the spice of an acciaccatura-like dissonance

Ex. 72

Ex. 72 (contd)

(caps in Ex. 72), technically suspension in semiquavers. A linear counterpoint is added by the 'cellos, but it dies out after eight bars. (In bars 27 to 39 the figuring gives the intervals above the subject (bass). Octaves are unfigured; figures above the countersubject are used when subject and countersubject have an octave. 'T' is used for tritone, whether augmented 4th or diminished 5th; from bar 41 the figuring is to be understood as normal figured bass.)

In its original form the 'Offertoire' included a short counterexposition (nine bars between 101 and 102; eight between 105 and 106: NBE 9, pp. 171–2). Berlioz may have considered it redundant because it reverts, fugue-like, to the original countersubject in full (with the wind parts of the exposition sustaining the subject's *sforzandi*); or he may have sensed a more general *longueur*. Much of the rest is freely contrapuntal (53ff; flowing semiquaver wind counterpoint, 67ff; a new counterpoint remaining around the cut passage, 96ff). This decrease in real fugal activity is seen in other movements of similar pattern, such as the 'Introduction' of *La damnation*, *Roméo* V, and, in *L'enfance*, the 'Marche nocturne' and overture to *La fuite*. All of these, and the 'Offertoire', have contrasting lyrical ideas, which in *Roméo* V and the 'Marche nocturne' are strongly periodic and suggests a mixed fugue and sonata form. In the 'Offertoire' it is the broad 'Canto espressivo', which bursts forth at bar 60 (see Ex. 21A) and again, after a sequentially extended middle entry (67ff), in bar 78. At its conclusion in B♭ (bar 85) the texture fragments to a low point, dynamically and in thinness of motivic content (reached by way of diminution of the subject's first three notes from bar 87; the low point is around bar 95). The music accumulates through the remains of the mostly cut counterexposition to an abrasive outburst, syncopated after the *sforzandi* of the subject (bar 106) and resolved in the second part of the lyrical idea to cadence in F (112). A characteristic pattern has emerged of stable and unstable (developmental) periods, like fugal entries and episodes; but actual fugue is in abeyance, and in contrast to normal fugue the subject-entries are mostly unstable, the other material stable. This is borne out from bar 112, the extraordinarily disorienting return to the tonic (summarized in Ex. 20); what follows is in effect a cadence with the tonic now major (the 'Quam olim Abrahae').

This is not a criticism intended to diminish the movement by pointing out its inconsistencies. I agree with the spirit, if not the letter, of Schumann's verdict: 'This Offertorium surpasses everything' (Mem51, 4th letter). Indeed, in weakening the fugal aspect by his cut Berlioz perceptibly strengthened the movement's overall proportions.[58] The 'Offertoire' is outstanding in its resourceful handling of its subject – fugally, as a refrain, symphonically developed in combination and conflict with the discrete pedal – within an overall design which owes hardly more to fugue than to sonata. It is music of multiple perspectives and its very form is expressive.

9 Concerning rhythm

'there remains one field in the musical estate which has not been explored, to which Beethoven and Weber have cleared the path and to which no active and intelligent member of the younger musical generation should delay his journey. This is the field of rhythm; it is vast and fertile, and all we need do is to cultivate it well.'

Berlioz (*Le journal des débats*, 10 November 1837)

One might think that rhythm, the musical domain in which Berlioz's success and originality have been most generally recognized, would inevitably figure in any discussion of his style; but this is not so, despite his own attention to it in published writings.[59] The very ubiquity of rhythm, which as duration is the inescapable component of any kind of music, makes it harder to isolate; a rhythmic invention is often in need of pitch or harmony for its full definition. Most of what I have to say will concern the most obvious manifestation of rhythm, as metre. But rhythm is an aspect of phrase-structure (which will be further discussed in Chapter 10) and is thus integral to the experience of musical form; on the largest scale form is concerned with durations of sections, or proportion (see Chapter 12). The vexed question of whether rhythm can exist as an independent element in polyphony cannot be answered by any nineteenth-century composer, but the variety of Berlioz's rhythmic invention is such that it can at least attract attention to itself *as rhythm*. Typically, however, he is not systematic and does not insistently follow up his inventions in later works; he had little interest in musical processes as such, but only in those suggested by his subject-matter.

That, at least, is what one must conclude from his works. His most striking pronouncement on rhythm, however, might lead one to look for innovation, even theory. I quote at length in order to be able to refer back from time to time, and to see how much is actually reflected in his music:

Many rhythmic effects exist independently of the even or odd number of bars or the symmetry of phrases. They can result from accenting weak beats at the expense of strong; from the more or less rapid succession of alternating triple and duple groups; from the simultaneity of different metres whose lesser divisions are irreconcilable and which have no other

127

point of contact than the first beat; from the occasional appearance of a melody in triple time introduced into a quadruple metre, and vice versa; or finally from the intermittent use of certain sounds independent of the principal melody and of the accompanimental rhythm, and separated from each other by expanding or contracting intervals in proportions which it is impossible to predict. These kinds of combination are probably as numerous as those of which melodic succession is capable. They form in rhythm groups or connections analogous to the connections and groups from which chords, melodies, or modulations result. *There are rhythmic dissonances, there are rhythmic consonances, there are rhythmic modulations*; nothing could be plainer.[59]

METRE

Paradoxically, overt metrical irregularity is least frequent in those works of the 1830s and 1840s which pulse most abundantly with rhythmic life (*Harold, Benvenuto, Roméo, La damnation*). It is with *L'enfance* and *Les troyens* that metrical peculiarity, like modality, rises most often to the surface. The conjuration of soothsayers in *L'enfance* has a relatively extended passage of septuple metre (ten bars of 7/4, then three of 4/4 and three of 3/4; the pattern repeats with four each of 4/4 and 3/4). For *Les troyens* Berlioz sketched a melody in 5/4 for a 'Danse des nègres', and began Aeneas's narration (No. 7) in 5/4, but he rejected both ideas (NBE 2c, pp. 935, 938). He retained, however, an attractive 5/8 section, only eight bars long, in the 'Combat de ceste' (No. 5). Berlioz was generally more interested in applying metrical freedom against a prevailing regularity. Once, in *La tempête* (Cat. 17/VI), he composed in quintuple metre for a whole section, notated in compound duple; 'bars' of 15/4 are defined by a recurring rhythmic pattern and by accents (six 'bars' covering bars 289–306 in the 6/4 notation). When the chorus enter to reprove Caliban they adhere to 6/4 (Ex. 73). Such conflicts between heard and conducted metres are used more extensively by Schumann (as in the Piano Concerto, third movement, 81–123: the ensemble is in 3/2, the notation 3/4).

Experimenting in stretched metres, like quintuple, has its precedent in Reicha, who described quintuple metre as 'one of the new metres which we need so much'.[60] Fieramosca's fencing-practice (*Benvenuto*, No. 7) is performed in shrinking units, carefully labelled by Berlioz (table 7). It seems that he did not follow Reicha in wanting to enrich the language permanently by the acquisition of new metres. Caliban and the soothsayers are grotesque, Fieramosca comic; there remain only the eight bars of 'Combat de ceste' to rival the second movement of Chaikovsky's 'Pathétique' in the natural and graceful application of such metres. If it were not for their almost total neglect by his contemporaries, Berlioz's interest in such regular irregularities would seem tepid.

Ex. 73

Table 7. *Benvenuto* No. 7, 130–46

The Caliban passage also includes metrical counterpoint of a kind Berlioz occasionally employed elsewhere. The procession of Pluto's priests (Cat. 40A/49) is given a bodeful twist from bar 50 when, in the prevailing 4/4, bass drum and violins mark every third crotchet. After seventeen such '3/4 bars' one entry is advanced by a beat (bars 62–3); then the '3/4' is resumed until the end. Thus there are two distinct metres, their first beats coinciding only every three notated bars (certainly a very faint adumbration of parts of *The Rite of Spring*).

Mixed metres more usually combine different prolations within the same time. Such combinations can be successive ('rapid succession of alternating triple and duple') or simultaneous (where 'lesser divisions are irreconcilable'). The shorter values are in a 4:3 or 3:2 ratio, and the point of contact is often every strong beat, not just the first. Indeed the slower combinations, like 3/4 with 4/4, are much rarer than the faster and more easily assimilable (also more conventional) combinations like 4/4 and 6/4, or 2/4 and 6/8.

Berlioz relished the syncopations and 'two-beat bars, thrown, by accentuation of weak beats, across bars of three beats' in Beethoven (AT, 23, 31/G, 41, 49). Such cross-accentuation occurs in *Fantastique* II (bar 272, with wind in 3/8, strings in 2/8; from 320, *tutti* in 2/8); and often when 3/4 notation is employed in movements in 6/8, for which Berlioz preferred the notation without ties (e.g. *Harold*, Cat. 19/III; Berlioz wrote ♩♩ ♩ but OBE prints ♩♩ ♪♩.). In *Fantastique* V the prevailing 6/8 gives way to 3/4 which is itself syncopated (from bar 395); indeed this happens twice, and the first time (bar 78ff) the impetuous descent leads to an inserted bar of ¢ (table 8; the note marked 'X' has a value of five semiquavers of the 6/8). Berlioz must also have liked Beethoven's arresting bars of 2/2 in the scherzos of the 'Eroica' and Ninth symphonies. The equivalent in 6/8 is 2/4; the slower quaver-values break the headlong impetus of *Le carnaval romain* – but to turn in new directions rather than, as with Beethoven, to cadence (bar 397ff). 2/4 recurs at bars 432–3, but the use of semiquavers makes the prevailing values faster – eight instead of six to the bar. The more usual introduction of triplets into a prevailing simple time lends impetus by accelerating values, as in the coda of the *Francs-juges* overture (bar 624ff). In *La tempête* Berlioz alternates 6/4 and 4/4 during the main section. In the final *animato*, ¢ is soon modified by triplets (bar 597), before the signature changes to 6/4 (at bar 615) to accommodate its characteristic rhythms. The 6/4 is repeatedly shivered by sudden bars of ¢ (strings, 651, etc.), and the whole orchestra finally reverts to ¢ .

These examples are of somewhat unsystematic combinations, both successive and simultaneous. Berlioz's boldest and most systematic combination of 2/4 and 6/8 is the union of 'Choeur de soldats' and 'Chanson d'étudiants' (Cat. 32B/8), but there are numerous, less ostentatious, instances of this technique, which has its origin in eighteenth-century

Table 8. *Fantastique* V, 78–82

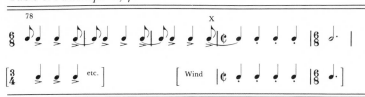

French opera. The elements are usually complete in themselves and are presented separately, then together. In this Berlioz is not particularly original, but he shows great skill and inventiveness; the listener can resolve the confusion of texture and hear with the lucidity of Mozart such breath-taking ensembles as the 3/4–9/8 passage in the great trio from *Benvenuto* (Cat. 23C/3).[61]

Shorter combinations of this kind can generate a very Berliozian type of climax. Usually the nineteenth-century orchestra works as a unit towards a single goal; this is even true when Wagner combines several motives and textures, wonderfully evoking both the scenic and emotional aspects of a dramatic climax, as at the end of *Die Walküre*. In Wagner the harmonies govern texture and motive and weld them into a unity. Berlioz was more concerned with simultaneity of the unlike than with unity, but his climaxes can be just as overwhelming. The 'last anguish' in *Roméo* (Cat. 25/VI) is represented by the abandonment of the exuberant 6/8, most of the wind throbbing in 3/4 and clarinets, sinuously low, in ¢ (from bar 158; the 6/8 is intermittently restored by the string basses, but when the whole orchestra turns to ¢ the violins at once divide it into triplets, effectively 6/8, bar 194). But the very premises of this remarkable movement are rhythmic, harmonic, and motivic dislocation.

It is otherwise with the 'Chasse royale' (Cat. 40A/29), which begins and ends with an idyll; yet at its climax is the *ne plus ultra* of metrical superimposition. The metres are associated with fanfares, heard from different directions and combined from bar 241 (see table 9). The fanfare in 6/8 uses mostly crotchets and quavers; that in 3/4 has minims and crotchets; that in   , minim, crotchet, and quaver values, the minim being equal to half a bar of 6/8. The confusion is increased from bar 246 by violin sestuplets in ¢ (quavers in 6/4 equivalent to semiquavers in 6/8), and by cross-accentuation in basses and bassoons, producing a 3/4 accentuation (cf. No. 49!) a third as fast again as the fanfare in 3/4. Add syncopation in ¢ and the spatial effect, and you have an exhilarating chaos unmatched before Ives. The neo-classical severity of *Les troyens* is seriously disturbed; but the music reflects, even though it does not try to embody, the emotional disorder of this dramatic turning-point. Dido yields to Aeneas in the cave, and the nymphs and satyrs scream the fateful 'Italie', its rhythm yet another element in the uproar, as well as a sort of *Leitmotiv*.

Table 9. 'Chasse royale', 245–8

COMBINED TEMPI

Berlioz's ideas of rhythmic consonance and dissonance, and of alternation
and combination of metres, are now accounted for. Examples could be
multiplied, in every period and mood. A very early example of superimposition is in the *Francs-juges* overture (Cat. 6), a subdued and sinister beat of the
drum in 3/4 against the prevailing ¢. But in fact the dominating impetus is
altogether slower, for the middle section (bars 193–336) is really Adagio,
notated in 4/1. It would be more natural to write this mournful melody in 4/4
(Ex. 74A). Various violin gestures struggle in vain to affect the essential
slowness; but the harmony, which in tonal music most controls our
experience of real speed, falls in with the melody and eventually subsides
onto a long pedal (bars 282–329). The famous combination of themes in
Roméo (Cat. 25/II) could be notated in the 3/4 of the first appearance of the
melody instead of 3/1 (Ex. 74B). Tovey points out that this passage 'reveals
what has already been open to suspicion, that the festive theme, for all its
leg-shakings and twitchings, never had any power of movement at all', and

Ex. 74

Cairns is recognizing the same musical facts when he says that the ball music 'deliberately creates a feeling of reckless gaiety, as the theme seems both to whirl forward and to remain in the same place'.[62] Not seems – it *does* remain, rooted in a pedal over which the few chord-changes are powerless to create a sense of movement or even articulate the periodicity of the dance.

The *Roméo* reunion shows a fundamental difference between Berlioz's rhythmic (and ultimately formal) language and that of the classical tradition, notably Beethoven. Tovey's observation is intended to underline the fact that when Beethoven introduced the slow 3/4 melody of the Adagio into the Allegro of *Leonora* no. 3, superimposition of tempi is precisely *not* his intention:

> he adapts it to the purposes of his second group . . . without slackening his pace . . . his semibreves not only maintain his allegro, but . . . lead to modulations of which the action is as rapid as anything the allegro can do; and you will not find it difficult to imagine the theme being cast in 3-bar rhythm so as to maintain its original adagio aspect; and, if you can imagine this, you will see at once that the allegro would from that moment have sagged beyond hope of recovery.[62]

To assist the imagination, Ex. 75A gives the adagio theme in bars of 3/1, superimposed upon Beethoven's actual rapid modulation by means of a sequential development (Ex. 75B). In *Roméo* II the most vital surface elements (including instrumentation – see Ex. 41) do not overcome the stasis in the medium term (i.e. the speed of Beethoven's modulations). This is not a weakness in Berlioz, whose intentions were quite different from Beethoven's; rhythm resumes its sway in the larger aspects of the music's form (see below, p. 194).

Ex. 75

'SPRUNG' RHYTHMS

The use of duple metre by cross-accentuation within a triple metre, or triple
within quadruple, is a form of compression; its converse, stretching what is
experienced as a rhythmic unit, may be related to the poetic idea of sprung
rhythm, in which a foot embraces several syllables rather than merely one or
two. I have pointed out the use of virtual 9/8 bars in the 6/8 of 'Chanson de
brigands' (above, p. 20). Similar extension marks the peroration of *Harold* I
(Cat. 19). Ex. 76 shows the unison line, in which *sforzando* markings, at first
on unexpected pitches, imply 9/8 and 12/8 bars (the *sforzando* C♯ in bar 378
retrospectively defines the preceeding '9/8 bar'; the distance to the G♯ is four
beats; and so on). The restoration of 6/8 is by no means sure even with the
regular rhythm of bar 389; only the fierce accents of bar 392 really redefine
the duple metre, and that mainly because we tend to experience an
undifferentiated series as duple. Taking a 6/8 bar as a crotchet, table 10

Ex. 76

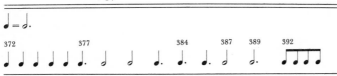

Table 10. *Harold* I, 372ff

shows the macrorhythm from the end of the stretto (bar 372) to the restoration of binary rhythm.

The best way to illustrate Berlioz's flexibility, his manipulation of asymmetrical 'feet' in sprung rhythm, is to examine music with one beat to a bar and convert it into the large bar-sizes that we hear, whose irregularity the one-beat notation disguises. Indeed Berlioz may have chosen one-beat notation precisely because it permits metrical compression, stretching, and counterpoint, without confusing the performers.

In 1829 Berlioz headed 'Chanson de Brander' (Cat. 32A/4) 'Ce morceau se bat à *un* temps', so that his 2/8 signature is in fact 1/4. The metrical counterpoint is between elements of irregular rhythm (table 11A). One might be tempted to postulate larger 4/4 'bars' (downward arrows), but the accentuation of the voice part, based on text and pitch contour, is more complex (line A). Line B is the intermittent *forte* of the orchestra; line C marks stabs of semiquavers in the 'cellos.[63] The voice rhythm is repeated exactly (bar 19ff), but with a different melody. Line C is repeated; line B has more attacks. The rest of the verse is more relaxed, implying 2/4 metre until the very end (shown in table 11B), and rhythmic counterpoint is dropped

Table 11. 'Chanson de Brander'

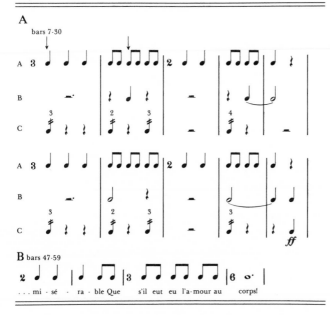

(two *forte* attacks, semiquaver groups in the violins on 'weak' bars of the vocal rhythms, were omitted in *La damnation*, Cat. 32B/6B).

Berlioz was partial to a fast 3/8, which again simplifies the notation of irregular metre. *Mab*, however, his largest movement in 3/8 (Cat. 25/IV), falls so much into four-bar groups that Liszt wrote: 'When I conduct it I like occasionally to use Beethoven's method of beating as if it were in 4/4 (*ritmo di quattro battute*, as in the Scherzo of the Ninth symphony), thus securing more response without affecting precision.'[64] The four-bar (or 12/8) metre prevails most of the way, and *Mab* is more remarkable for harmony and instrumentation than rhythm. There are, nevertheless, a few significant hiccups.[65]

Metrical stretching is doubtless the reason for the notation of a number of vocal pieces in 3/8; it occurs in the 'Chant des ciseleurs' (Cat. 23C/6B) and in the three G major 3/8 movements of *Béatrice* (Cat. 42/5, 7, and the 'Scherzo-duettino' which also begins the overture). The trio (No. 5) begins with 16 bars of duple groups (thus eight of 6/8), but forms a triple group (9/8) from bar 17 and alternates duple and triple to the E minor cadence (bar 33) (table 12A). Bars 34–66 repeat the rhythm of 1–33. Duple groups then predominate until another 9/8 'bar' (82–4) is defined by Benedick's upbeat 'D'une . . .' (table 12B). In bars 96–7 the orchestra compresses the metre with a 'hemiola', three 2/8 'bars' in two notated bars; a decisive $^6_4$ chord (bar 115) is approached by another sprung upbeat, a 9/8 after several 6/8 bars; and so on.

Table 12. *Béatrice* No. 5 (Trio)

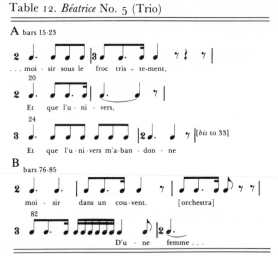

The 'Scherzo-duettino' is different in the nature of its irregularity, as it constantly reaccentuates motives in what is really an instrumental conception. Ex. 77 gives the melodic line in Berlioz's 3/8 notation. To this I add a proposed interpretation of the 'real' changing metre, in figures (3, 3, 2, etc.; cf. Friedheim's analysis, FriBR, 39). The accompaniment, however, has its own metrical implications. The attacks of its principal rhythm

Ex. 77

are indicated by downward strokes like crotchet stems. Its single quaver or semiquaver chords are shown by quaver stems. Friedheim's first duple group is supported by chords with the first off-beat attack in the accompaniment (bar 3); this projects forward to the undoubted duple groups of 5ff, until the opening rhythm returns in 9. From bar 12, however, accompanimental attack and implied melodic rhythm diverge. Friedheim's analysis assumes the melodic 𝅘𝅮𝅘𝅯 to be always an upbeat; but the accompaniment has accustomed us to hearing it as a downbeat from the start, and suggests that bar 12 is no different from bars 2 and 10. Certainly the G of bar 12 does not sound like the half-bar accent of a 4/8; but the F♯ of bar 13 must, by the same token, be a downbeat. The accompaniment is thrown onto the second beats of the 3/8 bars (this music would not be easy to perform in any notation), and proposes from the second quaver of bar 14 groups of 3, 2, 4, etc., a quaver ahead of Friedheim's melodic interpretation. Has the downbeat quality prevailed, or the upbeat? is the first beat of bar 13 downbeat, upbeat, or a 1/8 bar? In bars 19–20 the accompaniment again diverges from the melody and the barline. However from bar 19 the heard metre could simply be the written metre, or from bar 21 the accompaniment's 2–2–2, etc. The continuous rhythm from bar 23 implies nothing, unless an accent on chromatic pitches like E♭; if a duple metre is heard it is stretched in bar 25 by a final triple group – a more attractive interpretation, involving the whole of the polyphony, than Friedheim's symmetrical groups of 4/8. I propose no solution to these problems. They are insoluble ambiguities, indispensable to the music's charm.

INDEPENDENT RHYTHM

Another of Berlioz's ideas (above, p. 128) is the use of 'intermittent' sounds independent of other rhythmic and polyphonic elements. One candidate would be the discrete pedal; the 'Offertoire' was written only a few months before the 1837 article. However such ideas – the bells in *Harold* II, the psalmody of 'Convoi funèbre' – depend as much for their definition on pitch as on rhythm. The septet in *Les troyens* (Cat. 40A/36) adds to a continuous upper pedal an 'intermittent sound' (basses, horns, bass drum); this just escapes being a discrete pedal by one change of pitch, from F to A♭ (bar 27). However, in this piece, where the melody is periodic and the texture homophonic, the intermittent sound provides an irregular slow metre, mainly triple, against the almost consistent four-bar phrases; when there are longer gaps it is to allow the intermittent sound to coincide with a cadence or climax. The sounds appear in this series (semicolons mark gaps larger than three bars): bar 13 (cadence), 16, 19; 27, 30, 33, 36, 39; 47 (climax); 51 (cadence); 58; 62 (orchestral repeat of 47, 51). This too, however, impresses itself less as a rhythm than as intermittent colour, or as the breaking of waves on the nearby shore.

If we seek rhythms with a life of their own, we should look at Berlioz's accompaniments, for piquant accompanimental rhythms are themselves expressive, independently of the pitches to which they are applied. The idea is itself commonplace, but Berlioz's rhythm is particularly vital and varied at this level (see, for instance, Ex. 41). Rosen rightly traces to Gluck the 'conception of the dynamic accent' in such pieces as 'Lacrimosa' (Cat. 22/6; table 13A).[66] (This inheritance Berlioz shares with others such as Verdi.) Because of the accent on the sixth quaver the metre has been called 5/8 + 2/4 (FriBR, 25), but the cross-accent is soon dominated by the regularity of the melody, and the syncopations and off-beat accent sound just what they are. Another decidedly Gluckian displaced accent accompanies Dido's despairing 'Va, ma soeur, l'implorer' (Cat. 40A/45; table 13B).[67]

Just occasionally the musical texture is so fragmented that rhythm can emerge as the predominant element. Even an orchestral *tutti* may stagger on without melodic or tonal direction. From bar 106 the music of 'Scène aux

Table 13A. 'Lacrimosa'   Table 13B. *Les troyens* No. 45

champs' introduces prolonged values which remove smaller pulsations; when these recur it is to suggest 3/4 rather than 6/8 (bar 109), but the degeneration into a pulsation of semiquavers, alternately chord and silence, delays until bar 111 the revelation that the preceding notes were all syncopated. Another timeless note – an unresolved low Db, bar 112 – allows two possible interpretations of the scale (113–14); only with bar 115 is 6/8 perfectly clear again (table 14). Although it is remote in mood the precedent for such dislocation may be found in bars 176–80 of the first movement of Beethoven's Fifth Symphony.

Table 14. *Fantastique* III, 106ff

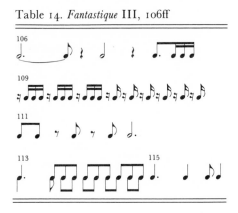

RHYTHMIC MODULATION

The notion of rhythmic modulation (see above, p. 128) could be realized in two ways: a gradual change of speed leading to a new tempo, or the gearing of successive metres and tempi by a fixed relationship. As a conductor Berlioz seems to have favoured strict tempi; he regarded Wagner's conducting as too free, Wagner thought Berlioz's insensitive.[68] Berlioz followed Beethoven in giving metronome marks, a practice Wagner abandoned. Wagner wanted his music flexibly interpreted; Berlioz, like Stravinsky, wanted *reading* rather than interpretation. This does not mean that his tempi are inflexible; only that his modifications of tempo are instructions rather than suggestions. Numerous *rallentandi* are marked – momentarily expressive effects which should not be allowed to break the continuity of metre (as they sometimes are; e.g. *Fantastique* II, 49–50, or *Roméo* III, 277). Berlioz used the metronome to prescribe modifications of speed; the 'Scène d'amour' is particularly rich in such indications.

However these hardly constitute *rhythmic* modulation. A nearer approach is the common marking of the type 'twice as fast', a precise tempo relationship; but this is a coordination of adjacent sections with no modulatory bridge. Such a marking is often associated with thematic transference. A very early instance, in the *Scène héroïque* (Cat. 4/4, bar 60), has both a verbal direction to double the speed and a metronome mark – an understandable precaution in a piece which was muffed at the first performance.[69] Sometimes the directions are less precise. At Cassandra's first entrance (Cat. 40A/2), 'This bar is equivalent to a little more than eight bars of the preceding movement' is reinforced by a metronome mark ♪ = 160; an exact equivalence would require 168. *Harold* (Cat. 19/I) has a controlled *accelerando* marked at critical points: Allegro, ♩. = 104; at bar 312, ♩. = 120; at bar 321 (the fugato), *animando*; at bar 350 (stretto), *animando*; at bar 438, 'approximately double the speed of the original Allegro', but ♩. = 160, which is in fact only about half again as fast as ♩. = 104; at bar 468 (just before the coda), ♩. = 168.

At least once, Berlioz did achieve a primitive form of the metric modulation developed to a high degree of complexity by Elliott Carter. *La damnation* (Cat. 32B) provides three examples of composed links, of which the one in the 'Introduction' is a true modulation. In No. 7B, the 6/8 Allegro (bar 61) is superimposed onto the 3/4 with ♩. = ♩. At the end the 3/4 virtually becomes 9/8 through violin triplets; these use the motive of the 'Ballet de sylphes' (No. 7C) which follows at once, with the ratio ♩. = ♩. In Margaret's 'Romance' in the *Huit scènes* (Cat. 32A/7), the drumtap in 2/4 overlaps with the Adagio in 3/4 in the ratio ♩ = ♩. The fanfare for the retreat is in 2/4, the soldiers' chorus superimposed on it is in 6/8, so the modulation is made in two easy stages, ♩ = ♩ = ♩. = 58, or, for the chorus, ♩. = 116. Berlioz wrote 'sans rallentir' near the end of the cor anglais melody, and gave no new tempo indications, nor any metronome mark. When the chorus was revised for *La damnation* (Cat. 32B/8) it was marked ♩. = 96 instead of 116; several such modifications were made for *La damnation*, including the slowing of the 'Romance' to ♩. = 50. At the end of the 'Romance' (Cat. 32B/15), the 'sans rallentir' and metric modulation remain; the reminiscence of the soldiers' chorus (at ♩ = ♩ = ♩. = 50) thus emerges at ♩. = 100, slower than in the *Huit scènes*, faster than in Part II of *La damnation*. Although Berlioz no longer combined drumtaps with the last strain of the 'Romance' itself, he put their rhythm, in halved note-values (and thus the identical speed), into the very last reminiscence of it (bar 192), on pizzicato strings. A rhythmic trick can seldom more evidently have been devoted to a poetic end.

It was in the 'Introduction' to Part I that Berlioz achieved his most felicitous rhythmic modulation. Foretastes of the 'Ronde de paysans' and 'Marche hongroise' mingle with the development of the opening idea, beneath the tonally dissonant pedals (Ex. 45 above). The 'Ronde' follows at once, marked 'le double plus vite'. Ex. 78A shows a phrase which is used exactly in the 'Introduction', cross-accented and in halved values. Two other motives from the 'Ronde', however, are markedly accelerated for the sake of a more pungent rhythm within the placid 6/8 of the 'Introduction'

Ex. 78

'Ronde de paysans'

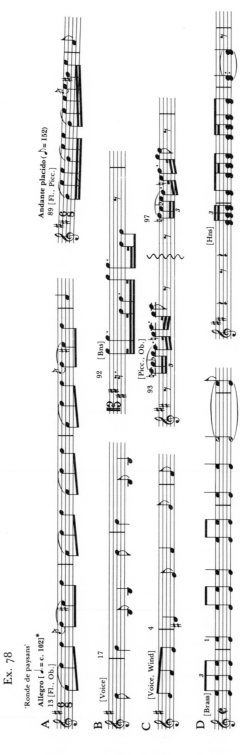

* Berlioz marks the 'Ronde' ♩= 110, a little faster than is implied by his proportional direction (see Ex. 79).

(Exx. 78B and C). The 'Marche' (Ex. 78D), however, appears rather slower in the 'Introduction', again cross-accented and in halved note-values. The 'Introduction' is then linked to the 'Ronde' by the reaccentuation within the first tempo of the common unit, to make it correspond to the second, a genuine metric modulation (Ex. 79); that a new movement has started should be heard from the change of instrumentation, not of speed. (Berlioz did not, however, calculate exactly; from the Andante's ♪ = 152, the 'Ronde' should be ♩. = c. 102, but it is marked 110.)

Ex. 79

Rhythm cannot be divorced from other elements, like melody and harmony, but it acquires in Berlioz a pronounced character which enables it to emerge from time to time as a structural force on its own. Rhythmic elements in general – hemiola, misplaced accent, syncopation – produce the floating effect in relation to a strict pulse which is Berlioz's hallmark, and in which none of his contemporaries can match him. It is perhaps the single most wholly original aspect of his music. Schumann, as so often, was the first to remark on it:

> The music of our day can offer no example in which metre and rhythm are more freely set to work in symmetrical and asymmetrical combinations, than in this one [the *Fantastique*]. Hardly ever does consequent correspond to antedecent, or answer to question . . . It seems that in the present instance music is trying to return to its origins, when it was not yet bound by the law of the downbeat, and to achieve on its own a prose style or a higher poetic articulation (ConFS, 237).

Berlioz's originality in rhythm lies less in any one significant innovation than in the profusion of his rhythmic ideas and their distinctness from the preoccupations of his contemporaries. Even at their most daring his rhythmic schemes still have much in common with Gluck's, and their background is post-classical periodicity and a melody-dominated style. This style was developed to some extent in instrumental music by Schubert and Mendelssohn, but it is still based in Italian and French opera (as will be seen in Chapter 10). Berlioz obviously has less in common with Schumann or Wagner, both of whom used wrongly to be considered deficient in rhythmic invention. Schumann's accumulation of impetus through the repetition of rhythmic cells results partly from a revival of interest in baroque music in which Berlioz did not participate. Berlioz's rhythmic pulsations, unlike Wagner's, usually aim to reinforce rather than obscure the beat, however displaced; his music is more naturally related to the dance. Yet we do not find in Berlioz the vast rhythmic schemes of Schubert's instrumental music, his obsessive repetition of cells, the extended rhythmic drive of, for instance, the finale of the 'Great' C major. Berlioz is always 'nerveux' – some might say jittery. His music does not accumulate; sections separated from each other inter-react in making a large structure. Rhythmic propulsion based on a short motive is used for casting the statue in *Benvenuto*, but it does not develop like one of Schubert's giant tarantellas; the rhythm is as unsettled as the harmony, forming periods on the smallest scale (by immediate repetition) and on the largest (by a long repeat), but not on the more cohesive intermediate levels of phrase-structure (indeed, the motive appears in two metres, triplets in ₵ becoming quavers in 6/8). Even the dashing tarantella of *Le carnaval romain* is adroitly broken up with all kinds of metric displacement, as well as by harmonic, orchestral, and melodic twists. At its fastest Berlioz's music is lithe and athletic, but it never becomes virtually self-propelling like Schubert's or Schumann's. It is the athleticism of the gymnast, a scheme of coordinated but unlike movements, not of the specialist runner. Nevertheless, in almost every category of rhythmic inventiveness Berlioz is peerless in the period between Beethoven and Stravinsky.

10 Melody

'If M. Fétis maintains that even Berlioz's warmest friends would not dare to defend him as a melodist, then I belong among Berlioz's enemies'

Robert Schumann (ConFS, 241)

The present chapter attempts a double task, of dealing with the nature of Berlioz's melodic idiom, and with melodic structure, a foundation of his musical form. Fortunately Berlioz requires no defence as a melodist; here at least the strictures of Fétis (ConFS, 219) and Vallas (ValG5, 663) can safely be ignored. Abundant melody is one of the most obvious qualities of his music. As Berlioz observed:

> One may well want to dispute the value of these melodies, their distinction, their novelty and charm; it is not for me to evaluate them. But to deny their existence is, I submit, bad faith or incompetence. However, as these melodies are often of very large span, childish minds, with a short vision, cannot clearly make out their shape . . . they are so unlike the little baubles called melodies by ordinary listeners, that they cannot bring themselves to give the same name to both (MemPS).

Schumann was the first to comment on the freedom and independence of Berlioz's melodic thought (see above, p. 99). He was also concerned to differentiate Berlioz's melodic ideas from 'melodies of the Italian type, which one knows by heart even before they have begun' (ConFS, 241). This deeply sympathetic and percipient critique, however, should not blind us to the real connection between Berlioz and Italian melody. Moreover, the quality that Schumann observed in Berlioz's melody need not preclude consideration of its harmonization in a stylistic analysis. The question of Berlioz's competence hangs on this in a number of ways. Dent attributed Berlioz's 'harmonic oddity' to 'the intensity of his melodic sense', and he observed that 'both Berlioz and Weber owe a great deal to the influence of Italian melody' (Dent, 1932–3, p. 92). Boulez draws a direct contrast with Schumann: '[Berlioz] invents melodies that contain certain references to Weber or to Beethoven, then harmonizes them in an extremely clumsy way; so in his case, melodic and harmonic invention do not coincide. We do not find, as in Schumann, the invention of a melody which carries its own harmony; that does not exist in Berlioz'.[70]

It is tempting, in the face of these remarks, to isolate melody from the other elements; but in tonal music it cannot be done. Reicha declared this intention when he subtitled his *Traité de mélodie* with the words 'abstraction faite de ses rapports avec l'harmonie'. In no time, however, he is discussing scales, modulations, and cadences, as the indispensable syntax of melody, together with intervals and durations. All he omits, therefore, is the contrapuntal realization of the harmony; the harmonic essence, as the basis of that periodicity on which he is so insistent, still lies behind his analyses. Berlioz's melodies often sound well unaccompanied; to most, however, the composer gives a framework of bass and harmony. Schumann did not say that Berlioz *ought* not to have harmonized his melodies, but that they defy *ordinary* harmonization. If they were better unharmonized, we could infer, then Berlioz should not have set them the way he did.

In fact, most of Berlioz's melodies have clear tonal and harmonic implications: some of these are fulfilled, others denied. But they are difficult to harmonize in an 'ordinary' way, for rhythmic reasons. Classic and romantic melody usually implies harmonic motion of some consistency and smoothness; Berlioz's aspiration to musical prose tends to resist such consistency, because, as Schumann observed, antecedent and consequent phrases are not always symmetrically balanced (see above, p. 142). The application of conventional, workmanlike harmony is therefore liable to jar, if it does not produce an efficient platitude. Whether Berlioz's harmonies always work is a matter on which critical opinion is likely to remain divided; but it is no use trying to defend him by denying their relevance. Moreover, they are often extraordinarily eloquent.

The withdrawal of periodicity, of consequent balancing antecedent, deprives the 'childish mind' of regular repose. Cone remarks that 'Berlioz's melodies forbid the easy comprehension that allows even the untutored to enjoy, though only superficially, the arias of Mozart and Verdi. You cannot appreciate a Berlioz melody superficially; you cannot grasp it at all unless you are willing to give it your undivided attention from beginning to end' (Cone, 1953, p. 141). The view may seem élitist, as was Berlioz's own; but the background to his melody is not the instrumental, motivically organized melody of his German contemporaries, but the popular vocal melody of France and Italy – which he was far from despising. As a preliminary example (Ex. 80) the first melody of the *Symphonie funèbre* (Cat. 26) will serve, as its second will for the final example in this chapter. Bars 7–8 could perfectly well close in A♭, a symmetrical consequent (lower staff). Instead Berlioz interrupts by a melodic rise in bars 6–7, and a D♮, with diminished 7th – a method he could have learned from Catel or Reicha. The indeterminacy of bar 8 projects it forward into bar 9; bar 9 picks up the

Ex. 80

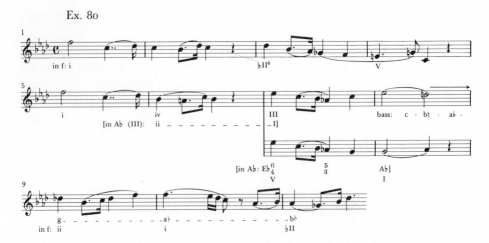

rhythm not of bars 1 and 5, but of 3 and 7; the end of bar 10 introduces the first anacrusis, using the rhythm occurring on five previous second beats; and the melody does not come to rest (in the dominant) until bar 23 of the movement. Reicha's symmetrical period, for him the foundation of true melody, is overthrown – in a piece in march tempo which Wagner acclaimed as truly popular.[71]

CHARACTERISTICS AND SOURCES

Two recent analyses of Berlioz's melodic style take opposite approaches. Primmer concentrates on phrase-structure and contour (PriBS, Chapter 2), while Schenkman's intention is apparent in his title 'Fixed ideas and recurring patterns' (1979). Schenkman uses the repetition of certain fundamental configurations to demonstrate, not the structural unity of a single composition (as in Réti's analytical system), but the stylistic unity of the composer's output.[72] The fingerprints detected by Schenkman (Ex. 81) are remarkably chromatic for so diatonic a composer; and four of them are grouped around the dominant, which has obvious advantages for potential richness of harmonic reference as well as for melodic tension, since it will tend to prolong a pitch requiring resolution within the melodic line. Each shape has one or more auxiliary note, and three fall to the mediant (cf. the F♯–G–F♮–E of the *Fantastique* 'idée fixe'). Schenkman compares these shapes to Schumann's 'Sphinxes' (*Carnaval*), but those are deliberately odd

Ex. 81

[all in C]

configurations derived from letters, whereas Berlioz's consist of clichés from the *lingua franca* of tonal music.

Schenkman's conclusion is curiously hostile: he suggests that Berlioz was 'less the conscious master than the helpless slave of his ever-present melodic formulae'. If not patent nonsense, this certainly confuses analytical ends with means. The analysis of whole melodies, as opposed to the isolation of certain building-blocks, shows, on the contrary, the mastery and diversity of Berlioz's melody. Schenkman's sample is relatively small (mainly the symphonies); a brief check through some other works suggests that these formulae are not always embedded in the principal melodic shapes, even if they occur from time to time in the course of melodic extension and development. Stylistic analysis of this kind, however, sheds some light upon Vallas's claims about the folk and liturgical sources of Berlioz's melodic invention (see note 3): one of Vallas's examples is the opening melody of *La damnation*, which has a prominent fingerprint, ♭6–♮6.[72]

One thing rings true – the hint of a vocal origin to Berlioz's melodic idiom. Schumann understood this when he said that the melodies of the *Fantastique* needed to be sung (if inwardly) to be comprehended (ConFS, 243). The textures and forms of song and aria are at the root of Berlioz's whole style – harmonic, polyphonic, and structural (see Chapter 11), as well as melodic. In melody his vocal and instrumental styles are the same, as is demonstrated by the vocal origins of several melodies which receive instrumental treatment: the opening of the *Fantastique*, for example (see NBE 16, p. 194), and its 'idée fixe', first heard in *Herminie*; the oboe solo in *Roméo* II, from *Sardanapale*; the cor anglais melody in *Le carnaval romain*, from *Cléopâtre* by way of *Benvenuto*; the 'Sicilienne' in *Béatrice*, from *Le dépit*; and the middle movement of the *Symphonie funèbre*, from *Les francs-juges*. Others may well have unknown vocal sources, even if their instrumental setting goes beyond the capabilities of the voice. This possibility is shown by a melody in *La tempête* (from bar 230), which occupies a range of nearly two octaves, whereas the vocal original in *Cléopâtre* covers only a 9th (Cat. 10B/4, bar 25ff); and by Ex. 82, from *Benvenuto*, in which the range of the instrumental version is only a little greater, but the end is changed by delaying, then precipitating, the descent in chuckling Rossinian quavers – a quite unvocal ornament (Ex. 82 is also an example of a melody transformed by its altered metre).

Ex. 82

Ex. 82 (contd)

Berlioz's ornaments include the portamento over a 4th, to extend a syllable in vocal music; besides Ex. 80, bar 10, and Ex. 83, it appears in *Le spectre de la rose* (Cat. 27B), *Petit oiseau* (Cat. 37B), and the 'Marche troyenne' (Cat. 40A/11). He is fond of turns, in both vocal and instrumental music (*Les nuits d'été* and the 'Scène d'amour' are full of them). He also uses sequence to tie up the ends of a melody; examples include *La captive* (Cat. 18) and the cor anglais melody of *Le carnaval romain* (alias Cat. 23C/3). All these features appear in the last stanza of a little-known song, *La belle Isabeau* (Ex. 83). Berlioz's melodies are the reverse of austere, but while they never disappear beneath ornamentation, as do Rossini's, they make plentiful use of

Ex. 83

auxiliaries which are ornamental by nature. An upper auxiliary appears in the first oboe solo of *Lear* (Cat. 15, bar 38); a lower one in *Roméo* (Cat. 25/II, bar 2) and in the clarinet solo in *Les troyens* (Cat. 40A/6), both of which give the impression of the melody completing a line of verse.

Typically vocal, too, is the appoggiatura, which Berlioz is often said to have disliked. In fact, as with fugue, he objected not to the appoggiatura but to its abuse. The appoggiatura cannot be dissociated from harmony, since a melodic shape contains one, or does not, if the chords precede it onto the point of resolution, or move with it. Berlioz certainly disliked such things as Ex. 84, from Adam's *Giselle*, an instrumental piece of *bel canto*; the upward and downward appoggiature (arrowed) are prolonged and frequent, on more than half the first beats. In his critique of Hérold's *Zampa* Berlioz refers to 'superfluity of sickly appoggiature . . . which de-nature all the chords'; they 'lend the harmony a vagueness, without definite character, which weakens the effect of certain dissonances or increases it towards discord; transforms softness into pallor, makes elegance into a simper, and in sum appears the most intolerable affectation of the Parisian school' (MM, 132, 136). This curiously anticipates his view of the *Tristan* prelude (AT, 311/G, 327). In his obituary of Bellini, however, Berlioz mentions that a profusion of appoggiature is a feature of Bellini's best and worst melodies; those he praises are full of them (MM, 167ff). Nor did he object to Gluck's appoggiature: Alceste's air 'Ah, divinités implacables' contains five in a row, and Berlioz called it 'a melodic shape of incomparable beauty' (AT, 188/G, 206).

Ex. 84

In his own music Berlioz uses appoggiature selectively, with some preference for the anticipated kind which, if the preparation is long enough, is properly called a suspension (expressively, however, the distinction is not great; and no-one who disliked appoggiature as such would make much use of suspensions). In *La tempête* (Cat. 17/VI) it is not an Italian text which causes them to proliferate from bar 230, for the melody came from *Cléopâtre*. Berlioz never uses appoggiature systematically, or perfunctorily; he has no habits, and often removes or adds them when reharmonizing (as in the *Cléopâtre–Tempête* melody, or Ex. 52). The elegantly yearning Italianate appoggiatura is part of his vocabulary (see Exx. 5A, 56, and 85A from *Roméo* II, which with its melting 3rds caused Macdonald to remark that it 'might almost have come from Bellini'; MacBO, 49). The same 4–3 appoggiatura, momentarily anticipated, is used as Aeneas utters the terrible truth: 'Je pars et je vous aime' (Ex. 85B); there are relatively so few appoggiature in *Les troyens* that this one has tremendous impact. But in some works Berlioz uses the anticipated appoggiatura more consistently; it forms the basis of the refrain of *La mort d'Ophélie*, assuredly one of his loveliest and most characteristic smaller pieces (Cat. 34B).

Ex. 85

With coloratura ornamentation, too, it is *abuse* to which Berlioz objected. His denunciation of the florid end to Donna Anna's 'Non mi dir' would have been less vehement if it were not by Mozart and if he had not been so deeply affected by the preceding Larghetto (Mem17). He supplied cadenzas in his operas, perhaps for the gratification of singers (Cat. 23C/2 and 14; Cat. 42/3, and 7 (later omitted) – see NBE 3, p. 305), perhaps, too, with a trace of irony, although there is manuscript evidence of his composing them with care. He did not take the opportunity to omit them when revising *Benvenuto* for performance in Weimar under the aegis of *Zukunftsmusik*. He ornamented the parts of Dido in the septet and Aeneas in the duet (Cat. 40A/36, 37), although he wrote *Les troyens* to please himself; and the regal Dido in her first air (No. 19) is positively flamboyant (Ex. 86). It is neither surprising nor vexatious to find such 'Italianisms' (if they are that) in Berlioz. Liszt, even at

Ex. 86

times Wagner, flirted with Italian melody as something gracious but foreign to their normal selves. For Berlioz, thanks to the 'Parisian school', it was hardly foreign; French music had been mixed up with Italian for decades. In any case, the melody of Weber, Bellini, and Berlioz, is as significant an aspect of musical romanticism as the harmony of Schumann, Liszt, or Wagner.

FOLK MUSIC SOURCES

Like other composers of his time, including Schumann, Berlioz took an interest in folk music and was open to its influence. We have already seen how its modal inflections fed his ideas for extending the range of normal tonal scales (see Chapter 4). At times he borrowed openly from folk and popular sources, the 'Marche hongroise' (Cat. 32B/3) having something of both; and several pieces owe their atmosphere to the natural grace of folksong. His partiality for 6/8 metre probably stems from folksong of Dauphiné, Auvergne, and Provence. Although its harmonic range is greater, the lovely *Petit oiseau* (Cat. 37B) is a close cousin to numerous folksongs, and their effect may be felt in such diverse places as *La belle voyageuse* (Cat. 12D) and the main theme of 'Scène aux champs'. Berlioz's most heart-felt music is often in a slowish 6/8: the 'Scène d'amour' (Cat. 25/III), the opening of *La damnation*, the love-duet in *Les troyens*, and the Duo-nocturne and women's trio in *Béatrice*. His lively 6/8 metres may also have their origins in folk music. Tiersot collected a 'Ronde de paysans' from Dauphiné, in 6/8 but with a 'Tra la la' refrain in 2/4; it is worth noting that Berlioz added the latter feature to his own 'Ronde de paysans' in 1846, for it does not appear in Goethe's verses and thus not in the *Huit scènes* (see Cat. 32).

The influence of traditional Noëls is obvious in the 'Adieu des bergers' (Cat. 38/8). For example, 'Noël du pauvre pâtre' from Auvergne has a Berliozian ambiguity of mode (it moves from F major to D minor). The familiar 'Un flambeau, Jeannette, Isabelle' feels very close to the atmosphere of *L'enfance* (a version appears in the collection of Saboly, a contemporary of the fictitious composer of the 'Adieu', 'Pierre Ducré, imaginary 17th-century chapelmaster', GM, 169ff/G, 185ff). The 'Adieu' is nevertheless introduced by the sound of *pifferari*. It is as if Berlioz wished to draw together round the crib a wider community represented by Italian bagpipes, French folksong, and the modern language of enharmony (the modulation from C♯ minor to C major, bars 25–32, is inconceivable from any seventeenth-century chapelmaster, even Charpentier). Berlioz used a livelier strain of *pifferari* on two occasions: *Harold* (Cat. 19/III), and the *Sérénade agreste à la Madone* (Cat. 30A), which is strikingly like a saltarello for mandoline or violin with guitar ostinato in Didier's collection of popular music from the Campagna (see also Mem39). A song from that area appears in *Benvenuto* (Cat. 23C/15); it is a mournful working song, despite its identity with the cheerful greeting of Berlioz's friend Crispino (Mem38). These last instances are of course undisguised imitation. Elsewhere Berlioz stylizes; despite its simple beauty, the sailor's song in *Les troyens* (Cat. 40A/38) could hardly be a folksong – any more than that in *Tristan* – and no cowherd could play the 'Ranz des vaches' in 'Scène aux champs'. Berlioz thought seriously about the aesthetic problems raised by such evocations (see his 'On Imitation in Music', ConFS, 36ff).[73]

MELODIC STRUCTURE

In the organization of long melodic paragraphs the primary influence on Berlioz was certainly Gluck. It may seem perverse that of the five melodies to be analysed here only two are by Berlioz, but it seems right to demonstrate the background from which he diverged in his own day, through Bellini, as well as the sources of such divergence which lie in Spontini as well as Gluck. It appears that the Spontini melody (Ex. 90) has much in common with the Bellini (Ex. 87). But certain elements in it diverge markedly from the Italian tradition to which Bellini adheres, and it is those elements which caused Berlioz to hear Spontini less as an Italian than as the successor to Gluck. Exx. 92 and 93 will help to show what Gluck and Berlioz have in common; then having begun the chapter with a glance at one melody from the *Symphonie funèbre*, I conclude with another (Ex. 95), for the sake of its extraordinary length and span.

Bellini may represent the Italianate ideal because his harmony is genuinely simple (whereas Berlioz's only seems so). His whole soul was in melody; he might be held to epitomize the vices of his school precisely because he has its virtues in unusual abundance. Ex. 87 gives one of his loveliest inspirations, from the second part of *I puritani* (1835), written for Paris. The melody is divided between Elvira, who at this point is out of her mind, and the orchestra. Ex. 87 conflates their roles; notes given to the orchestra alone are printed small.

The outline structure is of paired phrases with similar, rather than complementary, harmonic action. The third pair of phrases (C, C[1]) restores the upbeat structure of the first; the bar-count is 4–7: 4–4: 4–4 (a seven-bar phrase is unusual in this normally quadrilateral composer, but not unique: 'Casta diva' begins 4–4–7). Harmonically, both the antecedent and the consequent of period A, as so often in Mozart, end on the tonic. Melodically, both rise to eb^2 and fall through the octave. In the antecedent the harmony is simple, but not impoverished; the most expressive element is the 4–3 appoggiatura (arrowed here, although it seems superfluous to point out all the appoggiature). Before the voice begins the orchestra plays the melody

Ex. 87

(starting ten bars before Ex. 87), with a four-bar consequent almost identical to the antecedent; subsequently B[1] and C[1] prove almost identical to B and C. In A[1] of Ex. 87, however, the diminished 7th with appoggiatura (bar 6) breaks the symmetry (cf. Ex. 80). Similar interruptions occur, although over a tonic bass, in *Le spectre de la rose* (Ex. 88A, bar 11, transposed for comparison) and *Les troyens* (Narbal's air, No. 31; the version in Ex. 88B is from the prelude to the scene, No. 30). The sequel in Ex. 87 is the dissolution of the texture in a Berliozian chain of diminished 7ths; but Bellini, even with

Ex. 88

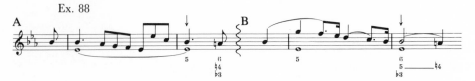

a mad heroine, keeps a hold on the main key, for the resolution in bar 9 onto a supertonic harmony clearly points to the tonic cadence which follows.

Period B falls into two parts, identical except for details of declamation, the harmony of the upbeat bars (11 and 15), and the vocal range (to g^2 in section B^1). The line is more constricted than in period A, its stepwise movement confined within the range of bb^1–g^2, and the harmony is mostly submediant. A brief dominant leads to the glorious melodic flowering of Period C. This also consists of two essentially identical four-bar phrases but it avoids the 2 + 2 of period B; and C^1, extended by its cadenza, rises to ab^2. Berlioz may have remembered this lovely phrase when composing his 'Scène d'amour'; the b6th is only the most obvious of the elements permutated in both melodies (contents of enclosures in Ex. 89; A by Bellini, B by Berlioz).

Ex. 89

When compared with Berlioz's most remarkable melodic spans, Bellini's seem repetitive and symmetrical. 'Qui la voce' projects its one seven-bar phrase against a background (already heard in the orchestra) of four bars. Bellini cadences more than Berlioz; every section departs from a tonic, and only B does not end with one. For these reasons Bellini's long spans are more illusory than Berlioz's, whose extensions rest upon varied repetition, running-together of phrases, more elaborate harmony, and a more consistent evasion of symmetry.

Nevertheless the kind of development that led to Bellini also led to Berlioz; this is at least a possible conclusion to be drawn from Ex. 90, the cantabile from the great *scena* in the second act of *La vestale* (1807). Spontini's melody has all the Italianate elegance of clear phrasing, predominantly stepwise movement, and delicately applied ornamentation, which indicates a descendant of Piccinni. Yet in contrast to the pure Italian line of descent through Cimarosa and Rossini to Bellini, Spontini's expressive irregularities and declamatory force derive from the tradition which his major works extend, the French operas of Gluck. The lesson was not lost upon Berlioz. Ex. 90 shares with Ex. 87 its outline structure (Eb with a C minor middle section); its opening curve, with a 4–3 appoggiatura over an Ab (here as part of a descent from eb^2 to g^1); and the harmonic scheme of its first phrase, going from the tonic via the supertonic to the dominant, and back (I–ii–V–I). The

Ex. 90

Ex. 90 (contd)

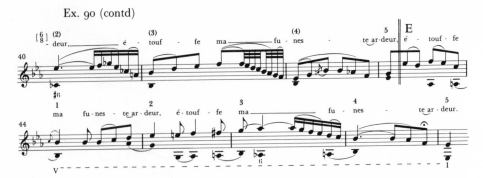

differences are instructive. Spontini makes his opening move only once, welding antecedent to consequent in a single seven-bar span, whereas Bellini does it twice, first in four then in seven bars. Spontini has a short-term tonic pedal (bars 1–2), and then declines to resolve the 7th in bar 3 (d^1–c^2) to the expected eb^1–bb^1 (cf. Ex. 87, bars 12–13, 16–17). Instead he takes the bass down to C and arpeggiates to Ab for the ii^6 chord (bar 5). The outline of the phrase is reduced in Ex. 91A, a counterpoint which suggests narrow avoidance of parallel 5ths onto C/g^1 (which contribute materially to the expression here but are 'corrected' at the reprise, bars 33–4, when the resolution is duly made onto eb/bb^1).

Such expedients might well have appealed to Berlioz, who liked such bass pedals as this, which Spontini extends into the fourth bar of period B. The outline of period B is similar to that of A, but similar melodic motives produce a very different tune (Ex. 91 B). The new phrase lasts nine bars, with the supertonic (bar 11, cf. bars 5–6) divided from the dominant at the point where the words are repeated, thus breaking the symmetry of 2 + 2 (bars 8–11). Word-repetition seems to throw emphasis on the half-bar (bar 11), making a 9/8 'bar'; the sprung rhythm projects onto the emphatic chromatic chord of bar 13.

Ex. 91

Period C opens remarkably like Bellini's period B, but the main sequence occurs only once, to be followed by another in single-bar units (from bar 23). These form an unbroken eight-bar phrase, driving to an ab² (from bar 27), which coincides with a change of direction in the bass, to Cb. Spontini then repeats his opening (period D), but modifies the antecedent and replaces the consequent (cf. bar 5) with period B (from bar 35). The coda (period E) makes a final thrust to ab² which causes a harmonic change on the second quaver of the bar, where a ⁶₄ would be expected (bar 46); this seems strikingly Berliozian.

By 1820 or so the Italian basis of Gluck's style can scarcely have been recognizable, and his influence on Spontini, Méhul, Cherubini, or Lesueur would seem, in the aftermath of Piccinnisme, to be Franco-German. Nevertheless Berlioz's roots are in a style Gluck developed in setting Italian words. In a letter of 1860 Berlioz quoted 'O malheureuse Iphigénie' (which he knew was originally composed to a Metastasio text, 'Se mai senti spirarti' in *La clemenza di Tito*), with four exclamation marks as sufficient comment. Elsewhere he said: 'The antique colouring, the solemn tone, the noble desolation of melody and accompaniment, recall the sublimities of Homer' (SO, 22). To a great extent the aria depends on dynamic accent, but it also has a melody phrased like noble but irregular verse (see Tovey's analysis).[74] The source of Berlioz's fluid, organic musical prose, wayward but always expressive, clearly lies in Gluck, whose 'prose' results from his determination, in both Italian and French operas, to reflect the proper declamation of the text in his melodic line, if necessary at the expense of the steady metres generally characteristic of the late 18th century.

Ex. 92, Gluck's 'Ah, malgré moi', is the perfect recomposition in French (which Berlioz will have known first) of an aria originally in the Italian version of *Alceste* ('Io non chiedo'). It is accompanied simply, without dynamic accents; and it leads directly into, and is harmonically completed by, an Allegro in 6/8 ('O ciel! quel supplice'). Berlioz called it 'this immortal adagio which in grandeur of style surpasses anything known in this kind of music . . . What melodic substance! what modulations! what control in the accents over this unrelenting orchestral accompaniment!' (AT, 183/G, 202).

Gluck proceeds in clearly defined periods, but displays his unique control over the long paragraph by projecting each phrase on to the next. Section I, to the A minor cadence (bar 21), consists of five phrases, the last two (repeating the text) being closely linked. Phrase A defines the tonic and the full melodic range, between the initial c² and f¹. Phrase B introduces an anacrusis and extends the range slightly to d², with a chromatic inflection (b♮¹) which gives a new significance to the bass F; otherwise the harmonic structure is virtually the same as in A. Phrase C establishes a new range (f²–bb¹), and moves through Bb to G minor, without implying a secure tonality. Each phrase in the voice ends on the 3rd of the chord; the melodic

Ex. 92

Ex. 92 (contd)

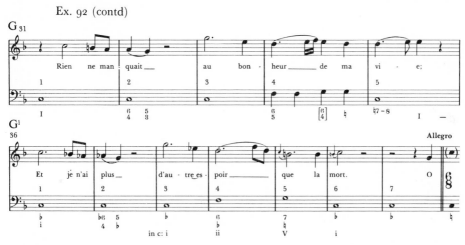

head-note is clearly c². The flatward move of phrase C heightens the expressive contrast of the subsequent sharper keys (up two 5ths, via D to A minor). Phrase D ascends within the same range as C and is linked to D¹ because it ends on a dominant; the cadence goes over from bar 16 to 17. It is, however, virtually interrupted by the diminished 7th on G♯, which is the more biting for being a syncopation. With no extension of range, phrase D¹ marks the climax by holding f² for three full beats and by modulating to the mediant; it is also the first phrase to exceed four bars, its underlying harmonies, i–ii–V–i (in A minor), being drawn out over its second to fifth bars (18–21).

Section II intensifies the modulation, ending in C *minor* instead of major. Phrases E and F are again of four bars, with a free sequence through F and G, preparing for C major (brackets in Ex. 92 show the interversion of motives). E slightly extends the range down, and F makes poignant use of minor inflections. In such a declaimed melody a variety of motives is bound to arise, which Gluck here puts under some measure of control: the next motive ('Rien ne manquait') is derived from bar 17 ('Que j'ai besoin') and returns for 'Et je n'ai plus' (bar 36), binding the whole melody together. Phrases G and G¹ have different texts but are otherwise virtually identical except for the change of mode and the cadence; G¹ is extended from 2 + 3 to 2 + 4 bars by a slower rate of chord-change, an extension corresponding to the end of section I. The dominant minor is turned back to major (as V of F) at the start of the Allegro.

The influence of this kind of melodic thought on Berlioz is made clear in his most Gluckian work, *Les troyens* (Cat. 40A). Aeneas's air (No. 41, Andante; Ex. 93), in the same key as Gluck's, has similarities of structure despite Berlioz's tendency to avoid even the intermediate perfect cadences that Gluck uses. Instead he multiplies imperfect cadances. In Dido's air (No. 48) the only perfect cadences are at bars 22 and 38, out of 42 bars; the first is in the supertonic, the second, at last, in the tonic, but in the orchestra only (the tonic is also used in bar 27, but with no cadence, for the parenthetical reference to the love-duet, No. 37). Yet this air affects us by its simplicity and purity, like Gluck's 'Che farò'.

Aeneas's air (Ex. 93) falls, like 'Ah, malgré moi', into two sections. Gluck's mediant and dominant cadences are replaced by the more closed form of dominant (bar 14) and tonic cadence (bar 33), but the action is still concluded by an Allegro. Berlioz's melody is also declamatory, but it is more lyrical, with more word-repetition. Simple phrase-lengths yield to ones of increasing complexity, and unity again depends on small motives. Berlioz makes most use of a pair of accented falling quavers: bar 2 (d^1–c^1) is reflected in bars 5 and 7 (f^1–e^1) and expanded in the d^1–$c\sharp^1$ of bar 8, a conventional

Ex. 93

Ex. 93 (contd)

half-close which returns in bars 17 and 21. The original form of the motive returns in bar 22, pointing the slight differences between phrases D and D¹. Phrase D¹ thus looks ahead to E, both by the rhythm ♪♪. 𝄾 and the recaptured motive, used in each of bars 24–7.

The gradually increasing complexity is best traced phrase by phrase. Phrase A moves from tonic to dominant in four bars. Phrase B introduces enharmony; the Db decorates a first-inversion tonic, the C♯ converts the bass A into a root (broken slur; cf. Gluck's enhancement of his bass F, Ex. 92, bar 6). But for the auxiliary note d¹, phrase A is confined to the range of a 5th; phrase B lies in the corresponding upper 4th of the scale, with bars 7–8 compressing the range of bars 5–6, which they partly echo. Echo is indeed built into this air; the solo horn countermelody uses echo from bar 6 (small notes on lower staff) and, by projecting bar 8 (a vocal phrase-ending) into bar 9, initiates the complication of phrase-lengths. Phrase B might be reckoned four, five, or four-and-a-half bars; phrase C has an apparent downbeat on the half-bar (see bar-numberings, and cf. Ex. 90). Metrical balance is restored by compressing the repetition of 'L'aspect affreux' into a three-note upbeat to bar 12, so that the following three bars plus echo complete the first section in 4–4–7 bars.

The play on the 6th degree (d^1 in bar 2; the enharmonic db^1–$c\sharp^1$; D as a local tonic in bar 8) is rationalized by the subdominant harmony in bar 9. The line seems freed to reach a half-close in F (bar 11), descending into a lower register whence it rises to interrupt the bass V–I by a minor 3rd, A♭. Projected up an octave, this becomes part of a D♭ chord which acts as a pivot between F minor and C (♭VI in F becoming ♭II, a Neapolitan 6th, in C); its function recalls Gluck's diminished 7th (Ex. 92, bar 17). Also like Gluck, Berlioz mixes dominant major and minor (cf. Ex. 92, phrases G–G^1). In bar 15 the horn echo is surmounted by A♭ as ♭6 of the C now established in the bass; this A♭ was picked up by the violin from the voice (bar 13), which returns there for the climax (bar 28) after a consonant reference (bar 20).

Having touched the tonic in phrase C, Berlioz does not return to it (as Gluck did in Ex. 92) during section II. He continues from the dominant, so that his final move can be a return to the tonic. Echo continues to bind phrases together. D^1 is a large-scale echo of D, but it is also a static area (in ♭III) including a reminiscence of the love-duet, though less exact than that in Dido's 'Adieu, fière cité' (No. 48). There is a half-close every two bars. The pre-echo of bar 23 thrusts the music into phrase E, which is extended to ten bars, beginning with indeterminate harmony and ending on the downbeat of the Allegro. It could be divided, using half-bar units, into 4–4–3–4–4, the irregularity arising from advancing 'En serai-je' to begin on the half-bar; its repetition is extended for the cadence. The bar-count (between the staves) also allows for an interpretation of phrase E as a background of eight bars expanded to ten by word-repetition and change of mode.

In tessitura, section II rises from a central C towards a central E♭ in phrase D^1, both 5ths of the tonic and ♭III respectively. The turning-point is the false relation e♭–e♮^{1} (bars 25–6), which Berlioz smoothes with one of his 'uncertain' basses, using both e♭ and e♮ before moving within the chord to g. The outer parts have effectively exchanged roles: in bar 28, over a root-position chord, the voice leaps to the climactic a♭^{1} from e♮^{1}, though the reverse was prepared (see Ex. 94, broken lines: the bass resolves its leading-note indirectly, the voice not at all). The harmony in bars 30–31 moves out of phase with the voice, forming its own periodicity (III–V–i), but the two come together when the cadence is echoed in the major. The interruption by the Allegro, which settles in A♭, means that the air never resolves in F major at all.

Where Gluck (Ex. 92) echoed major with minor, with obvious pathos, Berlioz, more dangerously, reverts to the major at the close; but where Gluck made a firm cadential fall, Berlioz is careful to leave the melodic head-note C unresolved. Nevertheless, we may feel a loss of intensity in Berlioz's major cadence, which seems less necessary because it is anyway expunged by the Allegro. Perhaps it deepens the surrounding shadows. Undoubtedly

Ex. 94

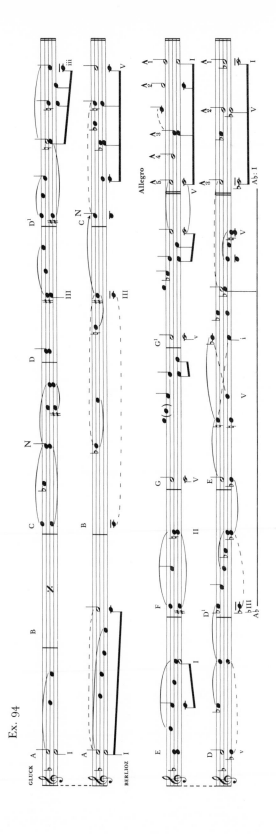

Ex. 95A

Ex. 95B

Gluck-like is Berlioz's choice of the major for both this air and 'Adieu, fière cité'. As Tovey observed: 'Gluck's highest pathos is expressed in the major mode. He uses the minor mode chiefly to express protest or energy.'[75] The choice of the major allows a resourceful composer to intensify by mixing elements of the minor, as in both Exx. 92 and 93.

Ex. 94 reduces the two melodies to their essential action, and shows the remarkable similarities and equally significant divergences between them. Gluck projects his move to the mediant (iii) over section I, while Berlioz uses his on the way to the dominant. Berlioz's manoeuvre is more elaborate, his goal more conventional. Much the same applies to section II. Gluck's repeated cadences create an impression of order against which his move to the dominant minor stands out the more powerfully, whereas Berlioz's simplicity is confined to the early stages (compare his period B with Gluck's C–D). Ex. 94 shows Gluck's consistent use of submotivic scales over a 3rd. Berlioz's section II seems indeterminate in direction, aiming both to return to F and to undermine it, with parallel minor, interrupted cadence, and lack of clear descent from 5th to tonic. In fact, of course, Gluck's open-ended form is resolved when the Allegro draws C down to F, projecting the last steps thrillingly into the top octave. Berlioz's is less open-ended, but F is not to be the final key; the head-note C will in fact fall only to A♭. This explains the prominence of A♭ within the Andante; the broad progression throughout the whole of No. 41 is from F *minor* to A♭.

My final example demonstrates the same sort of procedures in an instrumental melody, the second long tune of *Symphonie funèbre* (Cat. 26/I; Ex. 95). The tonic is presented in the first four bars, and no other key is used for a cadence; yet the divergence from the tonic is far more extensive than usual, while the phrases quickly cease to be discrete or symmetrical. There is no difficulty in imagining a banal consequent ending in A♭ or on E♭ in bar 8; instead the consequent covers fourteen bars, under the influence of the minor 6th (F♭), and of the telescoping whereby bars 7–8 take up not bars 3–4 but 5–6 (cf. Ex. 80). Even the key of F♭ is used in passing, an abrupt flatward move (bars 7–8) being neutralized by the return to A♭ (bar 9) and by further moves on the sharp side. The head-note E♭ is decorated from the opposite direction (D♮ instead of F♭), while enharmony in the bass (C♭–B♮) introduces a reference to C minor three bars after the reference to F♭, each being a major 3rd from the tonic.

A more significant feature of Berlioz's melodic idiom is the growth of the anacrusis, which begins from that same F♭ in bar 6. Its value amounts to a crotchet in bar 6, a minim in bar 8 and a dotted minim in bars 10 and 12, where its falling semitone is inverted. Repetition and sequence hold the thought together, springing anacruses drive it on; and the threatened symmetry is never completed. The anacrusis in bars 13–14 is reduced in value but increased from two notes to three. The range is extended by two chromatic thrusts, from g^2 to bb^2 (bar 13: touched on in bar 3) and c^3 (bar 14); the diatonic version which follows reaches the peak of the melody, db^3. There is complete chromatic filling from f^2 (bar 11) to db^3 (bar 15), but the Tristanesque yearning of the melody (appoggiature notwithstanding) is firmly based in the harmony, which even touches the tonic, preceded by its dominant (bars 13–14; the urgency of the melody prevents our mishearing this contrapuntal incident as a cadence). Before the clear division provided by the imperfect cadence (bar 18) the bass has resolved the active note, Fb, by treating it as $E\natural$. Appropriately this accompanies what proves to be a definitive fall of the head-note from Eb to Db, albeit projected into a higher octave (see Ex. 96).

The melody is thirty bars long (thirty-three in the recapitulation). The climax is at the mid-point, and the imperfect cadence is three-fifths of the way through. The rest unfolds in mournful downward progressions, with paired phrases which make it easier to grasp, like several other sequences appearing late in Berlioz's melodies. The portamento (bar 19) grows into a scale over a 7th; the repeat of the portamento (bar 21) has an anacrusis covering a minim value, which also passes to the scale and becomes the norm. The harmonic variation (bars 21–2) is most expressive. Except for passing chords (21, 23, which bears a 6th, and 25), the bass skilfully avoids the tonic; there is no question, however, of any other key. The scales spell out the broad final progression: IV–ii (23–4), II–ii (24–6), bII (26–7) – every variety of supertonic. A cadence in bII is only narrowly avoided by a diminished 7th (bar 28, figured 'X'). In the second ending (Ex. 95B, transposed from F) Berlioz makes the second descending scale minor, with more harmonic variation, and extends the cadence by a conventional but expressive interrupted cadence (bar 30), emphasizing the final close with a whole bar's appoggiatura (32).

Ex. 96 is a reduction which shows, behind the constantly varying motivic

Ex. 96

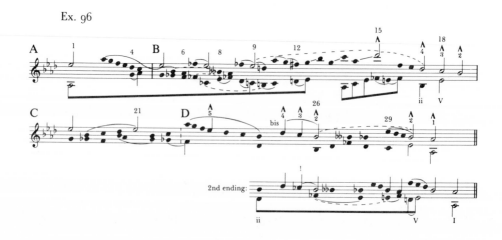

shapes of the melody, a single principal motive – a descending scale, which comes to the surface in bars 22–6. It contains the falling semitone, its first expressive interval (Ab–G), which is echoed in the crucial Fb–Eb. Parts of the scale also govern the cadences with the melodic fall from Eb to Bb; the scale over a 7th, extended to an octave, also binds together phrases A and B, which otherwise are the only pair separated by a perfect cadence. Then the semitone is reflected in the Bbb–Ab (bars 7–8), which reappears at the final cadence, expanded as a Neapolitan (from bar 27). The bass rises steadily through a maze of chromatic detail to the dominant (beamed in Ex. 96); in the second part it oscillates around Db, mediant to all the variegated supertonics. In the second ending the last progression to the dominant is made firmer by the anticipation of the bass Fb in bar 26 (not 27). At the earlier turning-point (bar 16), the bass resolved enharmonically; now Fb is properly resolved by a fall to Eb before another enharmonic interpretation as E♮ – a normalization of the previous rather elliptical progression.

Melody, for Berlioz, is the most vital agent of musical expression and the primary building-block of musical form. This factor is of great importance in considering his relationship to classical forms (see Chapters 12–13). The *Symphonie funèbre* presents no problem; it is a melodically conceived sonata form constructed from the alternation of huge melodies, with mercifully little development (Berlioz's symphonic forms are usually more complex and use short, pliable motives as well as sustained melodies). His command of these majestic paragraphs was unequalled in his time, as Gluck's had been in his; I hope to have demonstrated their organic qualities, even if what I have said is as much about harmonies and basses. The appeal of a melody is in any case not so fit a matter for discussion as its more abstract qualities, which inevitably lead to a discussion of the polyphony in which it belongs.

PART III

11 Vocal forms: *Satz* and *Ursatz*

'[In Mozart]: Each of the parts has its own movement, which, while still according with the others, keeps on with its own melody and follows it perfectly; *there* is your counterpoint . . . He [Chopin] told me that the custom now is to learn the harmonies before coming to counterpoint, that is to say, the succession of notes which lead to the harmonies. The harmonies of Berlioz are overlaid like a veneer; he fills in the intervals as best he can.'

Eugène Delacroix, reporting the views of Chopin
(*Journal*, 7 April 1849)

Musical form is sometimes considered as an abstraction, the result of sampling and comparison of a large number of pieces, sometimes even as a subject for legislation. Conversely it could be considered a synonym for a particular piece, the sum of its temporal and polyphonic structures. If the concept of form is to be critically useful, it must partake of both these extremes, for what a piece has in common with others is an important aspect of our experience of it, while what is unique deserves particular attention.

Those who consider form in terms of laws, like Hadow, have found it hard to be fair to Berlioz:

A more serious defect [than 'want of mastery' in counterpoint] is his almost invariable looseness of structure. The laws of form are as capable of extension and development as those of melody itself, but if any existing scheme is to be superseded something better must be put in its place. We cannot suffer a retrograde system of evolution from organic to inorganic, from order to chaos. And, unfortunately, Berlioz seems not to have been aware of this weakness (HadSM, 140).

One feels with any other composer, something as good as, but not better than, an existing scheme might have satisfied the critic, as it did Schumann (ConFS, 231). Unfortunately, too, we do have to suffer retrograde steps in evolution; the best music of the seventeenth century did not evolve from the best of the sixteenth. Finally, as I have suggested at the end of the last chapter, a search for what is organic, rather than an assumption that it must manifest itself in a prescribed way, can reveal it in Berlioz as much as in (say) Monteverdi. I shall try in the next chapters to offer a positive view, but the phenomena under observation are the same that Hadow and others criticized; nor is my point of view about musical form, defined as 'how it hangs together', different from theirs. It is only the angle of vision which changes.

On this subject Berlioz said: 'What is immensely difficult . . . is to find the musical *form*, that form without which music does not exist, or is only the humbled slave of the word.' The remark is perhaps enigmatic. It implies the existence of 'musical form' *as such* (even in vocal music – the context is *Les troyens*), but it cannot mean 'forms' in the sense of 'patterns' (binary, ternary, sonata). Rather it seems to be synonymous with 'idea': 'to find the means of being expressive, true, without ceasing to be a musician, and on the other hand to give the music new qualities, that is the problem'. This aesthetic statement resolves itself into a comment on the genesis of one work, *Les troyens*; the mature composer, whatever his earlier views, wanted expression to be inherent in the musical idea, which is subject to its own autonomous government. He explicitly rejected the continuous declamation which he assumed was Wagner's aim, and even the declared intentions of Gluck, 'who happily did not succeed in following his own impious theory'.[76] We shall learn more about Berlioz's attitude to form from his manipulation of musical material (not least from his revisions, which so often involve the reshaping of a design by cutting and the composition of new links: consider Ex. 14 above).

Berlioz's statements about the composition of *Les troyens* reflect his attitude to large-scale dramatic composition. The musical essence is explored, with no more than necessary intervention of what is musically recalcitrant: explanation, narrative, and so on. His aim is positive, and the right one given his own musical language; by omitting linking material, he invents a scheme, in the form of a dramatic symphony or of an opera, which consists almost entirely of self-contained musico-dramatic units. Even in *Les troyens*, which despite its statuesque aspect consists to a great extent of numbers which flow into each other without a break, narrative is reduced to a minimum. Years before, in the *Fantastique*, Berlioz said that the programme should connect the movements like 'the spoken text of an opera, serving to introduce the musical numbers whose character and expression it motivates' (ConFS, 20–21). The programme contributes to our understanding of an emotional sequence, not of the musical content of each movement, which remains autonomous. This is perhaps an oversimplification with respect to the *Fantastique*, but, as Meyer has observed, 'there is no causal nexus between successive connotations or moods . . . What the programme does is to provide the causal connection between the successive moods or connotations presented in the music.'[77] For a composer whose music all refers to something outside itself and who is not able or willing to rely on conventional expectations of the order of symphonic movements, an 'explanation' or a text is a necessity.

VOCAL FORMS

Berlioz's pieces very seldom conform to archetypes, although they may be described by reference to them. Once or twice, as with Benedick's Rondo (Cat. 42/7), the title identifies the form for us; but this only became such a clear ABACA (with B and C characteristically touching on the punned mediants, b/B♭ from G) when he cut a section after the third A, too extended to be considered a mere coda. The original form ran textually ABACAB, musically (despite some cross-reference to B) ABACAD; the cut removed more than a quarter of the piece (see NBE 3, p. 302).

Berlioz's manipulations usually go the other way: diversification from an archetype. The most natural medium for him in his early years was the strophic romance. Many works first published in that form were later modified to produce diverse types of strophic variation. Some were published with music for the first strophe and with the words only of the rest, an abbreviated form convenient for magazine publication, as with *Les champs* and *Je crois en vous*. The latter's history has been examined (Ex. 56); the former (Cat. 36B) was made into a through-composed song with strophic elements when it appeared in *Feuillets d'album*. But the strophic form was also used in major anthologies, such as the *Huit scènes* (Cat. 32A/2, 4, 6) and the first edition of *Irlande* (Cat. 12A, B, D, G, H). As early as *Le dépit* (Cat. 1A), however, Berlioz varied the mould by adding a coda to the last verse only (see NosFS, 93). This idea is followed up in the *Huit scènes* (No. 6), and retained in *La damnation*. The instrumental coda to *La belle voyageuse* (Cat. 12D) follows each verse in the first edition, but was later placed, asymmetrically, after verses 1 and 4. The 'Ronde de paysans' (Cat. 32A/2) became an elaborate structure with asymmetrically applied ritornelli and refrains (Cat. 32B/2). *La captive* (Cat. 18) went through various transformations before becoming a sort of 'symphonic mélodie' (a metamorphosis regretted by Noske: NosFS, 104–6).

Such diversification sometimes preceded the first published form of a work. The MS of *Villanelle* (Cat. 27A) shows that the simpler harmonies of the second verse were originally used for the first; the background to the variation is thus verse 2, not 1.[78] The 'Chant d'Iopas' (Cat. 40A/34) was more radically changed in the sketching stage.[79] Berlioz originally underlaid the words of the three verses to the same tune; he then developed an alternative setting for the second verse, in D minor (the submediant), but wrote 'En la mineur' over it before actually writing it out, almost unchanged, in that key (the mediant). At the end of this sketch he wrote 'Da capo'. It is not clear if he meant a return to the first tune, with the words of verse 3, or a return to the first text; but the revisions to the opening phrase include a variation applied to the words of verse 3. Berlioz must then have decided that a court musician would sing – even 'sur un mode simple et douce' as Dido requests – something altogether more sophisticated than strophic variations. He settled on a rondo form, both words and (varied) music of the first verse returning: ABA¹CA². Abandoning an already elaborated sketch, he wrote another series of sketches resulting in a completely new setting of verse 2, and another melody for verse 3, squeezed onto one staff without harmony. In the final score he began a fourth verse, or third episode, which Dido interrupts; but he then omitted the verse and with it the royal impoliteness, substituting a vocally elaborate coda and full close. Song has thus turned into aria.

Berlioz's attraction to rondo designs may also be seen in *Absence* (Cat. 27D), for which he set only three stanzas out of Gautier's eight, in the order ABACA (in the music, ABAB¹A). Margaret's 'Romance' (Cat. 32A/7), for which quite other forms are suggested by the poem (for instance that of Schubert's *Gretchen am Spinnrade*), also became a sort of rondo. Both strophic and ternary forms can thus give rise to a rondo, through strophic variation or multiplication of ternary forms. These two forms, vocal in origin, are fundamental not only to Berlioz's vocal music but to his instrumental music as well, where they compete with, and contribute to his interpretation of, classical forms (see Chapter 12).

'SATZ' AND 'URSATZ'

It should by now be clear that I do not claim for Berlioz any special immunity to academic criticism, whether made by an earnest appeal to 'laws' (Hadow), served with a dash of frivolity (Tovey), or contained, as with Schenker, within a devastating silence which effectively excludes Berlioz from the canon of composers of masterpieces. Berlioz worked in proximity to Chopin, the only non-German composer of the time whom Schenker wholeheartedly admired. We may choose to attribute the analyst's neglect to his blinkered attitude to whole areas of musical experience. We may not, however, dismiss the implications of this neglect, for they bear closely on the uniqueness of Berlioz's language.[80]

I have already employed an analytical notation derived from Schenker's (Chapter 10); its value for music outside Schenker's normal scope has been adequately tested, for instance with Debussy, and it proves itself able to reveal levels of structures in music that Schenker would have rejected.[81] Its use, therefore, implies no blanket acceptance of Schenker's views; nor does it imply that I think Berlioz should be considered, like Chopin, a 'Schenkerian' composer.

Schenker's analyses have two distinct aims. One is the study of the unique qualities of a masterpiece, relating the minutest details to the whole; the existence of such relationships is a criterion of mastery, for they show that a piece is truly organic.[82] The composer's genius is revealed in his control of the tensions inherent in the drive of the principal notes – which define the tonality – towards resolution. In the balance between fulfilment and creative frustration of drives lies the interest, and the unique form, of the composition (whatever structural blueprint – binary, rondo, sonata – may be used; Schenker disliked traditional formal analysis).

Schenker's second aim is nothing less than a theory of musical coherence. The *Ursatz* (fundamental structure) consists of the *Urlinie* (fundamental line), which descends to the tonic from the melodic head-note (5th, 3rd, or octave), and the bass arpeggiation, which defines the form harmonically. This structure is revealed by successive and scrupulous stripping down of the music, layer by layer, from the nearest and most ornamental foreground to the farthest background, in which lies its meaning. The absence, or obscurity, of an *Ursatz* inhibits perception of meaning, and in theory should produce musical incoherence.

Schenkerian analysis of Berlioz has not, to my knowledge, been often attempted, and its application to large-scale forms is certainly problematic; as Cone pertinently observes:

> [Berlioz's] elastic sense of phrase works hand in hand with his highly developed aptitude for sustaining long musical lines in order to create a special type of large-scale construction, conceived less as the development of one or more motivic or thematic ideas than as a wave-like series of motions towards a succession of proximate goals, each of which in turn initiates a further motion – and so on, until the final goal is reached . . . Hence this music often resists analysis in terms of standard systems, whether thematically or tonally oriented. That is why Schenker failed to appreciate Berlioz; the hierarchical structure of background, middle-ground, and foreground may not be entirely missing from his music, but it is often irrelevant to an understanding of what the composer is up to.[83]

Schenkerian analysis may, therefore, bring out what Schenker would have interpreted as negative signals, indicating ineptitude, lack of richness, a deplorably Rameau-based education – in short what Chopin saw (see epigraph: although he was wrong about Berlioz's training). Nevertheless, seen positively, these signals point to characteristic, and potentially expressive, features of Berlioz's music; hence my use of a Schenkerian system (if not its underlying philosophy) in the extended analyses of Chapters 13 and 14.

In the smaller forms, Berlioz did not diverge radically from the expectations of his time. Some sort of fundamental structure is always clearly present. As one might expect, it is melody-dominated; but analysing formal periods by a fundamental *line* was one of Schenker's most striking innovations, together with his emphasis on the contrapuntal derivation of many chords (there is a measure of coincidence here with Catel: see p. 53).

As Cone implies, Berlioz's longer movements are susceptible of subdivision into relatively short units. Even in Schenker's own longest analyses the most intense exploration is of the middle ground, and thus of drives to 'proximate goals' within sections. His demonstration of the relationship between shorter-term drives and the whole is intellectually impressive; but the longer the movement, the less the *Ursatz* can be heard and the more its significance becomes an act of faith.

CADENCES

Curiously enough it has even been held against Berlioz that he submitted to the melodic and harmonic urge towards completion. His cadences sometimes disappoint the most sympathetic hearers. Ernest Newman argues that the merits of Berlioz's melodies are to blame for their failure; when a melody is no longer in a conventional mould, but is 'the expression of something peculiar to the individual or to the moment or situation', it ought to have an ending in keeping with this exalted character.

> This new problem was often too much for Berlioz; in the body of his melody he could paint, and paint most convincingly, with his eye on the object, as it were, but he could not always maintain the individuality of his idea to the end, for there he came up against the natural limitations of cadence-material. And so it is that in the final phrase of a melody he frequently fails us (NewBR, 147).

Unfortunately Newman gives no examples of melodies in which Berlioz does *not* fail us, to compare with those in which, allegedly, he does; and without such models the question asked of the cited failures – is this the 'best ending conceivable'? – cannot be justified. In fact the only conceivable alternatives are not completed cadences at all; yet if every section were to end on an imperfect or interrupted cadence, the cure would be worse than the disease.[84]

Newman himself refers to 'natural limitations'. Berlioz accepts gracefully that there must be a fall to the tonic and a perfect cadence. Newman's dislike of the resulting frequency of resolution is perhaps another instance of the fallacy of hearing Berlioz with ears attuned to Wagner's 'endless melos'. Even the multiple 'Amen' of the *Requiem* ends with a V–I, as do virtually all Berlioz's pieces even if it is followed by some such joyous gesture as the iii–I 'cadence' of *Le carnaval romain*. Newman perhaps exaggerated the novelty of Berlioz's melodic language. Are his cadences really more disappointing than those of other melody-dominated composers – Mendelssohn, Bellini, Meyerbeer, Verdi, even Chopin? If so, it is certainly a tribute to the originality and scope of his melodic invention; but given a proper understanding of the framework of his language, this objection should very largely disappear.

AN EXAMPLE: CELLINI'S 'ROMANCE'

To reduce Berlioz to an *Urlinie* is obviously possible and appropriate. More surprisingly, in view of what Schumann and Tovey had to say about the limitations of his 'middle', reduction to an *Ursatz* does reveal interesting layers in the bass and inner parts (ConFS, 242; TovEM 4, p. 76). Even a simple piece like Cellini's 'Romance' (Cat. 23C/5) has an essentially three-part background. In order to display the rationale of the reduction, Ex. 97 gives a reduction of the piece to melodic line and bass, with figured

Ex. 97

Ex. 97 (contd)

harmony. Ex. 98 converts this into sketches of the fundamental structure.

There is some ambiguity at the opening. The woodwind chords suggest a head-note F; the voice has a sort of anacrusis D–Eb–F. If $\hat{5}$ (F) is the head-note the cadence (bar 40) establishes its upper neighbour, G, which returns near the end (bars 54, 57). This interpretation, however, requires a clear connection between G and F: there is none (bars 38–41, G goes direct to Eb; 54–5, G rises to Bb; 57–8, G descends by arpeggio). The arpeggio is an important motive (broken beams in Ex. 97). It cannot, however, establish direct linear connections such as G–F–Eb. When Eb is prominent, in bar 41,

Ex. 98

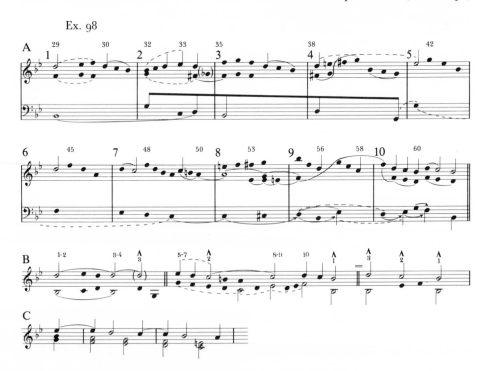

it is strongly connected to D; from 41 to 49 the chain Eb–D–C is very strong. It becomes clear that the emphasized neighbour is Eb, prolonging the head-note D ($\hat{3}$), an interpretation reinforced by the text; the nouns in the first line accent the D and form a miniature fall, $\hat{3}$–$\hat{2}$–$\hat{1}$.

The movement between Bb and G minor, taken over from the preceding recitative, means that the only intermediate cadences poise D as the root of dominants, in bars 34 and 38. D is enhanced by the Eb (bars 41–3), and moves decisively down to C in bar 47. This note next appears in the bass (bar 49); by the time the voice has again curved back to its C in bar 58 the bass has naturally moved up to Eb, forming the same supertonic 6th as at bar 47. The cadence repeats the $\hat{3}$–$\hat{2}$–$\hat{1}$ in diminution. All this can be seen in the middle ground (Ex. 98A), to which an *Ursatz* is appended (Ex. 98B).

The modest accompaniment produces a middle part which colours and adjusts the tonality, and occasionally appears to be motivic; in phrase 4 it emerges as the main melody at the cadence. This line is centred on F($\hat{5}$), enhanced by the natural and flattened 6ths (the latter as F$\sharp$). In phrases 5 to 7 this line goes underground (the texture is parallel $^6_3$ chords), and the form of the piece is partly clinched by its return. It is finally resolved by descending through Eb to D. The ambiguity of the head-note at the opening is thus fruitful; $\hat{3}$ (D) belongs to the top part, and $\hat{5}$ (F) to the middle part, and the ambiguity generates the right amount of tension for a simple strophe.

Noteworthy also are the inactivity of the bass (more than a third of the strophe is covered by an eight-bar pedal Bb and a five-bar pedal C) and the 'uncertainties' when it does move. One of the cadences in G minor (bars 39, 40) may seem redundant, and the harmonic goal is reached with the top of the melody, a bar before the cadence. This may serve, however, to underline the rhythmic caesura, an aspect of the binary form. It is precisely in the next, most harmonically vagrant, passage that the bass is most clearly directed, driving down a 5th (G–C). The 'uncertainty' resides in the parallelism and exists only in an interpretation by root movement (Eb–D–C–Bb–A). It is more positive to perceive it contrapuntally. The melody drives over a 3rd (Eb–C), establishing the fundamental descent $\hat{3}$–$\hat{2}$; the extension of the parallel bass movement (G–Eb) by a low-register Eb–C prepares for the interlocking upward drives of a 3rd (C–Eb, D–F: arrowed slurs in Ex. 98A). The $^6_3$ chords can then be appreciated for their expressive value. Berlioz could easily have written the passage as a chain of orthodox suspensions (Ex. 98C) and so put his technique beyond suspicion. In fact he uses only one suspension (bar 47), at the critical moment of the $\hat{3}$–$\hat{2}$ fall. The immediate goals, C in the melody, and in the bass, are embellished by the voice's further fall through B$\natural$ to A; the A minor chord (bar 50), aberrant in relation to Bb, falls into place not as harmonic vagary but as surface, colour, expression. The pedal C maintains suspense. It is quitted from a dissonance (diminished

7th) and its alteration to C♯ marks the harmonic climax, resolved as the voice reaches its highest pitch.

Berlioz originally emerged from the pedal with one of his unexpected root positions (Ex. 99). The pedal ended consonantly, as a root; the next chord was the tonic, another root. This is so obviously lame that it is surprising to find it entered in the full score prepared by a copyist.[85] Possibly Berlioz saw the way to rescue the cadence only when he revised *Benvenuto* for the Weimar performances of the 1850s; the 'Romance' was composed at the last moment before the original production and its text is not in the printed 1838 libretto.

Ex. 99

There is another unexpected root position near the cadence, with an 'uncertain' bass move, to G (bar 60). It does not affect the overall sense of the middle ground. 'Protège-la', sings Cellini, prayerfully, to Love, not God; in simple, pure counterpoint. By avoiding the directional force of dissonance, however, Berlioz suggests vertical understanding – not counterpoint but 'weak progression'; an 'uncertain bass', to ears unwilling (at this tempo) to distinguish between moments of passing sonority and those of real harmonic significance. In his search for expressive truth Berlioz thus lends weapons to his enemies.

Because Cellini's 'Romance' is simple and unpretentious, it is the more valuable as a pointer to characteristics of Berlioz's style. My analysis reveals no startling complexity; but surely it shows clear musical sense.

Berlioz's conformity with the principle of linear unfolding of a tonality, or at least his susceptibility to reductive analysis, will be further tested below. The fundamental line in Berlioz is normally clear; as the discussion of cadences suggests, perhaps too clear. In certain cases, however, its behaviour is as far from orthodox as is that of his bass; and in such cases it is striking how the resistance of the music to normal canons of behaviour supports the expression of a poetic idea (see also Faust's 'Invocation', discussed in Chapter 14). The results of a few other analyses (which it is not possible to reproduce in detail) support this conclusion.

In the two great laments in *Les nuits d'été* the fundamental line seems not to move at all. *Sur les lagunes* establishes $\hat{5}$ as head-note by its opening ostinato and the ascent of the vocal line over the first 25 bars; but the closing stages do not compose out any corresponding descent. (By contrast, in *L'île inconnue* a fall to the tonic is clearly in evidence, from bar 92, with the ambiguity of flattened 3rd and 2nd degrees; the failure to find a land where love lasts for ever is scarcely a disappointment, let alone a tragedy, and the sense of teased satisfaction conforms with the gentle descent of the fundamental line.) In *Sur les lagunes* a heart-rending outburst of tonic *major* (with cadence, bar 97) accompanies the words 'Never shall I love such another woman', but this resolution is as musically illusory as the despair is real. The voice ends on its eternally longing $\hat{5}$; the harmony is unresolved with it, fading out on the dominant. Still more immobile is the line in *Au cimetière*, which adheres to the tonic. Its frequent ascents to the mediant only suggest uncertainty as to whether this should be major or minor. The fundamental line could be a weakly articulated ($\flat$)$\hat{3}$–$\hat{2}$–$\hat{1}$ in D, but it is just as tenable to say that there is no fundamental line, only a prolonged $\hat{1}$ with auxiliary movement (particularly to notes outside the tonic scale, C$\natural$ and E$\flat$, conformant with moves to F$\natural$, B$\flat$, and even A$\flat$ (bars 39–40); and to E$\natural$, over a dominant, governing the middle section, bars 66–79). Chord-change is nearly all by side-slipping, scarcely ever functional; the resulting stagnation forms the character of the song, and is reflected in the immobility of the fundamental line.

None of this represents any judgment of Berlioz. If composing out a fundamental line is essential for musical communication, it follows that pieces which exhibit no such background (like the laments) or which exhibit it only perfunctorily (like *Villanelle*, which maintains its dominant prolongation virtually to the last) must be poor music. Yet to prefer Cellini's 'Romance', which composes out its fundamental line stage by stage, to any song of *Les nuits d'été* would be bizarre indeed.

All that is intended here is to show Berlioz's unique qualities from another angle. It was natural that Chopin, a keyboard genius and an instinctive master of counterpoint, should hear Berlioz's harmony as inorganic (see epigraph). Chopin's counterpoint is classical; his lines work in phase, the resultant harmonies emerge in a clear relation to the fundamental structure. Even those iridescent parentheses in which tonal connections seem to dissolve reveal their secrets under the Schenkerian microscope. With Berlioz we shall never achieve anything as elegant as Schenker's analysis of Chopin's *Etudes* (*Five Graphic Analyses*; see note 80). But as long as we are respectfully sceptical about the absolute nature of Schenker's doctrine, we can discover something about Berlioz's methods through a similar analytical approach. Berlioz's music appears less purely contrapuntal than Chopin's, but more independently linear; the strands operate on their own, and seem to function out of phase with each other. Consequently the harmonic events of expressive value adhere more to one line than another, like the A minor chord in Cellini's 'Romance', depending from the treble. Such chords stand perpendicular to the fundamental structure rather than being subsumed within it: *faits psychiques*, again.

We should not conclude that Berlioz is merely decorating a poetic idea; the music has organic qualities of its own. Individually they may seem like weak links in a chain (compared to the organic richness of middle- and background drives that Schenker reveals in Chopin). But they forge strikingly powerful lateral connections, and so illuminate the musical object (as well as the poetic idea) from several directions. We may recall here with sympathy Bockholdt's views (see above, pp. 24 and 73). It is true that Berlioz often does not reduce down to a cleanly classical *Satz*. This does not, however, invalidate reductive analysis, which reveals the positive as well as the negative qualities of the music. Such analysis even suggests why, from one point of view – a perfectly legitimate one – Berlioz's music is curiously unsatisfying. But it has qualities which prevent dissatisfaction from modulating to boredom or disgust and which, rather, increase the appetite to experience each work again.

12 Formal schemes in instrumental music

'They are showing one another why it ought not to have been written –
hunting out my consecutive fifths and sevenths, and my false relations –
looking for my first subject, my second subject, my working out, and the
rest of the childishness that could be taught to a poodle.'
Owen Jack in G. B. Shaw's *Love among the Artists*

It remains an open, and in the last resort insoluble problem whether the
general qualities of Berlioz's art referred to at the end of the previous chapter
are present by accident or design. Those who believe in accident can do little
more than say so; those who wish to believe the contrary can at least produce
some evidence. As far as musical forms are concerned, whatever the
deficiencies and deprivations of his early training, Berlioz, by the time he
came to write large-scale symphonic movements, knew a sufficient musical
repertory to identify those compositional routines for which he reserved his
bitterest scorn; he also knew some masterpieces worthy of emulation. Yet
originality always outstrips imitation. For all that early Berlioz is often
reminiscent of Weber and Beethoven, it is in the occasional melodic phrase
or sonority, rather than in any consistent formal pattern.

It is striking how little Berlioz actually imitated Beethoven's musical
forms. It is characteristic of him to prefer to find his own solutions; but it
turns out also that the whole dynamic of a Berliozian form is different from
the essentially classical rhythm of the instrumental composer he admired
above all others, and this lack of intimate involvement with Beethoven's
architecture had far-reaching implications. It is of a piece with Berlioz's
writings on Beethoven, which usually consist of a richly evocative and
enthusiastic appreciation of the whole of a movement, and minute dissection
of details which fascinate or repel him. Of structure he says next to nothing.
He may have identified formal archetypes behind such comparatively
uncategorizable movements as the Andante of the Fifth Symphony, or the
'Eroica' finale, but he does not mention them; what interests him is always
their uniqueness, never any relation to a pattern.

Three methods of formal classification may be distinguished, and I shall
discuss them briefly before attempting some kind of synthesis. The first

method is to distinguish formal types: variation, sonata, rondo. The second summarizes a musical form by a series of symbols: letters (as in ABA¹), each representing a theme, motive, or tonally defined unit. The third, concentrating on the temporal flow of the music, can be expressed numerically, in an attempt to understand the musical proportions.

Berlioz must have known about distinction between formal types, which preoccupied several of his contemporaries (see above, p. 169). Sonata form was classified during Berlioz's lifetime. Reicha describes it as 'La grande coupe binaire' (*Traité de haute composition*), and effectively places it on the eminence it occupied for the rest of the century, as the highest in value of instrumental forms. It is by no means useless to consider several Berlioz movements in relation to sonata form, but, like Haydn's, they seldom conform to any of the nineteenth century's formulae. Some critics, like Hadow, elevated the principles of sonata form to the level of fundamental laws, and argued that Berlioz broke them (in *Fantastique* I) 'not with the iconoclasm of a reformer, but with the awkwardness of a tyro'.[86] Tovey, however, while assuming that Berlioz intended to conform to some recipe or other, appreciated the qualities of his departure from it: his forms are 'totally different from (and much better than) anything they profess to be' (TovEM 4, p. 76). There is no evidence about Berlioz's intentions; but this open attitude is at least better than apparently trying to defend Berlioz's forms by distorting what he wrote until it fits a received framework (see note 11). The action of a sonata has its part to play in several movements to be discussed, but its absence, or the difficulty of reconciling a movement with it, has no direct bearing on quality.

There are equivalent dangers in the second approach – the depiction of a form by a letter-series or series of alleged tonal areas. The series usually identifies only one musical element; too often it suggests, or can be manipulated into, a wished-for pattern, which may well be at odds with other equally significant musical elements. Such an exercise can make the *Benvenuto* overture a rondo, which it is not in fact; to achieve this result sections are compressed or omitted, or sections of quite different structural weight in performance are given structural equivalence. Alternatively, a set of letters may emerge from the music – but from one element, key or motive – which produce no discernible pattern and which therefore may seem original; at least one critic has been seduced into proclaiming the logic of such more or less arbitrary patterns, although none can be demonstrated.[87]

The third method deals with the element most often ignored or distorted in the second. Units are counted out which represent time, or pulsation. Again the danger is that desired proportional schemes may be forced upon the music; notably the 'Golden Mean' and 'Fibonacci numbers'. Berlioz was acutely conscious of the temporal aspect of music. His tendency to cut (or more rarely to expand) his musical designs, in some cases quite drastically, is evidence of this. 'Long and diffuse' was his condemnation of *Rob Roy* (Mem39), a piece he then renounced; he might have said the same of the now unrecoverable original forms of *Fantastique* I and *Le corsaire* (as *La tour de Nice*: see note 95). The proper pacing of a work in performance mattered more to Berlioz than conformity to any pattern, even to tonal symmetries (see above, p. 34). For him the proper criteria for assessing form must have been whether, in performance, a piece continually engages the attention, and seems neither too short nor too long. As Tovey pointed out: 'From the two typical defects of bad highbrow music Berlioz is absolutely free; he never writes a piece consisting of introductions to introductions; and he never writes a piece consisting . . . entirely of impassioned ends' (TovEM 4, p. 76).

PROPORTIONS

The musical facts which feed our sense of proportion include tonality (definable by cadence-points or tonally stable and unstable areas); theme, subject, motive; textural changes; and points of intensity (climaxes and low points, either of which may define exact points or areas). These elements often work together, as when a new melodic idea is highlighted by textural change or by the establishment of a tonal area. The imposition of any pattern depends on the analyst's musical judgment. When points have been plotted, the distance between them defines the span, or spans, of musical architecture. In practice spans do not have to be the same length to be of equivalent structural weight, but it would require a more allusive, perhaps even a more eccentric style than Berlioz's to equate moments with extended paragraphs.

Unfortunately it is hardly possible to plot on a single chart all the elements which may affect the experience of music in time. If everything were included, the result would be equivalent to the score. A practical diagram is necessarily one cross-section out of many; those that follow are not complete analyses.

There is neither internal nor external evidence that Berlioz calculated the proportions of his music mathematically. Everything one knows of his temperament suggests that he would have been revolted by the idea of planning a form on a numerical system. I am not, therefore, talking about compositional method, but about the results of an intuitive feeling for balance and perspective in musical form. That the results can often be related, if only in a good approximation, to standard numerologies, is of interest but cannot be allowed to affect our judgment. I cannot here discuss the general principles or propriety of applying to the experience of time what appear to be well-established principles in the appreciation of visual art and nature. Appreciation of music in these terms is surely possible, even if only in a relatively simple way – simple because the mobility of music prevents the type of repeated and partial scrutiny which enhances appreciation of a solid object or a painting.

Proportion affects whole movements or sections within them; in the former, tempo changes can be reconciled because musical time is measured in pulsation, not by the clock. The simplest proportional schemes are the symmetrical division of a piece (into halves) and what Newman called the 'well-known law of two thirds', which, in his view, musicians follow instinctively.[88] Both proportions appear at the beginning of Fibonacci's series, in which each new number is the sum of the previous pair: 1:1, 1:2, 2:3, and so on through 5, 8, 13, 21, 34, etc. The higher the pairs of numbers, the closer their relationship becomes to the geometrical relationship of Golden Mean (hereafter GM), a division into unequal parts with the proportion of the smaller to the larger the same as the proportion of the larger to the whole (i.e. A + B = C, and A:B = B:C). Arithmetically the proportion is an irrational number which may be represented as 0.618, or 61.8 per cent (thus A + B = C; 0.382 + 0.618 = 1). On this basis rest the statements about GM that follow.

I will start with a simple vocal movement in order to show how points of articulation are chosen; it is also an interesting case of Berlioz's revision. In table 15 ('Chant de la fête de Pâques', Cat. 32B/4B) the choice of points is guided as follows. The piece is obviously in two verses. Period A is introductory, dominant in function; the verse begins with the downbeat of bar 6 (although bar 5 is also tonic). Period B is essentially an eight-bar tonic prolongation (see Ex. 40B) to the pause in bar 13 (in measuring musical units, the pause merely emphasizes a division; as it does not pulsate it is not counted). Period C begins with a sequential progression ('vers les gloires'), and suggests a 2 + 2 + 4 phrasing; but it reaches its climax on the sixth bar (bar 20), and this G major chord is extended beyond the eighth. The whole period thus extends to the A♭ cadence (bar 27); what might be an 8 + 5 (better, $7\frac{1}{2}$ + $5\frac{1}{2}$) becomes a larger unit of 13 bars. Similar patterns of growth in unit-lengths have emerged from the quite different criteria applied to melodic analyses (Chapter 10). Period D returns to the dominant in preparation for the second verse. Bar 48 is both the last syllable of verse 1 and the beginning of verse 2, with the return of the introductory bell-like figure.

The action of verse 1, however, concludes with bar 47, so that period D has 21 bars, subdivided 8 + 7 + 6. The links are stronger than the subdivisions: the 8 is 5 + 3, joined by continuity of text; the 8 is linked to the 7 by indeterminate harmony, an uncertain dominant quitted by backward resolution (E♮–E♭, bars 34–5); the 7 is bound to the 6 by word-repetition, a syncopated upbeat within bar 41, and the continuous triplets of the accompaniment.

The end of verse 1 makes a symmetrical division; the dominant arrives half-way through bar 47 (exactly $46\frac{1}{2}$ bars precede and follow). In the

Table 15. *Chant de la fête de Pâques*

Period *(bar no.)*	**VERSE 1**				**VERSE 2**			**CODA**	
	A (Intro.)	B (6)	C (14)	D (27)	A (48)	B (54)	C (62)	(79)	Hosanna (85)
Texture	Bells, Sops.	Chorus TTBB			Solo, full chorus				
Key	I–(V)–I	I	(II) V	bIII	(V) I	I I	I (II) V	I(V) I	I (III) I

VERSE 1 — Key continuation: (35) triplets (V):

VERSE 2 — pedal F — I; semiquavers ‑‑‑‑‑ (69) C; tonic prolonged

BARS

VERSE 1
- Subdivision: 5–3 (over 8)
- Division: 4 4 — 8 5 — 8 7 6
- Period: **5**   **8**   **13**   **21**

VERSE 2
- Subdivision: 4–2 (over 6)   4–4 (over 8)   6–2 (over 8) 9
- Period: **35**

CODA
- Subdivision: 4–2 (over 6)   4–5 (over 9)
- Period: **11**

Note: Texture: minimal indication, showing important changes.
    Key: numerals in parentheses represent significantly placed chords, not modulations.

original version (Cat. 32A/1) the dominant arrived on the first beat (see Ex. 40C–D). Within verse 1 the music follows a Fibonacci series: 5–8–13–21 (see table 15).

Verse 2 follows similar lines, but the internal subdivisions are much less marked. The motives of periods A, B, and C, are clear, but the pedals on F and C (see p. 114) and the continuous semiquavers flow over the divisions, as does the additional part for Faust. Verse 2 is thus a unit of 35 bars. Textural changes within it are modest, and out of phase with the harmony; the semiquavers migrate to the wind in bar 69, whereas the obvious harmonic divisions are in bars 68 (the supertonic, cf. bar 20) and 70 (the pedal C). Periodicity is blurred, flow enhanced. The texture alters markedly at the coda (bar 79), with a new melodic shape. The tonic arrives decisively at bar 85; the essential harmonic action thus lasts 82 bars (the following 'Hosanna' is not in the original version). Verse 2 from 48–82 is 35 bars; the next term in the Fibonacci series, unfortunately for seekers after conscious numerology, is 34, but it is an acceptable approximation, and this is still the best Fibonacci series I have found in Berlioz. Even so, it only arises in the revised form of the movement. Because its main idea is presented less succinctly (Ex. 40A), the original version is longer and divides asymmetrically (49:46). The individual sections show no clear arithmetical series. Berlioz probably considered his revisions mainly from the harmonic and melodic points of view; nevertheless the result is demonstrably tighter proportions, which may well contribute to the highly satisfying effect of the revised version in performance (see also note 58).

The counterpoint of proportions (in the above example, GM and exact symmetry) is a not uncommon extension of rhythmic counterpoint. More usually there is a cumulative scheme of roughly equal sections that works in counterpoint to some larger proportional approximation. This happens in *Harold* II, where the regular metre underlines a consistent periodicity of eleven-bar phrases; Berlioz himself referred to them as strophes (Mem51). But, as Berlioz also remarked, the overall form is crescendo–diminuendo; the high point of the first crescendo is bar 134, quite a good GM of the whole 334 bars. There is also a symmetrical division; the C major 'Canto religioso' begins after 168 bars.

More complex is the *Hamlet* march (Cat. 34C). In table 16 the equal units of eleven bars are calculated from combined thematic and dynamic points of emphasis. A series of such relatively short and equal spans may well be called an arcade form. *Hamlet* has a background of sonata form (see table 16); the arcade is compressed into ten-bar units in the recapitulation. Inevitably arcade construction recalls Cone's remarks about a series of proximate goals (see above, p. 173).

Of especial interest in *Hamlet* is the presence of an overall GM. The enormous climax (at which 'a peal of ordnance is shot off') comes at bar 84, a

Table 16. *Hamlet*

Section	Exposition				'Development'		Recapitulation				Coda
Bar no.	1	4	15	26	37	48	55	65	75	85 SILENCE fragments	101
Theme		A	A	B	B		A	B	B		(A)
Dynamic	*p*	*mf*	*mf*	*f*	*ff–p*	*ff*	*mf*	*ff*	*mf*	*fff* *pp*	
Key	a	a	a	C	B–eb–d etc.		a	a			a
Arcade	3	11	11	11	11	7	10	10	10	16	17 18 18

84

Original 51

Revised 34

good GM for 135. 135 is the number of bars in the original version. Berlioz seems never to have heard this piece; he must have made the cut of 17 bars (see OBE 6, p. ix; K 519, p. 166) after a careful reading. In performance the stunned silence after the climax and the fragmented music which follows, in which attention is concentrated on individual notes and pitch-relationships in the search for some sort of tonal orientation, make the revised version seem quite long enough in practice. The 'spoiled' proportions sound right, and the 'perfect' proportions of the original – in which the cut bars are hardly less intense that what remains – might seem unbearable.[89]

Marches are a single-minded sort of composition, even with a sonata form, and it is not surprising that they tend to show clearer overall proportions than more complex movements.[90] Berlioz's overtures and symphonic first movements nearly all have a slow first section, an integral part of the whole commonly related to the Allegro by the return of its music there in long note-values. This suggests an exact proportional relationship – not metronomic, but experienced – between the tempi.

OVERTURE FORMS

Berlioz had no direct roots in the mainly German symphonic tradition, and was probably unaware of its most interesting French extension in Méhul. His structural language is grounded in the shorter forms of song and of opera, and their grouping into larger entities – the arias in several tempi of Gluck and Weber, the massive tableaux of Gluck and Spontini. He had absorbed these before encountering the most potent influence on his symphonic outlook, Beethoven. Moreover, the programmes of the Société des Concerts tell us that the overtures of Beethoven were introduced at the same time as the symphonies, and were doubtless absorbed just as eagerly by Berlioz, who already knew such symphonic overtures as Cherubini's, and *Der Freischütz*. Many of Berlioz's symphonic movements are overtures; some of those which are not share overture characteristics. In a consideration of sonata form in Berlioz, therefore, an overture model with an integral slow section may be a more appropriate point of departure than a symphonic or string-quartet model.

The integration of slow and fast sections occurs in *Der Freischütz* and in Beethoven's *Egmont* and *Leonora* overtures (see Ex. 75). Berlioz follows a tendency of the nineteenth century (evident in *Der Freischütz* to some extent, and in Mendelssohn's 'Scotch' Symphony) in that properly speaking his slow sections are no longer introductions at all. They are too long for that; their relationship to the Allegro is too integral; above all, they are too stable. Rather than introducing, they *expose* lyrical material. This process often stabilizes what in Beethoven would be a parenthetical appearance of a submediant or mediant (see p. 32). The ♭VI of *Les francs-juges, Benvenuto,* and

Le corsaire, the ♭III of *Le carnaval romain* and *Lear*, are too fully displayed to be considered parenthetical. In Berlioz the true introduction is the occasional flourish of fast music before the slow section, which may enable the latter to begin in the 'wrong' key (♭VI, *Le corsaire*; ♭III, *Le carnaval romain*; IV, *Béatrice*). This fast preface is found in Rossini; but the obvious precedent is the E major *Fidelio* overture.

The overtures of Weber and Beethoven are also the sources of Berlioz's mighty perorations. The term 'coda' is properly reserved for prolongations of a final tonic beyond the last structural downbeat. With Berlioz this event usually comes quite near the end; his codas are thus mostly quite short. Nevertheless there is an immense amount of action in the closing stages, which cannot be construed as recapitulation, and which Tovey aptly calls 'peroration'.[91] The huge conclusion of the *Leonora* overture, the 'Symphony of Victory' in *Egmont* – a programmatic liberty Berlioz did not allow himself – the apotheosis of Agathe's melody in *Der Freischütz*, even the Rossini crescendo, are all ingredients turned by Berlioz into harmonically unresolved perorations.

Les francs-juges ambitiously combines a single super-Rossini crescendo (from bar 484) with a Weber apotheosis (bar 550). It is also the first of many pieces to introduce material from the slow section at this late stage (the D♭ interruption, bar 604; cf. bar 20); among others are *Harold* I and *Le carnaval romain*, which speed up the slow melody, and the *Benvenuto* overture. In other pieces the slow section is more extensively integrated. In *Lear* the regal bass-theme appears twice during the Allegro (see above, p. 91); in *Roméo* II the reunion of themes takes place comparatively early in the Allegro (see below, table 17), and the slow melody reappears in the coda; in *Le corsaire* the slow melody acquires an allegro character and appears in part in both tonic and dominant sections.

In this aspect of larger design Berlioz practically never repeated himself. Even movements which seem to be based on similar structural principles usually differ quite significantly in the way they are applied. Both *Roméo* II and *Benvenuto* have mighty climaxes which combine allegro material in ¢ with a slow melody in triple metre, but the reunions are at different structural points. Both the 'Offertoire' and 'Convoi funèbre' (*Roméo* V) combine fugue with a 'psalmody'; but in the 'Convoi' the orchestra and voices exchange roles, the major mode is deployed quite differently (the ostinato being tonic, not dominant), and there is a background of sonata form (on the 'Offertoire' see note 58).

The nearest Berlioz came to repeating a highly personal formula was in *Le carnaval romain*, which turns out very like *Harold* IV once the Allegro is under way. Both have what is virtually a written-out repeat of the exposition (*Harold*, bar 280, with a half-bar anomaly quickly resolved; *Le carnaval*, bar 176, with the alternative mediant, see above, p. 34). There follow short developments using fugato (*Harold*, 428; *Le carnaval*, 304); a recapitulation of the secondary exposition material only, in the tonic (*Harold*, 449; *Le carnaval*, 344); and a final peroration.[92] But there are differences; the fugato in *Le carnaval* is based on the slow section, speeded up (thus resembling *Harold* I), whereas *Harold* IV presents a last memory of the slow movement (bar 473) as a quotation, not integrated. A more exact, but conventional, pair are the overtures *Waverley* and *Béatrice*, which both lack integration between slow and fast sections, have virtually no development, and use an insouciant interruption of the tonic in full flood by ♭VI (derived perhaps from Rossini; *Waverley*, dominant section, bar 207; tonic section, bar 384; *Béatrice*, more wittily because only once, bar 195). But *Waverley* has a quite different sort of conclusion, with a diminution (bar 401) impossible in the already electric tempo of *Béatrice*, and a moment of mystery (bar 336ff) appropriate to its very different 'subject'. The pieces were written some 35 years apart, in any case, so Berlioz might be forgiven some relaxation from his austere rule of continual novelty.

SONATA FORM

A corollary of his extended slow sections and perorations is that Berlioz devotes a far smaller proportion of his movements to the essential action of the sonata than is normal, even in overtures. By 'sonata action' I mean: 1, the exposition of material in the tonic and a structurally significant modulation with a well-defined area in the complementary key; 2, the resolution of that structural tension, usually after some rapid modulatory activity, by the recapitulation, for which minimum requirements are restatement in the tonic of significant material previously exposed only in some other key, and substantial cadential activity in the tonic. This minimal definition has at least the merit of including all kinds of classical and romantic sonata; it is based on tonality as much as theme, and can assimilate the monothematic exposition which Berlioz approached in *Fantastique* I and *Le corsaire*, as well as movements with a multiplicity of thematic ideas.

I deliberately imply a binary basis to sonata form, as Berlioz can have heard the form defined only in this way.[93] His sonata forms do have characteristically nineteenth-century elements, notably the exposition of long melodies, usually in the complementary key (*Lear*; *Symphonie funèbre*, Ex. 95; *Benvenuto*) but in the tonic in *Fantastique* I. These do not, however, force one to consider the form in a ternary light – exposition, development, recapitulation – as the development is disproportionately small in most cases. The tonal, binary definition suits Berlioz better, for the most consistent element in his sonata and related forms is their rigid adherence to the principle of tonal resolution. However much he may omit to recapitulate material previously heard in the tonic (entirely in *Harold* IV and *Le carnaval*) he always resolves well-defined material exposed in another key. This compulsion occasionally causes him, in full recapitulatory flood, to revert to a comparatively slow harmonic rate and a lyrical impulse, so that the fires of peroration need vigorous stoking. Such alternation of pace (which concerns the alternation of dramatic and lyrical material, and not necessarily thematic transference from actual slow music) may be what Hadow means by structural looseness (see above, p. 169); yet it results from a structural rigour of a kind by no means always observed by contemporaries such as Chopin and Schumann.

Berlioz's tightest movements gain in impact by playing with the point of recapitulation. In *Fantastique* I he brings back the slender new idea exposed in the dominant (bar 152) after the double-bar, twice, in the tonic (bar 191 and, as the climax of the fugato which begins in iii, bar 322). Both resolutions precede the tonic restatement of the principal theme ('idée fixe') which blazes forth in rhythmic diminution (bar 410). This inspired combination of the point of recapitulation with a transformation, unrelated to any specific event in the programme, was often imitated by later composers. Berlioz himself only did it again in a context of thematic transference, the 'élan de joie délirante' of *Roméo* VI, which hysterically transforms the love-theme; it is the obvious model for the climax of Tristan's delirium (where Wagner forces his tenderest love-motive into an Allegro with bars of 5/4). Otherwise the procedure is bequeathed to the symphonic poem, while Berlioz, lacking 'esprit de suite' or simply possessing infinite curiosity, tried other structural economies.

Many features characteristic of Berlioz's most complex instrumental forms will emerge from the detailed study of the *Benvenuto* overture which follows (Chapter 13). That alone, however, cannot demonstrate the variety of his forms and their shifting relationship to traditional tonal, thematic, and proportional interpretations. I append here, therefore, a few comments on some other pieces.

The overture to *Les francs-juges* is by any standards a remarkable instrumental début. In it, however, Berlioz encountered, and did not quite resolve, the problem of combining fast music, lyrical music, and mixed tempi. The recall of the D♭ episode from the introduction is a masterly coup (bar 604); but the main use of slow music is the development of the opening phrase (bar 1) as an interlude (bars 194–336; see Ex. 74A). So tonally stable an interlude must be considered to lie outside the sonata action; and it is so long that it stretches the connections between the parts of the sonata to breaking-point. Moreover, it is followed by another interlude, in effect; the second statement of the lyrical melody in the aberrant key of E♭ (bar 344), a parenthesis within the C minor from which it comes (the slow interlude) and to which it returns by a V–vi (bar 390). Bar 344 is not, because of its key, a recapitulation, and Berlioz duly resolves the theme in the tonic at the apex of the brilliant crescendo (formed of its elements, bar 484ff; the apex is bar 550). The impressive main allegro material is much reduced in significance and the Eb statement appears a lyrical indulgence.

After the admirable but more conventional *Waverley*, a great stride is made by *Fantastique* I. It is, however, atypical in using a lengthy melody for its first allegro material; lyricism in the subsidiary key is therefore suppressed. The repeat of the whole 'idée fixe' in the dominant (bar 238) recalls the episodic procedure of *Les francs-juges*, but there is no slackening of tempo and the use of this key for this theme poses a question whose answer may lie in considering the whole movement outside any sonata framework.[94] A more promising archetype might be the rondo, but for that too the dominant statement remains anomalous (it would normally be tonic, but in that part of the movement the tonic is used for the two resolutions of the subsidiary material). The form of the movement depends most on the alternation of stable areas – with the repeat, the four statements of the 'idée fixe' in C, C, G, C, counterpointed to four of the secondary idea in G, G, C, C – separated by areas of tonal instability, either violently eruptive (exposition, bar 113ff; see above, p. 110) or more gently vagrant (like the developmental passage with solo oboe, bar 358ff). Other thematic details, like the one Cone calls the 'cadential phrase' (bar 119; ConFS, 251), are elegantly manipulated to produce a capricious form appropriate to its subject, musically obeying its own laws, possibly still a little loose (since its success in hanging together is still dependent, in a way Beethoven is not, on a sensitive performance), but perennially fascinating.

The rest of the symphony presents fewer problems, for while the forms preserve an element of ambiguity, they never feel anomalous. An equivalently complex discourse next appears in *Lear*, Berlioz's most overtly Beethovenian piece, in which, however, the clearly defined and quite orthodox sonata action is cut into by two references to the slow section. Both come after the point of recapitulation, so that the music hangs together as a sonata much better than *Les francs-juges*. The incursions of the opening theme are clearly identified with Lear's madness (MacBO, 18), but it is the lyrical theme (bar 151ff) which is subjected to the most remarkable fragmentation and distortion (violins, 396ff; *tutti*, 424ff). This melody is then, however, fully resolved by a tonic statement as long as its dominant exposition (446ff); this means a vast lyrical period – eighty bars – with its own ternary form. The piece has been criticized because its energetic conclusion does not smack of tragedy. This extra-musical defect, however, appears venial; what seems to me the one failing in a superb piece is this excess of lyricism in the recapitulation, almost as if Berlioz has deprived himself of structural economy in the interests of purity of form.

Twice Berlioz embraced a similar range of feeling in an overture and succeeded completely; in *Benvenuto* (see Chapter 13) and in *Le corsaire*. With the latter it is almost (but not quite) useless to think of sonatas. There is a monothematic exposition: the main theme in C (bar 90ff), then inverted; in Db, with 'canon' (bar 107), effecting the disruption of the tonic; then in the dominant, in a different texture and mood (bar 140). Yet Berlioz settles down, in the middle of the piece when structural tension 'ought' to be highest, to a full-scale reprise of his Adagio theme (Ex. 62), in the tonic. The exact mid-point of the Allegro is the end of this section; intensity declines still more towards the subdominant, whence energy is regenerated by the opening material (bar 256), brusquely developed. Decorum is apparently restored when the material takes the same form as the introductory flourish (bar 266), but its nature is so unstable – it has previously led into both Ab and C – that Berlioz is able to recapitulate the main theme in Eb (bar 284), like Schubert in the finale of the 'Great' C major symphony. The G major version of the main theme is resolved in the tonic (bar 313) to preserve sonata proprieties; but it is quickly expunged and for much of the rest of the movement cadences are continually evaded (notably bar 346). Bar 402, after a massive cadence, is a final reprise rather than a coda, with the effect of peroration (bar 447 will do for 'tail').

Le corsaire emphasizes how alien to the single-minded architecture of a classical sonata Berlioz's thinking is, for its whole rhythm is anti-classical. Instead of stable exposition and fully stable resolution of tensions at their highest in the centre, the music is most unstable at the opening, both of the whole overture and of the Allegro (including the capricious modulations of the monothematic exposition). The centre is relaxed, and in the tonic, albeit a necessary resolution of the Ab Adagio and thus as essential to the whole form as it is alien to the sonata dynamic. The tonic is never far away, yet the tonalities continue enjoyably vagrant right to the end. The very contrariness of the form keeps the listener alert (see note 87!) and leaves him satisfied. The piece is a remarkable tribute to Berlioz's compositional powers, especially considering how different its original form seems to have been.[95]

TONAL FORM WITHOUT MODULATION: *ROMÉO* II, *HAROLD* I

Tovey praised the final cadence of *Le corsaire*, a resounding series of triads: Ab–Eb–G–C (TovEM 6, p. 52). He did not remark that this final coup sums up the four principal tonalities of the piece; he might even have considered such an observation valueless. In several Berlioz movements we are confronted with another structural problem: the virtual absence of any key to contrast with the tonic. Instead of major departures from the tonic, Berlioz often devises a strategy of stable sections in the tonic (or in closely related keys), separated by episodes which disrupt tonal connections quickly, efficiently, and expressively. *Fantastique* I is based on tonic and dominant only. 'Scène aux champs' and 'Scène d'amour' similarly devote most time to immediately related keys – the former has the 'idée fixe' in the subdominant, the latter episodes in C♮ and F♯ minor (♭III, vi) – and through devotion to the tonic Berlioz can derive astonishing energy from a very late modulation to the dominant ('Scène d'amour', bar 367ff, the last passionate outburst).[96]

Although Berlioz does use unconventional modulations, his unconventional use of conventional key-relations has more structural impact. In *Roméo* II the dominant is used to expose a theme in a slow tempo (bar 81ff) which reappears in the Allegro at its mid-point (bar 226ff; see Ex. 74B). This, of course, is no still centre, like that of *Le corsaire*, but a climactic reunion which establishes a felt, if not metronomically exact, tempo-relation between Larghetto and Allegro (one crotchet = one bar). A proportional scheme arises which excludes the preceding F major Andante; the Larghetto begins the movement proper, and appears in the dominant because the tonic is 'exhausted . . . for the time being' by the Andante (Cone, 1953, p. 475). In *La tempête* Berlioz also begins his main action (bar 198, after the storm) in the dominant; there follows a loose sonata plan in which, after the recapitulation of this theme in the tonic (bar 453), a single structural economy is made by combining a reprise of the opening Andante with resolution of the lyrical theme taken from *Cléopâtre* (bar 491ff). *Roméo* II tightens up this plan considerably.

The form of this 'Concert et bal' has nothing to do with sonatas. Within the Allegro each section is comparatively brief (see table 17); both the Larghetto and reunion stand out by their length and stability. The music is organized in short waves: after the Larghetto, 22 bars preparation (bar 107), 27 theme, 31 episode, 20 theme, 19 episode. These fall into larger periods: 100 units (Larghetto crotchets, Allegro bars) to the fermata in bar 128; almost the same (97 bars) to the point of reunion.

But the reunion is not a final climax; it is only Romeo's appearance at the ball What follows is an extraordinary piece of legerdemain. Berlioz seems constantly about to cadence, but consistently avoids doing so. At bar 266 the ball-music is interrupted for the third time by capricious, slightly tipsy, episodic music (cf. 156ff, 207ff). The music dies away, and a new idea appears which proves to be no mere episode, for the main material is henceforth present only in fragments. This idea is a fugato, a texture used in the introduction to the symphony for squabbling; here too the subject is quite angular (bar 278ff). It settles into an ostinato (from bar 294) with a chromatic element, clearly associated in the original form of the Prologue with the indignant Tybalt.[97] Against this obstinate adherence to a chromatically inflected dominant prolongation, the festive mood struggles to reassert itself; it contrives to halt the ostinato, but on a dominant (bar 330). This fifty-two-bar period is the longest yet (equal to the reunion plus its sequel); and the dominant underpins a festive crescendo over the next

Table 17. *Roméo* II

	Larghetto	Allegro								
Bar nos.	81	107	129	156	187	207	226	278	330	375
Key	C	V	F	[#]	F	[b]	F	(V)	V	F
Theme	Oboe solo		Ball A^1	Episode	Ball A^2	Episode	Re-union	Episode Fugato Ostinato	Frag-ments	
Units per section	78	22	27	31	20	19	40–12	52	45	40
Symmetry	100	197		97	97		52	52 97		
			189		237			189		
GM			197					149		

forty-five bars, before resolving for the forty-bar coda. (The tonic at 367 is not attained by cadence, as is that of 375; only the wish not to disrupt the mood can have prevented Berlioz displacing it by something like ♭VI or a diminished 7th. Appropriately hollow and garish, it is another of his unexpected root positions.) The end of the reunion (bar 266), and thus of the main festivity before it is disrupted, comes close to GM of the Larghetto–Allegro, just as the beginning (bar 226) is close to the mid-point (table 17).

Finally, *Harold* I, a movement still more vexatious to the analyst, for there is more than a residue of sonata form; yet it flies in the face of convention by refusing to establish the complementary key in the exposition. It was à propos this movement that Tovey declared that Berlioz's sonata expositions 'are quite flat' (TovEM 4, p. 76); but in fact, *Harold* I is the only example. Hadow was sufficiently perturbed to call the movement 'a fortuitous concourse of phrases, without form and void' (HadSM, 141). If so, it is a bad piece; if, on the contrary, it appears effective and well-made in performance, the analyst at least has a point to prove. In fact, it is a complex example of arcade form, but the sonata angle is not neglected; rather its principles of resolution are treated in a new way – one more thematic than tonal – which, with quite different detail, proves to have some impact in the *Benvenuto* overture as well (see Chapter 13).

Some tempo-relation is felt to exist between the Adagio and Allegro, but it is not musically expressed, for the 'idée fixe' when it reappears in the Allegro is in a more wooden rhythm and roughly twice the speed (bar 323ff). Nevertheless if we equate a beat of Adagio with a bar of Allegro (table 18) it is apparent that the Adagio works in larger spans, and the Allegro's proportions make more sense without it. The Allegro is defined by the alternation of two principal motives, A and B in table 18. Clearly established keys are few, apart from the tonic. But relatively short periods – the arcade – are formed by alternation of theme and of tonal stability and movement (compare its elder sibling, *Fantastique* I).

An overall proportional scheme for the Allegro – not precise – has GM near the fermata and the start of the fugato, which is the combination of theme B with the 'idée fixe' (IF), an important moment for both the Allegro and the movement as a whole. In the tonal-thematic arcade form (table 18) the arches vary from 26 to 37 bars, an acceptable inequality given the clarity of the divisions. In common with other movements, the later sections are a little longer, notably the two huge strophes which combine the 'idée fixe' with theme A (if, however, the sprung metre is counted – see p. 134, above, table 10 – rather than the notated bars, the totals of 44 and 42 become 36 and 35 'bars').

There is also a larger arcade form consisting of double-arches, so to speak, where the variation is less (61 to 68, with 86 or 71 for the perorative strophe).

Table 18. *Harold* I

Section	Allegro	Exposition strophe		Repeat		'Development'	Strophe		Recap. A	Fugato	Stretto	Repeat	Recap. B	Coda
Bar nos.	94½	131	166	131bis	166bis	192bis	229	259	290	323	352	396	438	473
Theme	(A)	A	B	A	B	A	A	B	A	IF/B	IF/A	IF/A	B	(A)
Key	V	G		G	V	(Db)	C	G (Eb)	G	G	G	(b)	G	G
Units	36⅔	35	3¹	35	26	37	30	3¹	33	29	44 (36)	42 (35)	35	21
		66		61		37	61		62		86 (71)		56	
Large arcade				35		63				68				

Here, however, an ambiguity arises from the repeated exposition. This repeat is indispensable; the music drives towards the $^6_4$ chord (first-time bar, 192), which restores the tonic after a period of uncertainty. The second-time bar (192bis) is a splendid coup given the expectation of the $^6_4$, but if the repeat has not been made, and the $^6_4$ has not been heard, the A major substitute sounds wanton. (It is far more important than the repeat in *Fantastique* I, where the first-time bar is rather perfunctory.) The first time, the exposition produces a large strophe (bars 131–96); the repeat produces either a ninety-eight-bar period until stability is restored by the C major (bar 229), or a period of stability to bar 166bis and a period of instability, the longest in the movement, from there to 229. Certainly no good division falls at the second-time bar. The result is a massive sprung rhythm, which gives the music a forward impetus which more obviously sectionalized movements, such as *Fantastique* I or *Roméo* II, tend to lack.

The interesting points of the sonata aspect concern theme B. At its first appearance (Ex. 100A) it is hopelessly unstable; Berlioz follows a dominant with F♮ major and modulates capriciously; the B♭ phrase (bar 170) is cut to three bars, rebuked for its rudeness in being *forte*; D (bar 173) is no more established than the other keys; from 181 all the phrases are three bars, including the themeless oscillation on a diminished 7th which emerges blithely into the tonic $^6_4$. The next B is tonic (Ex. 100B), a sort of resolution,

Ex. 100

creating the impression (which I am not saying is false) of an arched recapitulation (A returns at 290). Yet B is still melodically nebulous, wandering into a sequential extension which debouches into a *tutti* in E♭, refreshing the tonic for the return of A. B next appears as countersubject to the 'idée fixe', still with no real thematic form (bar 329). The action of the sonata is not really over until B has been given a full resolution, a thematic shape with a consequent phrase (Ex. 100C; it had a relatively trivial consequent originally, in *Rob Roy*, Ex. 100D). At the same time the melody is fully assimilated into the solo viola part. The viola exposed both the 'idée fixe' and theme A, but hitherto it has shared theme B with the orchestra (mainly wind). Even here the viola's third phrase is a counterpoint to the bassoon; but the solo preserves overall melodic continuity through the resolution of the G♯ which links the central pair of the four five-bar phrases.

Ex. 100 (contd)

An ambiguity corresponding to the end of the exposition, and also affecting the larger arcade, concerns the point of recapitulation. One could identify this with the vigorous A (bar 229, subdominant) and subsequent B (bar 259), making a sixty-one-bar strophic variation of the exposition; there would be precedents for the IV–I in Schubert, unknown to Berlioz. Here, however, it corresponds to no previous I–V. If the recapitulation begins with B, reversing the thematic order, the strophe (259–322) is sixty-four bars. Besides Mozart, there is a precedent for the reversed order in *Fantastique* I (in *Benvenuto* it is clearer than in either). But bar 259 could also be heard, like the corresponding point in *Fantastique* I (bar 191), as a false reprise of the secondary material in the tonic, quickly swamped by the *tutti* in Eb. In that case the recapitulation is not reversed; it begins at 290, and extends to the end of the fully resolved B (bar 472), a sixty-eight-bar strophe (bars 290–322, 438–72) divided by the intruding 'idée fixe'. (This, my preferred interpretation, is given in table 18.)

It seems that Berlioz's rigorous adherence to the principle of tonal resolution does not imply that his forms are tonally conceived. Indeed, they appear curiously modest from this point of view. But just as his triadic preferences make his polyphony harder to analyse in terms of motion towards goals, so his tonal preferences make his structures more complicated, not less, for they depend for their sense of beginning, middle, and end on a combination of factors rather than on one or two. *Harold* I depends on a reunion of the 'idée fixe' with both Allegro themes; a sonata aspect in which resolution acquires a thematic as well as a tonal dimension; the concerto aspect, unique to this work, also affecting the sense of resolution; a controlled *accelerando* (see above, p. 139); and a double scheme of proportions including a GM (Allegro only) and, much more conspicuously, a strophic succession of spans of equivalent weight which ask to be treated in pairs and produce ambiguities thereby. This result certainly bears out Cone's observation (see above, p. 173): there is an overall goal, but it is less apparent throughout than the 'proximate' goals. It follows that the exposition may legitimately be 'flat' because its aspect as a double strophe, with a kink in the form at the repeat, is more important than tonal perspective.

I conclude by returning to my visual analogies of form. The uneven arcade, in which arches have equivalent weight if not exactly the same span, is familiar in mediaeval cathedrals; an arch may be slimmer, or cut off, as the nave reaches the crossing, in order to fit with some larger proportion. Changing the analogy, Berlioz's are not what Stravinsky called 'the great suspension bridge forms of classical music'.[98] Yet even these are compromised by their repeated expositions. Berlioz's bridges are not less attractive for being supported on many piers. They may be less brilliantly engineered; they do not defy gravity in the same way. But the same is true of the most advanced and characteristic musical forms of the generation which lived in Beethoven's shadow and matured with Berlioz in the 1830s – Schumann's piano cycles, Chopin's ballades – although it is true that these works do not even have the semblance of classical forms.[99]

I would like to risk one more visual analogy, which is, however, also temporal. Berlioz's most individual large forms are like a painting on a curved surface which cannot all be seen at once. The eye is led from point to point, encountering details whose significance can only be grasped by looking back or, in time, remembering from some distance what has already been traversed. It cannot comprehend the whole synoptically. The mode is a narrative one, novel-like, all of a piece with Berlioz's musical and extra-musical tendencies. But synoptic comprehension, the grasp of a work of art as a totality, is only possible in music by a sort of analogy, or cheat; the smallest piece cannot be heard and contemplated outside time, as even large paintings usually can. Certain very large works have never been susceptible of synoptic comprehension anyway; their stature is not diminished thereby.[100] But synoptic comprehension is very much what most forms of analysis are about: including Schenker's, and the tabular methods outlined above (p. 182ff). To all these Berlioz is highly resistant (so is Wagner, but for reasons of sheer length as much as style). His long movements are an accumulation of short-term drives in which overall symmetries, GM, or sonata forms have a reduced impact even where they exist; hence my analogy of the curved surface. His longer dramatic works consist of complete tableaux, often interlocked by lack of cadence or by theme but essentially detachable, not organically growing from each other – a series of related frescoes. If in performance Berlioz relies on memory for understanding, so, in other ways, do Beethoven and Wagner. Where Wagner controlled a dramatic work symphonically, however, Berlioz derived instrumental forms from vocal models and so avoided the academicism which bedevils all but the very best post-Beethoven symphonic music. His designs are his own, richly imaginative and strongly controlled.

13 The Overture *Benvenuto Cellini*: an analysis

'Depuis Beethoven, depuis Weber, aucun musicien, en 1838, n'avait écrit une telle ouverture.'

Adolphe Boschot (1908, p. 244)

The *Benvenuto* Overture (Cat. 23D) embodies in large measure the paradoxes, and the rewards, of Berlioz's large-scale structural methods. It lasts about ten minutes, and consists of a fast introduction which also exposes the principal material; a slow section; and an Allegro which includes a sonata action, a lengthy lyrical melody, and material from the slow section. It is not programmatic but it evidently foreshadows not only themes from the opera but the personality of its hero. The opening idea, full of Cellinian impetuosity, includes a conspicuous triplet ('X' in Ex. 101) which recurs in the opera almost like a *Leitmotiv*. The slow section employs Harlequin's arietta (see Ex. 56) and the Pope's theme, which marks a crucial point in the opera as well as the overture (reunion of themes). The lyrical melody drawn from the great trio (see Ex. 82) has some resemblance to the Harlequin melody (see Ex. 101, C–D). The main idea of the Allegro spawns two continuations and a bridging idea.

Most of the thematic material of the overture is summarized in Ex. 101. A and B belong initially to the tonic group; this material forms the basis of the short development, and is recapitulated in the order B^2–A^1–B^1(combined with E)–B^3. This is active, dynamic material, constantly mobile, especially in the extraordinary opening (A^1); rhythm and harmony are steadied in A^2, and the B material is active mostly on the surface. In contrast, the C and D melodies present together a succession of lyrical interludes in the keys I–V–I (cf. the 'idée fixe' in *Fantastique* I); D is exposed in the dominant and requires a tonic resolution. E, on the other hand, has something of the character of a bass; it is most fully exposed in ♭VI (E♭) and thus is also resolved when it returns in the tonic in the Allegro.

Ex. 101 also shows some variants, uses, and interrelationships of the material. A^1 and A^2 are the forms in which the main material is exposed in full; they are compared in Ex. 102, which indicates the harmonic differences

Ex. 101

Ex. 101 (contd)

and tries to suggest their differences of character. In A^1 the accents mark the brass chords (bars 1–4), suggesting a mixture of 3/4 and 2/4 metres. When the harmony becomes mobile in the next four bars the brass settle into a more regular rhythm. The third four-bar group shows a melodic divergence where the harmony is the same; where the melody again coincides the bass moves in the opposite direction and in A^2 lands securely on a dominant. The open-endedness of A^1 seems almost inherent; A^2 is closed, preparatory to the entry of B.

In Ex. 101 various repositions of the motive are called A^3. A^{3a} and A^5 (derived from A^2) belong in the development, which ends with A^{3b}, a version shorn of triplets which in turn relates to the perorative A^{3c}. A^4 is a countermelody, really based on motive 'X', to the lyrical melody D.

Ex. 102

Ex. 102 (contd)

The remaining tonic and bridge material is called B. Motive 'X' is again in evidence, but as quavers, not as a triplet. Bar 97 (in A², see Ex. 102) begets the falling scale reproduced in B¹ᵇ. More significant is that both B¹ᵃ and B² are based on a rising tonic arpeggio (cf. A). B¹ is flexible material for development and combination with E at the climax; at its first appearance it makes a good deal of noise and goes nowhere, in the interests of securing the tonic and its own character. B³ is formed of descending arpeggiation, an equivalence difficult to hear but one which may account for its following B² coherently enough. It finally assimilates motive 'X' (bar 146); it also spawns the rhetorical trombone figure at bar 394ff (a slight variant metrically displaced; see Ex. 101, vertical strokes).

Motive 'Y' in the A material (see Ex. 102) resembles the upbeat structures which link melodies C and D. The reductions (Ex. 101, C¹, D¹) reveal underlying shapes which justify Berlioz's choice of them, out of all the profusion of melody in his opera, for symphonic treatment. The overall structure of cadences and *Urlinie* is the same, and both make much use of the 6th degree despite the fact that $\hat{5}$ does not form part of their fundamental lines ($\hat{5}$ is never linked to $\hat{3}$ through $\hat{4}$). Both also employ a pincer-like approach to the final tonic, a sort of counterpoint of the $\hat{3}$–$\hat{2}$–$\hat{1}$ by 6–7–8. These coincidences are summarized in CD².

The fundamental line of the A material is also $\hat{3}$–$\hat{2}$–$\hat{1}$, frustrated in A¹ by the move to the dominant, and in A² by evasion of the cadence in the sixteenth bar (Ex. 102, bar 106). With the repetition of the last four bars of A² the cadence is completed (bar 110); but an upper part attempts to restore b² as the headnote $\hat{3}$, in readiness for the B material. The mediant emphasis in the A material, as well as in B², is obvious. In A¹ it is harmonic as well as melodic; the bass drives to B for the cadence in E minor (bar 4) and for an odd cadence on B minor (bar 8; the context suggests a B major chord, V of e, which actually appears in A²). In bar 13 the brass bass – ophicleide – diverges from the strings, accenting B again.

In this overture, as in other works of Berlioz, it is the interaction of procedures which counts; no single elements, not even tonality, predominates. Loosely interlinked themes, their reordering in the recapitulation, rhythm, instrumentation, even a fundamental line – all contribute to define the 'proximate goals' towards which the music so energetically works, but they also lead us to anticipate the ultimate goal. The proximate goals are continually frustrated – by incomplete statements, overlappings, tonal parentheses, and, near the end, two massive interrupted cadences. I hope the blow-by-blow account which follows does not seem too heavy for such musical buoyancy.

PROPORTIONS

The tempo-relation of Larghetto to Allegro is experienced as ♩ = 𝅝 ; this is implied by the appearance of the Pope's theme in 3/4 and 3/1. Metronomically it is a good approximation, with the 3/1 statement a little slower (Allegro ♩ = 112, thus 𝅝 = 56, against the Larghetto ♩ = 60). Table 19 indicates the broad proportions, which are remarkably exact. Discounting the fermata in bar 22, and counting the 66 Larghetto bars as 198 units, the 220 units before the sonata action begins are exactly double the exposition's 110 bars. These divisions – the launching of the Allegro, and the interruption of its cadence which begins the development – are the most marked in the piece. For most of the rest, uncertainties predominate, as with the point of recapitulation, its mode, the entries of main material, and the conclusive cadences. Of the 222 bars from bar 199 to the end, the last two are a tonic chord. The overall proportional scheme, therefore, is 2:1:2 (preface: exposition: development, recapitulation, peroration). The 'law' of two thirds (see above, p. 184) is replaced by a higher law (closer to GM), that of three fifths.

There is no clear 'arcade' form. Only the central points of the division into fifths are marked out (one fifth would be the middle of bar 52; four fifths bar 310, near, but not on, important joins at 303 and 318). This precision of form, very rare in Berlioz, was obtained by four separate cuts in the Allegro.[101]

Table 19

Bar nos.	1	23	89	159	199	228	273	303	318	355	388	419
Section	Allegro	Larghetto	Exposition Allegro		Development	Recapitulation			Peroration	Reunion [coda]		
Key	G	G(D)G:Eb (E):C	V G	D	b etc.: V	g–G	G	(a)G	Int.	G	Int.	G
Motive	A¹	E	(C)A²B¹⁻³	D(A⁴)	A³ᵃB¹A⁵A³ᵇ	D (bis)	B²(B¹A³ᵃ)	A¹	A³ᶜ(B¹B³)	EB¹(B²B³)	(B³) E	
Units	22	123: 75	70	40	29	45	45		37	47	17	2
	└ 2 2 0		└ 1 1 0			2 2 0 ┘					2 ┘	

Note: Int. = Interrupted cadence.

RHYTHMIC AND INSTRUMENTAL FACTORS

Besides the motivic layers to which I have attached labels (Ex. 101 and table 19), there is a pitchless rhythmic motive: syncopation. It first arises in A^1 (bar 2). It is banished from most of the Larghetto, but reappears almost jarringly at bar 80 (horns), at the moment when the bass E♭ sinks to the dominant note; cornet and trumpet are added to the crescendo in the rhythm ♪ ♩ ♩. The Allegro begins with the accompaniment in bass crotchets while the other parts have the rhythm ♪ ♩ ♪. The Allegro syncopation comes out almost twice as fast, however, which makes it difficult to hear this as a direct link between sections.

Minim syncopation remains in the melody (A^2). B^1 begins *fortissimo* on the half-bar, reinforced by brass and drum entries, but the rhythmic structure is an extended upbeat (three quavers in A^2, five in B^1); the downbeat accents (bars 118, 122, 123) are hardly threatened even by the half-bar accent in 122. B^2, however, is always accented on the half-bar, forming a large semibreve syncopation; the metrical structure is thus thrown out before the modulation, which begins with B^3 also on a half-bar accent. The crotchet syncopation returns at the development, and persists from bars 199 to 221; it returns at the last reference to A^{3a} (the texture of A^2), just before the return of A^1 (303). Minim syncopation is important at bar 266ff, where melody D is cut off, and it precedes the resumed semibreve syncopation of B^2 at bar 273; it is used in the accompaniment (bar 248) and appears in the first and third statements of D (first 168–9, 177; third, 237, 240–2, 246–7). Most of the orchestra syncopates minims just before the end (bars 394–401).

Another rhythmic stratum is the introduction of triple metres in the duple Allegro, culminating in the massive 3/1 bars of the reunion. This forms a rhythmic resolution, since triple metre is reconciled to the whole bar of the Allegro; earlier triple rhythms appear destructive. The details are considered below, as they arise.

While not an obviously constructive force, instrumentation is another stratum. Berlioz begins with a massive *tutti*, gradually dismantles his orchestra, and, while providing a myriad of combinations, withholds the full *tutti* until A^1 returns, as late as bar 303. The trombones, whose delayed entry in the Larghetto marks its point of GM, are withheld in the Allegro until they punctuate the brittle, stratified orchestration of the development. They join the reprise of B^2 only in bar 278, when the percussion stops. The *tutti* appears momentarily at bar 281, but quickly decays; once fully launched (bar 303), it is maintained almost to the end, in varied forms. This breaking and reassembling of the *tutti* corresponds to tonal and thematic elements, and thus plays its part in reinforcing the overall design in more than the obvious way (the need to withhold something for a final climax). The *tutti* chord at bar 281, for instance, underlines a harmony (supertonic) which postpones a proximate, even a fairly long-term, goal (the return of A^1).

The prefatory Allegro (bars 1–22; Exx. 102–3)

The need to recover A^1 is one of the mainsprings of the action – and not just the sonata action. For A^1 does not begin the sonata; it is only used as its recapitulation, a striking economy of structure. Gräbner proposes that these opening bars give rise to most of the rhythmically significant events of the piece.[102] The melody which in A^2 is lucidly harmonized in G major, is as ambiguously harmonized here as it is rhythmically suggestive; the mediant and submediant emphasis proves important throughout (see Ex. 102). Ex. 103 is the first of a series of examples which if read continuously reduce the whole overture (Exx. 103 and 105–12). It shows the strong presentation of b^2 as head-note, prolonged by c^3 and falling locally to the $\hat{2}$ at the half-close. The harmonic adventures are an intensification of the head-note, making it a mediant, a 5th, a root, and the resolution of the c^3 whose instability is underlined by ending the third phrase on a $^6_3$ with chromatic bass counterpoint. The fourth phrase seems to settle the rhythm for the moment, and from bar 16 the dominant crashes forth; the section ends with a third-inversion dominant 7th, and the basses hold their dissonant C into the silence. The dissonance is thus left hanging in isolation, for later resolution.

Ex. 103

The Larghetto (bars 23–88; Exx. 105–6)

The Larghetto begins with what appears to be a tonic exposition of melody E. It falls, however, into four-bar phrases, and the rhythms are redisposed (Ex. 104). This is a limping version, restrained in colour, and it ends with a

Ex. 104

move to the dominant which occurs nowhere else in the overture (although it appears in the first phrase of the sextet, Cat. 23C/12). Above this cadence comes the 'Y' motive growing out of amorphous woodwind comments and leading to melody C. 'Y' is here harmonically an upbeat, as in melody D. The orchestral mass is broken into separated groups: woodwind, pizzicato basses, timpani. Within the six-bar dominant passage (Ex. 105, bars 36–41) the three groups are woodwind, horns (somewhat syncopated) and pizzicato strings, the last carried over into the double-basses from bar 42.

Ex. 105

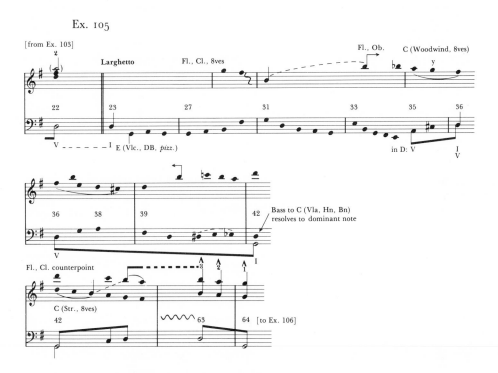

Again what sounds like an exposition (in V) is interrupted, by the reverse modulation through the ♭7th which appears in the melody. There follows a full statement of melody C (bars 42–64), summarized in Ex. 105 (see Ex. 101, C, and Ex. 56). It appears to be almost a parenthetical tonic (another Berliozian paradox). A flute counterpoint underlines the principal melodic events (motive 'Y', 42–5; the 3̂–2̂–1̂, 50–52) before joining the melody at the cadence. Motive 'Y' feels like an upbeat melodically, in bar 42; but the harmony is already tonic. The completed 3̂–2̂–1̂ is the first of several diminutions of the fundamental line that are not interrupted; although various factors – here tempo, elsewhere rhythm and instrumentation – detract somewhat from the sense of closure, we have here a piered rather than suspension-bridge form (see above, p. 200).

The whole Larghetto is enclosed by dominants (bars 22, 88), so Gräbner calls it all parenthetical (GraAR, 22). The closure at bar 64 marks the point of GM, and is also the most relaxed moment; it is that extreme stability which should make us suspicious, as in *Roméo* II. My reductive examples may appear to enhance the sense of repeated closure by their necessary concentration on pitch factors, but I do not consider these necessarily more important than other factors commented on in the text. (I have certainly not attained Schenker's ideal of wordless analysis.)

The trombone entry (bar 64) leads to a shift of harmonic perspective (it is hardly a modulation) to ♭VI (Ex. 106). In the prefatory Allegro Berlioz passed from I to V by way of the natural submediant; here he chooses the punned flat submediant. The melody sings forth in the register of the Pope's voice, although it does not function as the bass. The activity of the treble instruments is outlined in Ex. 106; the melody is the inner part. The mixture of solemnity (bass clarinet) and delicacy (muted violins) is as refreshing as the new key. In fact, violins and wind alternate in the treble counterpoint with a pattern corresponding to the phrase-length of melody E: twice 2 + 1 bars. It retains its own internal consistency in the two-bar phrase (73–4), the 6:3 beat proportion replaced by 4:2; then the pattern breaks, the wind taking over bar 76 and the violins hastily clearing the air in bar 77 before the cadence. This counterpoint prepares a ȝ̂–2̂–1̂ in E♭, but fails to complete it. At the cadence the double-basses (arco in bar 77) join the last phrase of E, a doubling which might arise because the bass clarinet cannot descend to B♭.

Ex. 106

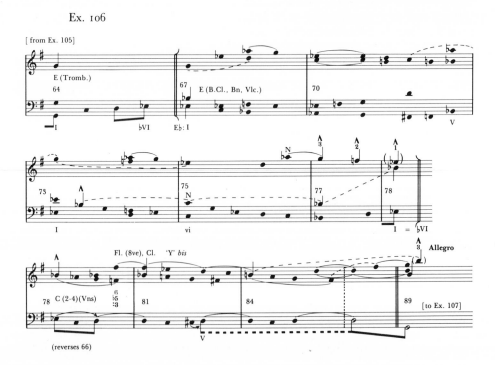

Rather than lose sonority by putting it up an octave, Berlioz adds the string basses to the melody and gives the bass clarinet a very low independent part.

There is something equivocal about this cadence, but E♭ has been sufficiently established to require resolution, for which reason the Larghetto is not parenthetical within the whole form, even if the statements of C and E may be considered so. The rest of the Larghetto returns to melody C (bar 78), but as if influenced by E, for it falls into three-bar phrases by omitting its first bar (motive 'Y'). The fragment of C is harmonically displaced, beginning on the dominant note (B♭); this follows naturally from the strong $\hat{5}$ projected throughout melody E. However B♭ is next heard as a mediant, for it moves up to the true $\hat{3}$ in bar 84, at the same time merging with a double statement of motive 'Y' in the flute-clarinet counterpoint (it was this sonority which introduced 'Y' above the fragmentary E at the beginning of the Larghetto).

Equivocation continues in the harmony. The bass falls to the dominant (D), which is accented and even made quite assertive by the appearance of the syncopated horns; yet the chord remains the dominant of E♭. Only the second time (with suitable inflections in the melody) does a dominant chord appear; the bass D falls non-functionally to C, then pushes chromatically to D which is thus enclosed in a pincer (arrows in Ex. 106) before it can assert itself as a dominant root. In bar 84 the 'cellos and timpani seem to resist interpretation of the chord as a $^6_4$, but the dominant feeling grows with the crescendo, which culminates with a timpani roll, now on D, to explode into a forceful allegro downbeat.

The Allegro: tonic area and bridge (bars 89–159; Ex. 107)

Two bars of tonic introduce a third form of accompanimental syncopation and permit the upbeat feeling of the end of the Larghetto to be duplicated by the quaver upbeat to A² (Ex. 107). There are no lurches to the mediant; the tonic persists for four more bars, the dominant for three, and the mediant major is composed out by chromatic alteration in the third phrase. The sonata action thus begins with a fresh look at the main idea, which will not be heard in full again. A² does, however, spawn ideas for the development and for the prolonged anticipation of return. Its cadence (bar 110) is at once interrupted by the bustling anacrusis of B¹, disturbing, but not destroying, the sense of downbeat, while confirming the tonic (which may seem hardly necessary). It is also a sort of *tutti*, and the full stable tonic bass from which B² begins to depart. B¹ here is not exactly what Berlioz later fits with E; it has its independent shape, and notably uses a strong pattern of descending 3rds in the bass, inverting the G–B melodic movement which is shared by A and B¹ (see Ex. 101). The violins twice rise to f♯³, the replacement of the diminished 7th (bar 122) by F♯ minor (126) contributes to the excitement and

Ex. 107

Implied bass from 155 (or even 146) to 159

anticipates several later cadences. B¹ is sequentially treated in the supertonic (B^{1b}, bar 118), the first use of a key which is important later on.

B¹ also cadences strongly, but repose is avoided by the emphatic treble note B and syncopated accent of B² (bar 130). The motivic 3rd G–B is now moved up to B–D, and the arpeggiation is completed on the top G (bar 134) at the exact moment of tonal disruption, which is also the moment of metrical disruption – the bridge (B³). B³ suggests C minor and E♭ chords, settling on the latter; again, a strong passing E minor (B¹ and B²) is more decisively succeeded by E♭. Having completely obliterated the tonic, by a chord which does not belong to the dominant and is therefore not a direct route to it, Berlioz has recourse to ambiguity to reach his complementary key. A diminished 7th crisply interrupts at bar 146, still accenting the half-bar; the violins adapt the falling interval of B³ – diminished 4th, perfect 4th – as a diminished 5th, decorated by motive 'X'. It is this diminished 7th which evades the dominant in *Harold* I (bar 98), by resolving onto the tonic $^6_4$. Here Berlioz does reach D from it, but only after still further destroying G by the use of a G♯ implying a C♯ chord. The chromatic G–G♯–A–B♭ otherwise only changes the position of the diminished 7th. At bar 155 it falls to the dominant of D; a chromatic passage, implying D minor, flows into the newly established D at bar 159. Functions are, however, blurred, as both dominant and tonic of D are in first inversion.

Interesting as the pitches are, most of the excitement of the bridge comes from the rhythm, which works closely with the harmonic outline. B³ reiterates the half-bar accent of B² (134, 136); then the accents at a breve's distance are closed to a 3/4 'bar'. A moment of ambiguity at bar 142 (5/4, or 2/4 + 3/4) leads to five clear 3/4 'bars'. Table 20 shows this macrorhythm, with values reduced to a quarter. From the tritone with 'X' (bar 146) the music seems all animation on the surface, all suspense beneath. From bar 151 longer values (2/2 and 3/2 'bars') precede the restoration of order with the minims of bar 155.

Table 20

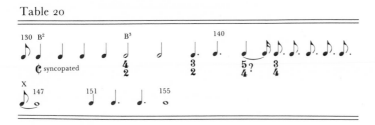

The dominant area (bars 159–228; Ex. 108A)

The fourfold statement of the lyrical melody D is interrupted only by the twenty-nine-bar development. D is not, however, a self-indulgent intermezzo. The first and third statements are harmonically unstable; the second and fourth in some sense resolve them. The first two statements form the exposition of the dominant; the second pair resolves them. There is thus no question of a central, symmetrical arch over the development. Indeed, as the only statement in the tonic major, the fourth resolves the previous three, and is accordingly extended at its cadence. Each repetition adds something; each is necessary.

Ex. 108A

[from Ex. 107]
Melody D (see Ex. 101): bars 179-198 repeat 159-178; only the outline and significant differences are shown.

Ex. 108 B
Pincer movements

Normally the resolution in the tonic would follow the recapitulation of elements of A and B. The apparently premature resolution proves to be Berlioz's first step in an elaborate series of postponements of expected goals; he allows one exception, the tonic key, which is not postponed but arrives unexpectedly early and unassumingly – itself perhaps a ploy to keep us guessing.

The first postponement is of the dominant chord. Bar 159 is D major, but the counterpoint of bars 155–8 has rearranged the diminished 7th so that G is in the bass; bar 159 is a first inversion. After a rest, F♯ is still the bass in bar 161. The bass is sustained by motion to and from G, passed down an octave to return to F♯ in bar 171. The first solid root-position D major chord is in bar 179, where a cadence is completed, or even bar 181; in bar 179 the floating violins seem to deny the solidity of the chord, whereas bar 181 is the first hearty D major, over a bass reminiscent of the solid tonic at bar 89. To this concealed reconciliation of material is added a direct reference, through motive 'X' (A⁴ in Ex. 101).

At this point some remarks of Gräbner concerning the use of sonata form demand to be considered:

> If this overture were a sonata movement the resolution at bar 110 would be the last tonic *tutti* in the exposition before the move to the dominant area and an extremely long piece could be expected. In fact it has little to do with sonatas, external appearances apart. A dominant second subject does appear (bar 159) but its power to create tension is dissipated during the 'development' partly because there is no final dominant cadence as a reference point for the modulations in the 'development' . . . Furthermore, the return to the tonic (bar 248) is preceded by a passage in the tonic minor. Nothing could be less dramatic in a sonata context since the tonic is neither properly withheld nor properly resolved. (GraAR, 22–3)

But how should sonata be defined for a mid-nineteenth-century style? Gräbner is obviously right to describe the return to tonic minor as undramatic; its values are lyric, poetic. But Berlioz is not writing in a dramatic (classical) language. Schumann described not only *Fantastique* I but the 'traditional model' in terms of theme as much as key (ConFS, 231); this may be quite unclassical, but it is the interpretation of one of the most sensitive musical minds of the time. The 'arched' form of the *Fantastique* is even more apparent in *Benvenuto*, in which the asymmetries already pointed out are not so obvious. Many nineteenth-century sonatas are oriented by melody as much as key; they need not be accounted weak merely because they do not measure up well to criteria appropriate for Haydn or Beethoven. I find Gräbner's argument convincing and enormously valuable where he discovers other criteria for discussion of the form; but I do not think we can ignore anything as important as the overture's external appearance.

Even if the whole of melody D were heard as a little unfocussed – 'flou', like the G major statement of melody C (see Ex. 56) – its sheer length and repetition forces us to consider it a structural point of reference. The interruption of a well-prepared cadence by a V–i in B minor (bars 198–9) does not alter this; melody D is too relaxed to create tension anyway. The incomplete cadence at this point is common practice in overtures and allows us to anticipate the resolution of the development on a dominant chord, sufficiently clearly to permit the chord itself to sound quite apologetic (bar 227). The blurred edges of the tonal areas are part of Berlioz's strategy for maintaining tension in the face of so undramatic a tonal scheme.

The proportional significance of bar 199 is adequately reflected in the suddenness of the interruption; the new texture and motives actually overlap the end of the melody in the violins. Ex. 108A goes through this moment to the brief dominant of bar 227. Motive 'Y' begins the melody; a^2 is the head-note, both as $\hat{5}$ of D and $\hat{2}$ of G, and it returns explicitly at the end of the development. (In Ex. 108A the line of melody D is simplified from Ex. 101, D^1, and the bass is added.)

From bar 199, Ex. 108A shows how symmetrical and clear is the background to the intense surface activity of the development. Each of the four-bar groups up to bar 214 has a single harmony, although some ambiguity of chord-position results from motivic activity in the bass register. The 'true' bass is defined by the trombones; there is an inner line, and bass arpeggiation (slurred in Ex. 108A). The triadic shape of the motivic material makes combination possible, although B^1 is here arpeggiated in quavers. The texture, with crotchet syncopations, suggests A^2; motive A^{3a} is used, and has nine notes identical with the form of B^1 used here. A^5 is tossed in to cover each chord-change, and the motives all change register for the second and fourth four-bar groups.

The trombones underline the symmetry of the four-bar groups, which enhance the acceleration from bar 215. It is the premature entry of the trombones half-way through this bar which marks a departure, rather than the factitious canon on A^{3a}. The texture is compressed, and B^1 necessarily omitted. The trombone chords reinforce the bass in $\frac{6}{3}$ position until bar 220, when they adhere to their position while the double-basses move within the chord to join the fourth horn on D before moving to A$\sharp$ in bar 222. The succession of $\frac{6}{3}$ chords adds to the instability, and the dominant of A in bar 221 has a decidedly eccentric contrapuntal motivation. It is however resolved by supertonic preparation for the dominant (arrow in Ex. 108A). The *fortissimo* diminished 7th (bar 222) halts the progression which has gained a great deal of excitement in very little time, partly through the use of a 'drunken walrus' technique (see p. 92), with 'no particular bass'. The dominant is reached by semitonal slides – pincer movements (Ex. 108B) – after the supertonic has been underlined by A^{3b} (see Ex. 101). The dominant is stroked in bar 227 and resolves onto a first-inversion tonic without the $\hat{2}$ descending to $\hat{1}$ (flute rests, 228); it is a deliberate anticlimax or, as Tovey might have put it, a hollowness in the centre of the form, part of a larger strategy, and of excellent effect in itself.

Resolution of D (bars 228–73; Ex. 109)

Berlioz underlines the contrariness of his minor tonic by only half-resolving the development (the $\frac{6}{3}$ chord recalls that of bar 159). The texture is the stillest of the overture, with barely shifting string chords, above which Berlioz's favoured solo instrument adapts D to a mood of heart-ache – the anguish of Teresa, who uses this melody's first appearance in the trio (Cat. 23C/3) for 'O Cellini, se peut-il faire que je laisse ainsi mon père'. In the overture, therefore, the relaxation is tonal, not emotional; the structure, accordingly, does not sag. Berlioz preserves this equilibrium between immediate excitement, anticipation of resolution, and actual degree of resolution, through to his grandest climax. The oboe solo is only slightly

Ex. 109

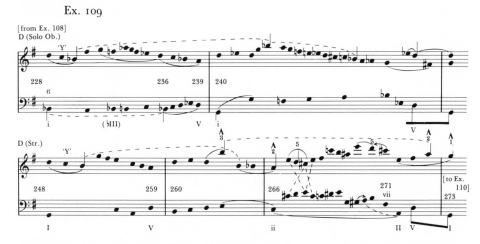

chromatic, but it includes the only use in the overture of Berlioz's favourite ♭III (here a natural mediant of G minor, bars 233 and 243, the latter a second inversion reached contrapuntally).

The repeat of the melody in the major, from bar 248, is the third major version, and the third reharmonization. The chord-changes are texturally induced. At bar 159 the texture required minimal motion and unstable chord-positions; bar 179 had no accompaniment, as if, by delaying the downbeat to bar 181, to highlight both the denial of a cadence and the subsequent combination of D with the accompanimental texture of A^2. Different chord-positions inevitably result from such structurally significant textural choices. At bar 228 the instability of the texture enables the melody to be stretched and its rhythmic certainties undermined without actually altering its structure (except for merging two four-bar groups by the inverted 7th of bar 235). The choice at bar 248 is dictated by a wish to parallel, but not crudely, the setting at bar 179. Momentum is gathered by the quaver ornaments (the upbeat recalls bar 179); by gentle minim syncopations in the wind stabilized by a pedal bass; and by the felicitous imitation (see Ex. 64). The bass remains quiet, moving to C and A in a single progression towards the dividing dominant of bar 259. The contrast makes the texture almost plush, with its string octaves, yet there is little figuration and the orchestration is light. Motive 'X' returns discreetly in bar 260 to influence, as before, the last fall of the melody.

Berlioz then completes the cadence to melody D by a striking supertonic prolongation, through a series of syncopated chords, mostly diminished; the melodic outline of the cadence remains clear (Ex. 109, from bar 266; cf. Ex. 101, D). The chords are contrapuntal in origin; there is another enhancement of the leading-note when a C♯ (bar 271) is harmonized by vii. The passage sounds almost like Chaikovsky, mingling ascending syncopations with a descending scale (over four octaves, chromatically a^3–A, then diatonically A–D). It restores allegro motion, which melody D tended to resist, and launches a full and emphatic tonic for the return of first-group material.

Recapitulation of B^2 (bars 273–303; Ex. 110)

There is some recall, but much that is inevitable is still withheld: the tonic major, and all first-group material but the most insignificant, B^2. As Gräbner excellently says: 'It becomes increasingly apparent that the large-scale tension to be resolved does not concern dominant and tonic in absolute terms but has more to do with the expectation that the opening theme must reappear and the delaying of its reappearance' (GraAR, 23). Berlioz is not so literal-minded as to provide a retrograde of all his material (see table 19). The value of choosing B^2 at bar 273 is its emphasis on the head-note B, which was largely in abeyance during the dominant area and, while not prominent during the reprise of D, formed part of a completed melodic fall through A to G in the previous cadence. The strident b^2, followed by supporting E minor and B minor chords, allows us to drown that melodic fall and to hear it as a local event. The procedure is more brutal than organic, perhaps, but effective in performance.

Moreover, the syncopation of B^2 weakens the metre just when the tonic is reinforced. From now on various factors, such as the metric indeterminacy of bar 281ff, the inherent ambiguities of A^1, and the recollections of B^3 with its

Ex. 110

triple-metre inclination, keep the metre uncertain except where the harmony is vagrant, at bar 318. No coincidence of metric and harmonic stability is permitted until bar 355, the reunion, and even there the very stable metre is 3/1.

B^2 is slightly developed, rising to another chord on the 7th, vigorously repeated with its own dominant (bars 279-80), before its pent-up energy overflows through another massive third-inversion dominant into a passage which leads to a supertonic (bar 299). Only a half-bar of dominant intervenes before the last necessary stage of recapitulation, the recall of A. The four-octave chromatic scale of the first supertonic prolongation (from bar 266) is matched by a swirling three-octave diatonic scale (strings) which incorporates elements of B^1 (the climax on a^3, bar 281; cf. bar 123) and of D (the two bars of triplets, 283–4; cf. 263–5). But despite its powerful bass C♮, bar 281 is not a supertonic, and the point of the passage seems to be the indirect 'resolution' of this $^6_2$ onto a simple $^6_3$ on C (broken beam in Ex. 110). The long-term significance of this will be discussed later. The passage is also a small second development, bridging areas of tonic.

The material of harmonic dissolution includes the rhythm (timpani, bar 285) and motivic shape ('cellos, bar 288) of B^1, secure elements within an indeterminate progression governed by side-slipping semitones. The timpani, however, remain obstinately on the dominant note. The idea may have been suggested by the bridge to the last movement of Beethoven's Fifth Symphony, of which Berlioz wrote: 'the A♭ chord . . . seems to introduce a new key; on the other hand isolated hammering of the timpani on C tends to preserve the ambiance of the original tonic. The ear hesitates . . . one cannot see the outcome of this harmonic mystery' (AT, 35–6/G, 53). Berlioz too uses a motivic 'isolated hammering' and his dominant, like Beethoven's C, is the goal of the passage, beyond which lies a very loud assertion of tonic major. Like Beethoven, Berlioz retains his D against chords to which it does not belong (the supertonic and its dominant, bars 289 and 293). However, unlike Beethoven's, Berlioz's timpani do not win; when the air clears it is on the supertonic, and as at the end of the development the 'inevitable' dominant scarcely happens at all (bar 302). The chief harmony of Berlioz's mystery is the diminished 7th, but the bass is characteristically ambiguous; in bar 285 the string bass B naturally follows its C, but the bassoons enter on F♮. The same diminished 7th finally debouches into the supertonic in bar 299, but it is repositioned (cf. bar 146ff, Ex. 107), with G♯ in the bass and F♮ in the treble (broken lines in Ex. 110; the bass and treble E, despite their apparent significance, are not part of a V of A but of another diminished 7th, bar 298). The recovery of A minor in bar 299 is a release, but even here functions are carefully confused, and the contrapuntally obtained root position (bassoons, double-bass) yields to a $^6_3$ with 'cellos in the bass. The tune is a sort of false reprise, deliciously impertinent; it is Berlioz's consonant version of the 'wrong' horn entry in the 'Eroica', a sort of practical criticism (see above, p. 27). It is also the reprise of the texture of A² (bar 89) but the melodic shape is A³ᵃ.

Reprise of A¹ and peroration (bars 303–55; Ex. 111).

After this miraculously balanced passage expectations are at last, and rudely, fulfilled. Although the upbeat in bar 302 belongs to A², it leads to the uproarious A¹, restless and syncopated, altered only by filling in the silences between each four-bar group (one of these fillings, in bar 310, suggests the filling motive of the development, A⁵). Again b² is restored as the head-note after a fall to a²; and resolution is firmly opposed by the first of two huge interrupted cadences. The splendid peroration, from bar 318, is based on A³ᶜ and B¹, and thus looks back obliquely to the development; it epitomizes Berlioz's power to deploy rich harmonies, pseudo-modulations, without losing touch with his tonic.

This peroration includes a reminder (rather than reprise) of the bridge-passage on B³. The compression of four-bar units into threes itself recalls the processes of the earlier bridge (already the interruption in bar 318 cuts a four-bar phrase down to three). The abrupt shift to a 3/4 metre at bar 337 (cf. bar 142) is thus prepared, although it remains, because of the dynamic drop, quite startling. Table 21 presents a macrorhythm of the passage, reduced like table 20 to quartered values. Beneath the regular 3/4 Berlioz introduces a counterpoint in 3/1 which describes a single rhythm twice (slurs in table 21). From bar 345 the woodwind (with bassoons) propose an alternative 3/4 in heterophonic anticipation of the strings, and the ophicleide replaces the bassoon on the slow rhythm, describing a whole diminished 7th which this time *does* debouch onto the tonic $^6_4$ (cf. Ex. 107). Bar 349, marked by a sudden *piano* in the strings to let through the low-pitched beginning of the woodwind scale, is the massive $^6_4$ we expect at the climax of a peroration; another goal attained, another frustration ended. But the trombones drop out, and the *tutti* is briefly withheld until bar 355. This huge six-bar dominant retrospectively explains the near-absence of any previous dominant preparation since the last ten bars of the Larghetto (before bars 228 and 303 the supertonic is given more space than the dominant). Berlioz points the cadence by non-motivic woodwind skirling and a colossal crescendo; it is the main cadence, the definitive fall of the fundamental line to g^2, the close of the harmonic action and the sonata. In short, what follows is (for Berlioz) a large coda.

Table 21

Reunion, coda (bars 355 to the end; Ex. 112)

Or is it? Coda it may be to the sonata, but the reunion is indispensable to the action of the whole overture. It is the resolution of the Pope's theme, exposed in ♭VI, and of the triple metres. Less important, perhaps, it is also the only

Ex. 112

Rhythmic proportions are indicated in quartered note-values as in tables 20-1

true recapitulation of B¹. The passage is one of those exhilarating pieces of simultaneity. Against the huge 3/1 bars which impose a larger pattern through the phrasing of the majestic melody E (see notation in 3/4 in Ex. 112), B¹ struggles to establish its own duple-bar system; the percussion crashes, largely avoiding the first beats of the 3/1 bars (with a consistency doubtless puzzling to contemporary bass-drum players, if Berlioz's portrait of them in SO, passim, is to be believed), tend to reinforce the phrasing of B¹. Berlioz flings in B² (bar 375ff) and B³ (381–2) in frantic efforts to halt the inexorable stride of the pontiff.

It is halted only by another massive interrupted cadence (bar 388), with E♮ in the bass (as one might expect after the E♭ of bar 318). A strong two-bar metre is then established which obtains through the silent bars (macro-rhythm superimposed in Ex. 112), before the Pope's theme is heard alone, in its original register (of bar 23ff); for the first time it is allowed a tonic cadence with its emphatic $\hat{2}$–$\hat{1}$. Thus if we view the form thematically as well as tonally, there is not a bar without its structural function; a principal theme is completed only in bar 419 (it is of course only its first phrase, but it sounds cadential, as other appearances of the first phrase have not). This last postponement, then, from bar 388, reverses the order of natural and flat 6th degrees; restores the readily assimilable minim syncopation; provides a last fling of the minor mode (trombones, 394ff) and an upward string scale matching that of the wind in bar 349; and concludes with a vast I–ii–V–I progression (bars 402 to the end).

SOME CONCLUSIONS

The whole overture is constructed on a large proportional scheme (of which Berlioz may have been unaware), and with a variety of actions embracing one, not necessarily dominant, element – a sonata. Most important is the succession of proximate goals, variously frustrated to preserve other expectations intact. Because he operates with musical elements other than tonality, Berlioz plays with the tonic by giving it prematurely, in stages; its recovery does not therefore detract from the significance of other resolutions. Any feeling of tonic saturation is prevented by the judicious placing of interrupted cadences, and by bridges which, among other harmonic details, tend to destroy the tonic and revolve around other degrees, notably the supertonic and flat 6th, while not actually establishing any other key. Besides this, a wealth of instrumental, thematic, and rhythmic detail maintains the liveliness of the musical surface and prepares for the culmination of the work, after the sonata has closed, in the papal intervention.

I have summarized much of this in the long-drawn but thin line of an *Ursatz* (Ex. 113). But this is not a Schenkerian study; it attempts to convey something of the life of other dimensions oblique to the fundamental and very simple conclusions drawn from an *Ursatz*. Counterpoint is of the essence in many highly original short-term progressions and prolongations; but the main objectives are not reached in that way. One may well ask where the bass tonic comes from, in bars 42 and 303. In bar 42, I have tried to suggest a theoretical way (see Ex. 105), but it cannot be readily heard. In bar 303 the very irrationality of the root position undermines the stability of the tonic even at the recovery of A^1 for which we have been waiting; for there are further objectives ahead, and the stability of a full cadence, or of A^2, would be premature.

In such overlaps and ambiguities lie the heady qualities of this music – intoxicating, not (as Bax suggested; see epigraph to Chapter 7) intoxicated. The simple fundamental line is obscured (desirably so) by other strata. The emphatic mediant and submediant chords sustain the head-note b^2 against the threatened cadences; both are attacked by their flat equivalents, the note Bb (as $\hat{5}$ of Eb and $\hat{3}$ of G minor) rather than the key, and by both the note and key Eb. These minor-mode inflections, despite the G minor recapitulation, intervene most powerfully through the enharmonic resolution of Eb with sharp 6th (C♯–Db, bar 318) onto Ab, after which the

Ex. 113

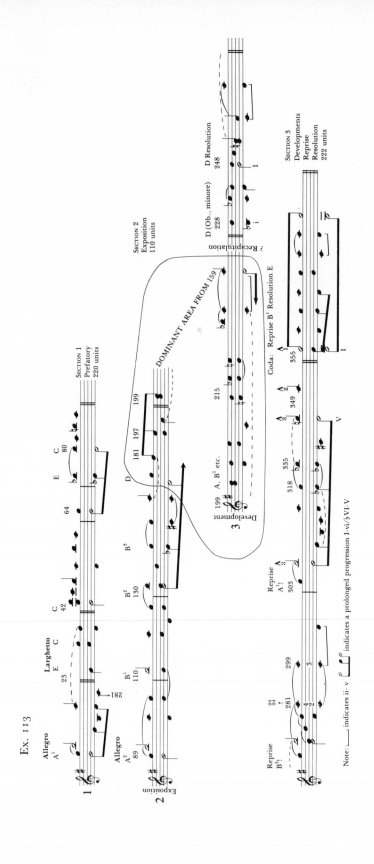

Note: ⌣ indicates ii · v   ♩ indicates a prolonged progression I-vi/♭VI-V

sequence underlines the flat relations of the tonic – B♭, c – and flat non-relations – D♭, G♭, E♭. The minor elements are integrated in their last fling from bar 394. Another element, more prolonging than disturbing, is the natural supertonic. The third-inversion dominant 7th left hanging in bar 22 relates to the supertonics with C in the bass; the connection actually seems to be the point of the episode from bar 281 to 299, a backward resolution which clears the air for an important cadence (which then, properly, does not happen). The supertonic appears prominently in the sequence of B^{1b} (from bar 115, on a bass C); the pitch of B^{1b} is not dictated by the need to combine B^1 with E, for the pitch is not used during the reunion. The supertonic is dominant of V, and its root is the only structurally dissonant note of the fundamental line. It has a thematic basis at bars 224 (A^{3b}) and 299 (A^{3a}), and receives massive prolongation from 266 to 272, still mostly in first inversion. Finally, the supertonic 7th in bar 406, with bass C, is followed, like bar 22, with silence, allowing the last resonances of the enigmatic $^6_4{}_2$ to be absorbed. The C bass is at last consonant; the dissonance is in an upper part. The Pope's theme and the last cadence describe only dominant (without 7th) and tonic.

We may add to these links in the chain various motivic intertwinings (unobtrusive reunions by metre or by means of motives 'X' and 'Y'), the *Urlinie*, harmonic strata, motivic links, instrumentation, an arcade-like adherence to the tonic, continual postponement of thematic resolution, and extraordinarily exact proportions – a veritable armoury of connections which unify the work without the aid of the classical 'suspension bridge' so alien to Berlioz's upbringing. One might argue that some of these elements are surface; the work is more unified when played by an orchestra (Berlioz never asked for it to be played otherwise). But I hope to have shown that even its 'black-and-white' elements have a fascination which in performance makes this overture a brilliant kaleidoscopic display, and to have suggested that so many links forge a chain that is scarcely weaker, as 'form', than the Beethovenian single link. All this is unique, yet typical of Berlioz, and if it is not precisely 'satisfying' in the sense that Mendelssohn is, it is hardly the worse for that. The myriad reflections of ideas in unexpected places, the treatment of stable harmony with little contrast to the tonic, present a clear yet shifting picture in which may be found a true anticipation of Debussy's perpetual variation and unexpectedness: 'organic vegetable inexactness', as Eimert calls it, to add to the idea of pre-Stravinskian stratification.[103] Perhaps after all, cliché as it is, and rooted in his time as he was, Berlioz is the first of the moderns.

14 The figure and the background: Faust in *La damnation*

'Berlioz, Français avant tout (il n'était pas vieux jeu à son époque!) en mettait-il de la variété, de la couleur, du rythme dans *la Damnation*, *Roméo*, *l'Enfance du Christ* – ça manque d'unité, vous répond-on! – Moi je réponds Merde!'

Emmanuel Chabrier, letter to Costallat (J. Desaymard, ed., *Chabrier d'après ses lettres*, Paris, 1934, p. 117)

In the music of *Huit scènes de Faust*, Faust plays no part. His musical depiction in *La damnation* is, therefore, exclusively the work of 1845–6. Monologues for Faust begin Parts I, II, and III; another occupies second place in Part IV, immediately before the sequence of scenes leading him to Hell. It is clear that Berlioz conceived the work's overall structure very much in terms of his hero's states of mind. The four monologues, and their relationship, bear on the musical design as a whole. Manuscript and other evidence, incidentally, makes it clear that the first, third, and fourth, at least, were composed fairly early in the genesis of the work, while Berlioz was on tour in Germany (Mem54; Rushton, 1975; NBE 8b).

I have already discussed several aspects of the 'Introduction pastorale', 'Le vieil hiver' (RusBL; and above, Exx. 69C, 71, 45, 78, 79). From the point of view of the whole work, it is noteworthy that Faust begins his role in the introduction in F♯ minor (bar 9) and ends in B♭ (bar 74), although the movement is in D. This runs counter to his expressed delight in the spring sunrise, the breeze, waters, birds, and growing plants, which inspire this remarkable orchestral canvas. The orchestra's first climax in D overwhelms the related minor keys of the fugal exposition (bar 28). Later the music meanders round B♭ and twice moves back to D by a creeping chromaticism: B♭–B♮–C♯–D in the bass (61–3, D minor, which Faust frustrates; 8off, to D major, when Faust is silent). There follows a purely orchestral development, and from the sounds of humanity ('Ronde de paysans' and 'Marche hongroise') Faust retreats, not in disgust but out of *ennui*.

The introduction to Part II (No. 4A) is closely modelled on Goethe; *ennui* drives Faust to the brink of suicide, but he is interrupted by the sound of Easter bells. This time the key of the monologue is F♯ minor; there is no exterior framework. The texture is again fugal, with a winding subject which ascends a minor 9th (F♯–g♮, suggesting a tonal descent to the subdominant). This fugue is more scholastic, answering at the 5th, not the 3rd; Faust himself only sings fragments of the subject, but his declamation avoids simple recitative. Broken off at his impassioned cry 'Je souffre!', the fugue resumes in C♯ minor (bar 23), to be broken again by Faust's intervention ('O terre, pour moi seul Tu n'as donc pas de fleurs'). It winds to an indeterminate halt, but the true recitative which follows still has motivic significance (see Ex. 114A[7] below); it leads into 'Chant de la fête de Pâques', taken over from the *Huit scènes* with a line for Faust added.

When Mephistopheles appears, he dominates Faust; the philosopher's morale is weakened by his failure to complete his last experiment, and by nostalgia for the simple faith of childhood. This is no conversion; although the text reads 'Heaven has won me back' (in Goethe 'Earth has won me back', a subtlety unsuited to music-drama), Berlioz's Faust deceives himself. He agrees to whatever will restore his youth; the devil finds him ripe for corruption. It is not an edifying spectacle; in that respect Berlioz's conception is closer to Marlowe's or to his friend Heine's, than to Goethe's. Faust says little in the next scenes (but see Ex. 114C[5]); when he joins in the 'Choeur de sylphes' (No. 7B), it is at the crucial moment when the music shifts to F♯ minor from D (the modulation existed, however, in the *Huit scènes*).

Faust's first demand of Mephistopheles is to be given Margaret, and this wish to possess, and hence to violate, innocent beauty, is his real fall from grace. Yet in Part III he comes near to redemption; the atmosphere of Margaret's room turns his thoughts heavenwards, if perhaps in the spirit of 'let me have this and then I will be good' (No. 9B; see below, 'Air de Faust'). Her physical presence, however, in an atmosphere of evil conjured by Mephistopheles, is too much; Faust is intent on seduction when the demon, the better to feed his lust, frustrates him by bursting in ahead of the neighbours (Mephistopheles admits, without apology, to having aroused them by his serenade). The E major duet (No. 13) is perhaps in Margaret's domain rather than Faust's, and the operatic finale, after the marvellous moment where her mingled desire and shame lead her nearly to faint (a descending slide of diminished 7ths), externalizes and makes the hero not a little ridiculous.[104]

Before Part IV begins, Faust has finished with Margaret; the operatic stuff of intrigue, and of Valentine, does not attract Berlioz (it is a pity, though, that he did not set the Cathedral scene). The 'Invocation à la nature' (No. 16) indirectly expresses this final break with humanity, the more forcibly as it follows only the slenderest of bridges from Margaret's 'Romance'; a single G♯, enharmonically the minor 3rd of the previous F, becomes the dominant of the subsequent C♯ minor, suggesting more successfully than an elaborate

bridge the immeasurable distance (physical and moral) between the two characters.[105] Even in this last utterance Faust (for all his protestations) is out of tune with his surroundings, the wild natural counterpart to the rural peace of Part I. The piece begins in C♯ but he begins once more in F♯ minor (see Ex. 114), with a falling figure which makes the most obvious of many correspondences with other places in his role.

Ex. 114 is a classification of the principal motives associated with or (mostly) sung by Faust. Figures on the left indicate Part/scene (see Cat. 32B) and bar number; those on the right refer to another part of Ex. 114 in which the line is continued.

Ex. 114A shows no fewer than seventeen shapes falling from $\hat{5}$ to $\hat{3}$ or $\hat{2}$. All come at significant points in the role; of the main numbers in which Faust participates substantially, only the E major duet is missing. These phrases come in the following sequence of keys (colon at the end of a Part, semicolon of a scene): f♯ f♯ f♯/A c♯ B♭: b; F: F F A♭; F F F: f♯ A F F. The preponderance of the 'punned' keys, f♯ and F, is obvious.

Ex. 114B shows rather similar shapes, falling from the tonic, in F D F; G G♭: F F; G G. The last two introduce the duet; B[4-9] are directly concerned with Margaret.

Ex. 114C shows shapes falling from other degrees. All seem associated with *ennui*: C[1] 'far from the crowds'; C[2-3] 'without pleasure I see again'; C[4] 'my black sorrows'; C[5] 'enough; let us away'; C[6] 'what do I care for tomorrow when I am suffering now', the self-destructive moment of signing the pact. By contrast the shapes in Ex. 114B appeared positive; even B[1], the suicide ('verse-moi le poison'), is at least decisive. Margaret may be the agent intended by the demon for Faust's destruction, but she is also his good angel. But the quest for precise meaning to these shapes is fraught with danger. The most important shape, Ex. 114A, is neither positive nor negative, but a structural link serving a variety of expressive ends.

Much of the rest of Faust's role is shown in Ex. 114D–G. The rising and falling arpeggiations of D and E, and the characteristic flat and natural 6ths of F[1-2] are noticeable; F[2-3] connect the air with the duet in Part III; G completes the tally of downward arpeggiation. I have not attempted to incorporate anything into this example which is merely the result of Faust singing a subsidiary counterpoint. All are significant utterances; and nearly all his significant utterances are included. Another element associated with Faust is a pronounced chromaticism. Harmonically it appears early in Part II. From 'je souffre' (Ex. 114A[6]) B minor is succeeded by a circle of 5ths: A–D–G♮–C♮ ('son silence et ses voiles'). Ex. 114C[4] is the modulation from there to the punned C♯ minor. Equally recondite modulations occur in the monologues of Parts III and IV (see below). Ex. 114G[3] is part of a rising sequence, C–D♭–d. In the wonderful recitative framed by Ex. 114B[2-3] every interval except one from bar 98 to bar 111 is a semitone.

Ex. 114 (contd)

Ex. 114 (contd)

Ex. 114 (contd)

THE 'AIR DE FAUST' (NO. 9B)

It is noticeable that Faust takes no part in the several strophic or otherwise
simple forms which make up a good part of *La damnation*; he is added only to
the most complex, and most extensively revised, of the *Huit scènes*. His first
two monologues are orchestral fugati with beautifully composed vocal
arioso. The only piece headed 'Air' is in no obviously classifiable form; it is,
however, a very characteristic piece of word-setting and polyphony, well
suited to study in black and white. It is not extreme in sentiment, is largely
homophonic, and is scored very simply: strings in four parts throughout,
with minimal use of double-basses (and only one independent bar, 28). Two
flutes, two clarinets, and cor anglais provide the gentlest touches of colour.[106]

   The verse is irregular, and one element of repetition offered by the poet is
not used.[107] I give it as Berlioz set it; italicized syllables receive especial
emphasis in the music. The section letters correspond to Ex. 115 and
numbers identify the lines.

A   1   Merci, doux crépus*cu*le! *Oh*! sois le bienvenu!
B   2   E*claire* enfin ces lieux, santu*aire* inconnu,
     3   Où je sens à mon front glisser comme un beau rêve,
     4   Comme le frais baiser d'un ma*tin* qui se lève.
     5   C'est de l'amour, j'es*père* . . .

C | Oh! comme on sent i*ci*
6 | S'envoler le sou*ci*!
7 | Que j'aime ce si*lence*, et comme je res*pire*
8 | Un air pur!
D 9 | O jeune fille! O ma charmante!
10 | O ma trop idéale a*mante*!
11 | Quel sentiment j'éprouve en ce mo*ment* fatal!
12 | Que *j'ai*me à contempler ton che*vet* virginal!
E 13 | Quel air pur je res*pire*!
14 | Sei*gneur*! Sei*gneur*!
15 | Après ce long mar*tyre* ⎫ [repeated]
16 | Que de bon*heur*! ⎭

(Faust, marchant lentement, examine avec une
curiosité passionnée l'intérieur de la chambre de Marguerite)

The only elements of melodic repetition are the use of line 1 as an
instrumental introduction; the (varied) repeat of the last three lines; and the
echo of line 12 during the instrumental coda (stage direction).

Ex. 115 is a preliminary reduction, sectionalized and with an analytical
line. First, some Berliozian quirks (see note 106). Bars 3–5 are virtually in G

Ex. 115

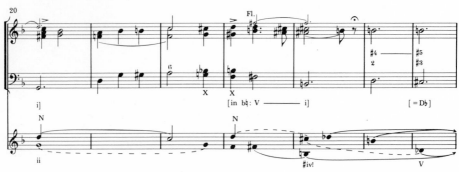

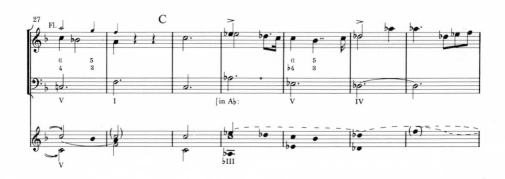

Ex. 115 (contd)

minor, blurring the bass counterpoint F–D–E–F by a bass arpeggio identical in rhythm to the melody; there are no appoggiature. The second three-bar phrase is adroitly overlapped by line 1, where the reharmonization removes all the supertonic, corrects the part-writing by removing the similar motion onto B♭ (bar 3), and gives the bass its own rhythmic values so that it strongly defines a functional progression. The vocal version is surely the model, the introduction the variation; why did Berlioz begin with a version so much less certain in direction?

Period A is closed in the tonic, a common procedure with Berlioz (e.g. Ex. 95). Period B, however, goes tonally as far as possible, to B. There is no tonic chord until bar 28 (except for two very unstable first inversions, bars 18 and 22). The progressions are entirely 'weak' – roots up a 3rd, down a 4th or tone – but the mediant and submediant (on emphasized syllables) take most weight, and the passage feels like counterpoint rather than harmonic progression. The first minor inflections of F follow the half-close (bar 16); but the Db (17) is possibly a disguised C♯ pointing to the dominant of G minor, the next objective (which may explain the emphasis on G minor in the introduction).

The return to F follows a modulation to B minor. It would have been easy to cadence in the dominant; Ex. 116A treats the first of Berlioz's diminished 7ths as an approach to the supertonic of C, and cadences there with minimal alteration of the notes. This seems to be the background to Ex. 116B; D minor is replaced by a second diminished 7th, which is the one best suited to approach the dominant of B (with F standing for E♯ in the bass). Friedheim (see note 106) is surely correct to maintain that the modulation is brought about by smooth part-writing, mainly by semitones, rather than by a functional progression that treats the diminished 7ths as rootless minor 9ths (beneath staff in Ex. 116B); although the functional explanation works well theoretically for the second chord (C♯ as II of B), it does so rather poorly for the first.

This modulation to B minor poses a large question mark over the whole composition, and the very swiftness of the return to F only poses it again. Bars 25–7 are perfectly clear, albeit bold; from B minor to E⁷ (inverted, 25) is a commonplace step, from there to C♯⁷ (26) merely relates the dominants of A and its relative minor (chords with two notes in common); C♯⁷ then becomes Db♯⁶, a strong, orthodox preparation for the dominant of F. The brevity of this return conveys the wishfulness, the transience of Faust's hope: 'C'est de l'amour, j'espère'. The cadence to F is completed and even bland, although in bar 28 the wind add a sort of shiver; but the music moves at once to Ab.

Ex. 116

Period C is all in A♭. Since the B minor, for all its cadence, is obviously alien and delusory, ♭III is the only substantial divergence from the tonic (to which, for Berlioz, it is closely related). Apparently new in contour and rhythm, period C when reduced to its outline is a transposition of period A (Ex. 117; cf. Ex. 115). The progression of bars 7–10 is compressed in 30–32;

Ex. 117

the subdominant is then prolonged for two bars. The melodic 6th is barely present in the voice (F, bar 33; bracketed), but appears in the violins. Period C is open-ended, but the harmonic progression is completed in bar 38. The rhythms of period C relate to period B; it is thus a synthesis of the previous sections (see table 22). Period C also reintroduces a triplet (bar 34, cf. 21), which from bar 38 becomes the main smaller value for six bars.

Table 22

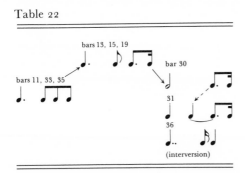

Period D is a transition from A♭, making the chord unstable by bass counterpoint (bars 38–41) and returning to F very rapidly (41–2) for a new melodic flowering. (In bar 41 D♭ is taken by the voice as C♯, but is resolved down to C♮ by the violins; the backward resolution is seen rather than heard.) In bar 42 F major is in root position, instead of the normal recovery point, a $\frac{6}{4}$ (cf. bar 27). The melodic expansion of bar 42 would conform readily to the usual procedure (Ex. 118). Instead Berlioz reaches F by a

Ex. 118

sliding bass and retains it as a short pedal; F is even anticipated on the first beat of bar 41. (I shall return to this point below.)

The rest of period D (lines 11–12) is nevertheless grouped around the dominant (bars 44, 48). The $^6_4$ on Ab (bar 47) has no function; it might be held to replace a tonic minor $^6_3$ but its effect is pure colour. The rather lame linking chromatic slide in the wind (bar 48) may have its origin in the diatonic flute scale (bar 14), accelerated in values but compressed in range.

Period E is purposefully directed in harmony, ending with a double cadence (interrupted by the favourite diminished 7th method, bar 59; completed in bar 66). Like period B, E begins on an A minor chord (these characteristically offset the stable area in the punned key, Ab). The dominant of A (bar 51) is resolved backwards for another contrapuntal approach to a tonic root, quickly suppressed by D minor (bar 53). In the double cadence phrases, major-minor mixture is extraordinarily rich, but the most startling progressions are smoothed by the melodic flow and intervening applied dominants (e.g. between D minor and Bb minor, the first hemiola, bars 53–4; between Bb minor and C minor, the second hemiola, 60–61). The first cadence uses the tonic minor $^6_4$ (bar 57), the second another backward resolution. The harmonies may be usefully superimposed (table 23). Variation is achieved by compressing the bass D–C–Bb to Db–C–B♮, with the salient notes picked out by pizzicato basses. This is surely one of Berlioz's most admirable cadences, and its final tonic is lovingly prolonged for no less than 34 bars, during which the violin line, unaccompanied, suggests but never completes remote modulations (E minor, bar 75; Db, bar 84).

Table 23

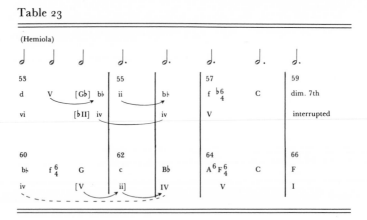

There remain questions about the overall structure of the air. The harmony makes an irregular periodicity: F returns twice, before and after the stable area in Ab, so that other excursions are incidents within a ternary F–Ab–F. The Ab material is in a sense a variant of period A (see Ex. 117); so too is the tonal recapitulation within D (Ex. 119). The identity of the bass

Ex. 119

outline is clear, with the addition of a passing B♮, and the proportions are the same (three bars to the subdominant). Perhaps this correspondence explains Berlioz's choice of a root position in bar 42; although the music feels to be in motion, this is also a point of reprise. The harmonic parallel extends to the dominant (bars 11 and 48). The second version is longer here, with more emphasis on the 6th degree, both natural and flat. Like period C, period D is left open, so that cadential activity belongs to period E. It happens, however, that both periods A and D are followed by A minor chords.

Hence the F–A♭–F design takes on the appearance of three strophes. It would be a mistake to insist on one category or the other, however; the form of the air 'is' the implied counterpoint of these larger designs and its smaller sectional divisions. Or it 'is' the *Ursatz* distilled from the 'analytical line' of Ex. 115; this (Ex. 120) shows that the main prolonging agent is contrapuntal activity around the dominant note, in both treble and bass (Ex. 120A summarizes the middle ground; Ex. 120B the remote background).

Ex. 120

The air has 100 bars, divided 65:35 at the structural arrival at the tonic, a good approximation to 'the law of two thirds' which makes both introduction – cadentially overlapped with period A – and instrumental coda integral to the form.[108] In contrast to the Da Capo and classical aria forms of the previous century, where the middle is the most expressive, agitated (modulatory, developmental) part, Berlioz has a still centre at 'Que j'aime ce silence': slow-moving, with simple motives, dropping to triple *piano* for the Db chord which (bars 32–3) is almost exactly the mid-point of the vocal part. The other marked articulations – the B minor cadence and the reprise at bar 42, marked by the first *sforzando* – are near enough to three and five eighths. Clearly these symmetries were not calculated, but they exist.

The first really strange event, the B minor cadence, is more than a mark of originality. There are plenty of examples, anyway, of tritone modulation in nineteenth-century music: Schumann goes away from c♯ to G and back in a few bars of the first variation of Op. 13, Wagner from Ab to D and back in a periodic phrase in *Lohengrin* (Elsa's entrance in Act I), Schubert from d back to Ab at the end of *Viola*. Remarkable as these are, none gives us the sense of alien intrusion that arises in Faust's air, least of all the Wagner, where both keys also bear cadences. Is it a response to the 'frais baiser' of the text? If so, it is surely rather extreme. Or is its justification its own beauty, the aura it sheds over the remainder? (Its remoteness is enhanced by the very orthodoxy, even glibness, of the return to F; in harmonic function the modulation to B minor may seem the weak link in the chain, but in the chain of thought it is the modulation back to F that sags – as, perhaps, does the impious hope of the text!)

As for the proportionately corresponding root position in bar 42, its function as disguised reprise demands stability but its symmetrical complementation of the B minor modulation requires instability. This is actually achieved by the root position; for it is gained by counterpoint, and not by functional harmony, and thus actually sounds less stable than would be a second inversion.

To what does all this idiosyncratic polyphony contribute? To a piece balanced on a knife-edge between tranquillity and anxiety, musically achieved by just these apparently irresolute or paradoxical elements in its structure. It has neither the sombre introspection nor the profound agitation which are found elsewhere in the role, but nor has it merely a Gounodesque blandness. It cannot achieve calm; Faust (despite his invocation, 'Seigneur . . .') has been led here by the devil and he can only accomplish his desire by destroying for ever the very calm which he is savouring. Hence the 'uncertainties' of harmony which are not inept; the main ineptitude is the greatest certitude, the return from B minor to F. Hence the chill of the 'frais baiser', the restless shift to Ab after two tonic bars, the ambiguity of mode in the ardent final prayer. Gluck employed rhythmic agitation when Orestes sings of calm returning to his heart (see note 67). Berlioz's harmonic agitation is subtler, but as Gluck said of Orestes, so we can say of Faust: 'Il ment'.

'INVOCATION À LA NATURE' (NO. 16)

Before his final monologue, Faust has abandoned the betrayed innocent; he turns to the roughest aspects of nature (the scene is 'Forests and caverns') to assuage his misery. The text is by Berlioz himself, the first he wrote for *La damnation* (Mem54); a turning-point, for hereafter he ceased to employ librettists.

A	a¹	1	Nature im*me*nse, impénétrable et *fiè*re,
	a²	2	Toi seule donnes *trê*ve à mon ennui sans *fin*;
	a³	3	Sur ton sein tout-puissant je sens *moins* ma misère,
		4	Je retrouve ma *for*ce, et je crois vivre enfin.
B	b¹	5	Oui, souf*flez*, ouragans! Criez, forêts pro*fon*des!
		6	Crou*lez*, rochers! Tor*rents*, précipitez vos *on*des!
		7	A vos bruits souve*rains* ma voix *ai*me à s'unir.
	b²	8	*Forêts*, ro*chers*, tor*rents*, je vous a*dore*! Mondes
		9	Qui scintil*lez*, vers *vous* s'élance le dé*sir*
		10	D'un coeur trop *va*ste et d'une *â*me altérée
		11	D'un bonheur qui la *fuit*.

Of the words indicated as having a musically accented syllable, some are picked out by decisive harmonic change as well as melodic contour (e.g. the $^6_4$ chords on 'aime', 'adore', 'vaste'). This irregularity of accent contrasts with the regularity of the verse, which can be read with an iambic metre in lines of five feet (lines 1 and 10), six feet (Alexandrine: lines 2–9), and the final three feet, completed by Mephistopheles ('A la voûte azurée'). It is noticeable that Berlioz is already closer than the poet of 'Air de Faust' (see note 107) to the Racinian inspiration which so obviously lies behind the text of *Les troyens*. The last line alone is difficult to scan; there is only one *enjambement* ('Mondes/Qui scintillez').[109]

The music is again an arioso, with no overt melodic form and harmonies as vagrant as any in Berlioz. It is not that the chordal vocabulary is extended; with such enharmony and elliptical resolution, who needs dissonances? But the very ease of vertically understanding diminished 7ths (these are unusually rare here), augmented 6ths, and dominant 7ths, may disguise longer-range progressions. The unhelpfulness of vertical analysis may be illustrated from the introductory eight bars (Ex. 121). Most of the chords are triads or simple 7ths. The only one difficult to classify is in bar 6, the 7th on G♯ (first inversion) which proves to be a supertonic, measured from F♯ minor, the problem being its intermediate resolution onto a second-inversion F minor (bar 7). Tonally, neither this nor the B♭ minor chord of bar 2 has any business here, and their bald identification in the analysis in Ex. 121 is unhelpful, or actually perverse. Certainly they both create a *frisson* by their tonal remoteness, especially the F minor which is

Ex. 121

underlined by the entry of wind instruments. Their contrapuntal origin – or better, contrapuntal justification – is clear, for their 'meaning' is not the counterpoint but the *frisson* (see below, Ex. 122).

The linear manipulation in the introduction has the remarkable harmonic aim of closing in the subdominant (hence the alternative analyses in Ex. 121). This will be commented upon further below. The other harmonic points which seem worth singling out are the curious chord in bar 26 (D♮/F♮/G♮/B♭), which sounds less like an inverted 7th on G than an 'added 6th', with B♭ as the root (the previous bar being V of B♭; the resolution, however, suggests that G is the root, a supertonic leading to a dominant of F); and the 'weak' progressions such as bars 29–30 (V–iv in E minor) and from bar 34 (b–D, then A–c♯), which in context expand horizons within the longer contrapuntal progressions.

It is worth consulting the two pages of sketches which show what were the principal pitches in Berlioz's conception.[110] From them it is clear that the voice is the structural top part, and the structural bass is the lowest note of the chords in the sketch, regardless of which is the lowest note in the orchestral realization. The first page of sketches (sketch A) has no key-signature, accidentals being added as needed (leaving some lacunae). It begins as a three-stave short score, but Berlioz wrote the chords on a single treble-clef staff with the bass an octave above its proper register, beneath the tenor G-clef; he used the blank staff for corrections, then compressed his working onto two staves. He then made a second sketch (sketch B), on three staves. The accompaniment is little more than chords, with a few passing-notes and slurs. This sketch goes only to bar 26. Berlioz may have decided that it added little to sketch A, and proceeded at once to full score (in which there are still many corrections); or a continuation page may be lost.

The sketches are considered here only for the light they can shed on the musical structure. I am aware that there is a paradox, in that my interpretation of the piece is mainly linear, while Berlioz's notations are chordal; but many of the changes in the sketches are clearly aimed as much at smooth bass-progression, with consequential changes in chord-structure, as at altering the harmony itself.

In the reduction (Ex. 122) the first step, less drastic than it may seem, is to omit the principal orchestral motive, a bass-figure heard nine times, which Berlioz sketched at the edge of a leaf (sketch B) but did not fit into the harmonic frame. It is one of those flexible figures which are readily adapted to changing harmonic contexts, and it can never have dictated the progressions (although it may help to smooth them as at bars 28 and 38). In Ex. 122 its point of climax is indicated by 'M', and I have noted the

Ex. 122

Ex. 122 (contd)

remarkable sonority which results, in bars 26–32, from its proposing a different bass to that of the sketch (middle line). The second step is to distinguish elements within the chords which seem to embody submotivic drives, and thus – on the basis of the score, not of the sketch – seem to control progressions. These are included; harmonic filling is shown by figured bass.

The division into sections A and B is implicit in the text, as is the division b¹–b². The music divides A from B by the only cadence to govern as many as three bars (until the tonic cadence of bars 47–9), and by a change of texture; but also by a general change in the counterpoint, from bold diatonicism to pure chromaticism. Within section A each subsection ends with a perfect cadence (in C♯/D♭, D♮, and F♮). Within subsection a³ a slight caesura corresponds to the end of a line of text (bar 21). Section B is longer than A but falls into only two subsections (a common phraseological pattern, as we have seen); they are divided by another C♯ major cadence.

Ex. 122 employs the following conventions: 'V⁷', dominant 7th resolved normally; 'V⁶', dominant 7th resolved as augmented 6th; 'X', diminished 7th; arrows (straight or curved) indicate functional resolution of a dominant; slurs show the direction of other important resolutions (e.g. augmented 6ths, auxiliary notes); dotted slurs indicate a surface or submotivic scalar motive; 'M' refers to the bass-motive (see above); 'en' indicates where my notation is the enharmonic equivalent of Berlioz's. Ex. 122 is written in 3/4 rather than the original 9/8. Notes are placed proportionately within each bar, and the rhythm signs (minim, crotchet), while corresponding proportionately to those of the score, are suggestive of hierarchical value.

It emerges that the main motive is a falling scale, diatonic, semichromatic, even whole-tone (bassoon, bar 11), over a 3rd (see Ex. 114A¹⁴), 4th (Ex. 114A¹⁵⁻¹⁷) or 5th. This, the first notated thought that Berlioz retained, provides not only the vocal ideas but the bass for half the instrumental introduction; it occurs as late as the coda (for which there are no sketches, incidentally). It appears on the surface in vocal ornament ('profondes . . . ondes') and as the dying fall of the bass-motive (bar 37). Its higher purpose is the connection of remote harmonies, by its operation as an inner part (bar 11) or bass (bar 26ff, 45–7). Another similarly amorphous element is the 4th- and 5th-movement of the bass (bars 9–11; 14–17; 34–5; 39–41; 44–6, F♯–B–G♮–C♮, with passing-notes) – amorphous in that it is never the same twice, important through its occupying the beginnings of subsections a¹ and a², and the bars before the three returns to the tonic, of which only the last is completed.

The following are the significant divergences, with some relevance to the final structure, between the sketches and the score:

Bars 1–2. Sketch B: the bass-note B♮ occupies bar 2, so there was a more regular rhythm, no pun b♭–A, a less disturbed initial tonic.

Bar 9. Both sketches: rhythm of 'Nature immense' foreshortened. But the first notation (sketch A) is also the final version, broader, and effectively overlapping the end of the introductory modulation.

Bar 11. Both sketches: the goal is always clear, but the route to it gave trouble (sketch A first notated D♭ major as C♯, incidentally).

Bars 13–15. The last reading of sketch B, and the first of the autograph score, made these three bars into two, foreshortening 'fière' to accommodate the upbeat 'Toi'. Again Berlioz reverts to his original thought, more spacious, better oriented in harmony, and matching a¹ and a² in length of phrase.

Bars 22–5. Sketch A shows that Berlioz first planned a more ordinary modulation, to E (III), but never harmonized it; he then apparently tried F *minor* on 'force' (pun to

E). The final form, a cadence in F major with minor mixture, is far more directed. *Bars 40–41.* Sketch A: the inner part (violas, broken slur in Ex. 122, bar 40) is in the bass.

Instrumentation

The scoring of the 'Invocation' is based on the continuum of string tone; from the central cadence in F (bar 25) to bar 42 it is tremolo. The wind dispositions underline the tonal flux. At the start the wind play: trombone c♯, cor anglais e¹, flute c♯³; the space between is partly occupied by the lugubrious clarinet notes, with independent dynamics. The timpani play E rather than C♯ (bars 1, 3, 5). The other drum is tuned to F♯, used for D and b chords (bars 10, 17, 39, 40, 44–5) but not for chords of f♯ although this is apparently the tonic for much of the movement. The E drum is used as a root (bar 21, of a dominant), and as mediant to C♮ (bars 42, 46) and c♯ (bar 47, at the top of a rolled crescendo); only the last coincides with an important tonal event, such as these instruments traditionally emphasize. Equally odd is the horn tuning to D♭ (ostensibly tonic *major*; E would be usual), and the trumpets to F♮. The brass is used sparingly, and tends to pick out tonally aberrant chords (bar 7, f, horns; bar 12, D♭, horns, trumpets; bar 17, D♮, trumpets, playing the mediant and 5th respectively). The trumpets also pick out an A chord (root, bar 20) and play A and C♮ in the F ⁶₄ (bar 23). The brass rests from bars 24 to 34. In bar 36 the trumpets again pick out the mediant (F♮/E♯), and they add a root to the vagrant C♮ of bar 42; there is nothing they can play at the last climax. Horns and trombones glow at the last C♯ major cadence (bar 36) but they only reinforce the final tonic recovery at bar 47.

The orchestration is thus pretty consistently anti-functional. The brass appears to underline cadential goals but adds little to the most important of all. This reticence is not caused by mechanical limitations. Berlioz had four horns in his orchestra, and he could have used a pair in E or F as seemed appropriate; he might also have included chromatic cornets, especially as it is the trumpets who are off stage during the retreat at the end of No. 15. The woodwind are more flexibly handled, now echoing the voice, now joining the strings, completing the cadence in f♯ (bars 8–9) and reinforcing (sometimes with trumpets) the arrivals in bars 12, 17, 20 and 23. The ubiquitous strings outweigh this conformist element, however. There is no pizzicato (the isolated drum strokes stand out all the more) and the tremolo is a continuum, not an effect (the timpani pursue it further, with a roll).

The coda

Ex. 122 (like the sketches) stops short of the coda, which prolongs the C♯ minor chord. It is, however, replete with interesting detail (Ex. 123A reduces

Ex. 123

the coda to three parts; Ex. 123B is its basic structure). The string line, doubled in three octaves, is acoustically above the trombone bass only in bars 51, beat 3, and 52, beats 1–2; but it functions as an inner part, a fact made clear by Berlioz when he detaches the bassoons from the strings to play a bass G♯ in bar 54. The flute and cor anglais provide a treble. The coda is a harmonically static counterpart to the introduction. It is one bar shorter, and has neither modulation nor real change of harmony; even its cadence is equivocal, with its flat leading-note (the only 'modal' element in the piece) and its lightly scored bass (G♯ on four bassoons, all strings on B♮). The hemiola (bars 53–4; see Ex. 123A) corresponds to bars 7–8 in the introduction.

Tonal questions in the 'Invocation'

Already, in the introduction, where the chordal vocabulary is nothing extraordinary, the syntax goes so far that the tonic, C♯ minor, is effectively obliterated, or compressed into the single upper pedal C♯; this moves a little and returns as head-note for period A, but it is now a $\hat{5}$. At this point, to analyse the music in terms of C♯ minor would produce hopeless contortion; and this is true at least for bars 9 to 38. *After bar 1 no chord of C♯ minor is heard until bar 47.*

One might well infer from the music what is obvious from sketch A, that Berlioz began composing in F♯ minor (actually F minor, quickly modified). When he had finished his voice part he found himself in C♯. There could be no question of abandoning that supreme inspiration; accordingly an introduction which begins in C♯ minor appears at the top of sketch B.

The first question when we hear the piece, therefore, is: is the C♯ major towards which period a¹ moves a tonic or a dominant? Berlioz actually modified his notation to D♭, which perhaps gives no answer. What is certain, though, is that the fall back to F♯ minor (bar 14) does not feel like a modulation, but like a relaxation from a dominant to a tonic – whence the move to D♮ (period a²) is a simple i–VI, not a flat supertonic. The same is true after the C♯ major cadence in bar 37, for all the greater weight of its preparation and orchestration. From an F♯ tonic period a² follows naturally, and the first move in a³ is back to F♯ minor. The aberrant F♮ major is pun to f♯; a resolution into the latter at this point would not only be possible, but easy (Ex. 124A). Period B is organized symmetrically around the cadence in C♯ major and the return to F♯ minor in bar 38.

Ex. 124

Period B is also asymmetrical, however, in that its predominant pitch element is the chromatic ascent of the voice which covers only a minor 3rd in b¹, but a 5th in b². This gives rise to, and controls, the most vagrant harmony of the movement. In b¹ the chromatic line is set against a descending bass rather suggestive of the introduction; the strongly projected D♮–C♯ is now in the bass, and C♯ is reached at the same time in the top part (bar 32, cf. 8). This is a half-close in F♯ minor, a caesura; but the bass pushes on by using the motive (bar 33). Then the bass 4ths, accelerating the harmonic rate of change, direct the music to the next $^6_4$, on G♯. Thus the second part of period b¹, like a¹, goes from a clear F♯ minor (bars 32–3) to an ambiguous C♯ (bar 37) which falls back to F♯. In this passage the upper part is a local rise and fall from C♯, with a 3̂–2̂–1̂ cadence which, however, is not part of a governing fundamental line (see Ex. 125 below).

Period B follows a pattern already observed in that its longer phrases are less clearly separated. The F♯ minor in bar 38 precedes the vocal entry, and the new text coincides with the move to D♮ (wider considerations define bar 38 as the start of b²; the bass F♯ is consonant with the head-note C♯, and the harmonic move from C♯ to F♯ seems to initiate the second phase of the chromatic ascent in the top part, beginning C♯–D♮). Period b² can almost be reduced to a single structural part. Of the chromatic upper notes, only the D♮ and E♮ are not doubled by the bass (cf. Ex. 90, by Spontini, bars 22–6). Usually consecutive octaves and 5ths in the middle ground result from elegantly composed suspensions; but Berlioz is here using a sophisticated form of his unison doubling (see above, p. 110). Like the passage in *Fantastique* I (bar 143ff), the basslessness of this passage contributes to its frenzy, its neurosis. It is, however, still more strongly directed to the next, most important goal, the C♯ minor which Berlioz decided was not to be a dominant minor but an elusive tonic. Hence perhaps his use of C♮ major in bar 42, where C♯ minor would not only be easily reached, but would follow its own dominant on the third beat of bar 41 (see Ex. 124B). The resolution of the dominant 7th as an augmented 6th to the punned key postpones the tonic still further, while strongly suggesting its imminence and immanence.

From this point a short series of contrary-motion thrusts makes a pincer-like approach to the bass G♯ which is necessary to the proper recovery of C♯ minor (slurs in Ex. 122; see the arrowed slurs in Ex. 125 below). The broad upward movement is F♯–G♮–G♯. F♯, however, is first approached from both F♮ and G♮ (bars 42–4); thus marked out, the B minor is strong enough to obliterate the preceding dominants of C♯ and C♮. Both G♮ and G♯ are approached by strong descending motives, the second (bar 46) a diminution of the first. The voice, which reached its previous highest point (F♮) in the remote region of F minor, attains G♯ exactly as the pincer movement in the bass reaches its G♯; the cadence follows at once.

Ex. 125 attempts a reduction to a middle ground, showing the principal harmonic and linear events and the main submotivic drives, including the characteristic pincer movements. Ex. 126 reduces this further, picking out the main bass prolongations, which prove to move mainly in 4ths, and the prolonged head-note, C♯, which begins as î and has to be reinterpreted as 5̂.

Ex. 125

Ex. 125 (contd)

Ex. 126

In section b² the treble line rises to G♯ and falls rapidly at the cadence, although the top note is retained by the treble part in the coda.

So what is the fundamental structure? Ex. 127A shows C♯ not, after all, as the head-note but as a prolonged overtone of the C♯ and (mainly) the F♯; the head-note is the $\hat{5}$ reached only in bar 47, to fall by 49 (or be retained in the coda, Ex. 127A¹). But in that case it would initiate nothing. Musical

Ex. 127

experience tells us that C♯ is indeed the head-note, and that the final ascent and 5̂–4̂–3̂–2̂–î in C♯ minor is, like the 3̂–2̂–î in C♯ major of bars 36–7, a local event. A more correct representation of the fundamental structure is Ex. 127B; for the treble C♯undoubtedly governs it (whereas Ex. 127A tries to fit the facts to suit the theory). The C♯ is modified from î to 5̂ and back; this *is* the motion of the piece, paradoxically embodied in the motionlessness of its head-note. The coda reinforces this interpretation, for its prolongation of C♯ minor contains no structural action and it too, retains its head-note (G♯; Ex. 126), thereby clarifying the introduction and acting – with its subdominant inclinations, D♮ and B♮ – as a microcosm of the whole.

This ambiguity suggested by Ex. 127 is a fruitful source of tension. To describe the opening (introduction and a¹) as an extended plagal cadence (PriBS, 169) feels wrong because of the amount of tonal disruption between the establishment of F♯ minor and the cadence in C♯/D♭, and because we accept the latter as a dominant. But to describe the whole piece that way (Ex. 127B) is by no means the *reductio ad absurdum* it might seem. The *Ursatz* lacks movement; this fortifies the expression of the situation. Faust aspires to completeness, through reconciliation with nature; the music also aspires. Its achievements of a tonic major are however immediately negated by falling back to F♯ minor, a key which in bar 9 is strongly experienced as a tonic (the sketches, while strictly irrelevant, bear this out). On three occasions the music achieves the illusory glow of another major key; a² ends in D♮, a³ in F♮, and C♮ is proposed at bar 42 where pressure of events overwhelms the ⁶₄ before it can cadence. The last two keys may be considered to 'replace' f♯ and c♯ (Ex. 124; Berlioz's conscious use of this particular substitution is well attested, see above, p. 34). Faust's aspiration is continually thwarted, the glow is a delusion. The music completes itself in C♯ minor with the only minor cadence; after such aspiration, such glow, this is the most depressing thing possible, as well as, in another sense, the most powerful. (The depressed effect of a dominant minor, if we may so consider c♯ for a moment, is echoed in the 'modal' cadence of the coda.) Faust cannot obtain more than the most fleeting happiness from union with nature. As in Part II, when he heard the Easter music and believed himself once more pious, he is vulnerable through his delusion to the wiles of the demon – who duly appears (No. 17), pact in hand, 'gravissant les rochers', to the ironic sound of hunting horns.

TONALITY IN *LA DAMNATION*

It remains to consider any larger context these pieces may have, apart from the strictly dramatic one. I have already pointed out Faust's adherence, in three pieces not in that key, to F♯ minor (Nos. 1, 7B, 16), the key of the opening of Part II. His excursion to its pun, F♮, in his air, might symbolize his entry into Margaret's domain, even the heavenly domain; it is the key of 'Chant de la fête de Pâques' (4B) and Margaret's two songs (11B, 15). But 'Le roi de Thulé' (11B) was transposed merely for the convenience of a singer; if Berlioz had cared so much for key-identification he would surely have transposed the two quotations from it, before Margaret's first entrance and before her meeting with Faust. His modulatory sleight-of-hand would easily have contrived this (see Ex. 14!), but they remain in G. And F, in any case, is also the key of 'Chanson de Méphistophélès' (6C) and the decidedly terrestrial end to Part III. Even the key of B, used for Mephistopheles's entrance, his 'Sérénade', and 'Pandaemonium', is not simply the opposite pole to heavenly F; it appears strikingly not only in Faust's air, but in the citations of Margaret's 'Romance' which precede 'Le roi de Thulé'. At times Berlioz seems to be using tritone relationships for devilishness. This is most conspicuous in the huge B and F chords of 'Pandaemonium', and in the appearance of Mephistopheles in B major after so much F (No. 5). But not all such modulations are devil's work: the move from Gb (citation of 'Sérénade') to C minor at Margaret's entrance, possibly; Ex. 14B, surely not. The melodic tritone appears stridently in Mephistopheles's 'Evocation', but it is also in 'Le roi de Thulé'.

There is other evidence which could be called in here, but I do not think a consistent pattern of key-symbolism exists; if it does it is so enigmatic that it can hardly communicate anything. Can we, then, consider the keys as forming an abstract structure – and say that *La damnation* is 'in' a key, as *Roméo* is 'in' B?

At best, one might find a scheme of interlocking tonalities.[111] The most often-used keys are D and F; but the work ends in Db. Table 24 indicates the main keys in order and shows their relative frequency. I have taken D as the centre because it is the first key and because its opposite pole, Ab, is not used for any whole movement. Keys in bold type are sustained over a whole movement, or very decisively cadenced. An asterisk denotes significant use of a key in passing. Square braces indicate successive sections in the same key or its equivalent (relative); it is noticeable that these link the successive parts into which the work is divided. Broken lines indicate punned keys (P) and tritone juxtapositions (T). I have not included all keys, but only those which appear significant – inevitably a matter of judgment when there are passing references within music which is occasionally chromatic and includes recitatives.

In table 24, as in all such analyses of broad tonal plans, some caution is needed in drawing conclusions. It is open to question whether keys ostensibly identical, but in different contexts, with music as different as, say, 'Chanson de Brander' (No. 6B) and 'Ballet de sylphes' (7C), can really be considered building-blocks in any kind of form. There are only irregular cross-references of motive (mostly shown in Ex. 114) or instrumentation –

Table 24

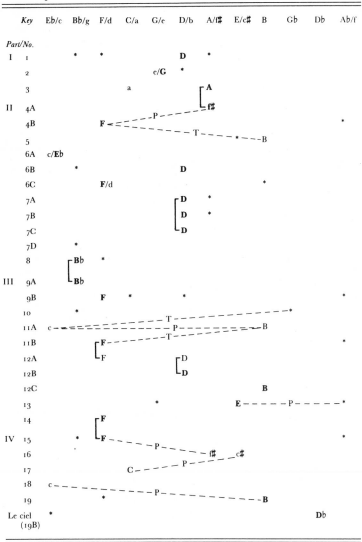

Key	Eb/c	Bb/g	F/d	C/a	G/e	D/b	A/f♯	E/c♯	B	Gb	Db	Ab/f
Part/No.												
I 1		*	*			D	*					
2					c/G	*						
3				a			A / f♯					
II 4A					P		f♯					
4B			F				T		B			*
5								*	B			
6A	c/Eb											
6B		*				D						
6C			F/d						*			
7A						D	*					
7B						D	*					
7C						D						
7D	*											
8		Bb	*									
III 9A		Bb										
9B			F	*		*						*
10		*							*			
11A	c				T	P		B				
11B			F		T							*
12A			F									
12B						D						
12C								B				
13					*		E — P — *					
14			F									
IV 15		*	F		P		f♯	c♯				*
16					P		f♯	c♯				
17				C	P							
18	c			P					B			
19		*							B			
Le ciel (19B)	*										Db	

that 'collateral evidence' which Tovey reasonably enough demanded for the existence in musical experience of such long-range relationships (as opposed to their existence on paper).[112] Even numbers apparently adjacent are often connected by modulatory interludes or recitatives; there can be little significance, for instance, in the departure from and return to D between Nos. 6B and 7A (the D minor of No. 6C, like the asterisked E of No. 5, refers only to the taking-off point in a scintillating bridge-passage). The tritone relations indicated in table 24 are pretty direct; the puns, it must be admitted, are not.

Nothing, therefore, it seems, permits us to allocate a tonality to *La damnation* as a whole, or even to regard as of much significance the relatively frequent occurrence of stable sections in D and F. *La damnation* is not 'in' any key or keys, even in the strictly limited sense in which *Don Giovanni* is 'in' D, *Roméo* 'in' B, or *Tristan* (according to Lorenz) 'in' E.[113] *Les troyens* and *L'enfance* confirm that Berlioz did not necessarily require the appearance of tonal unity in a dramatic composition, although both his comic operas (*Benvenuto*, *Béatrice*) are 'in' G. The *Requiem* too is 'in' g/G; and these last three works all return near the end to music heard earlier, like *Don Giovanni* or *Der Freischütz*. *Roméo* may seem to earn its symphonic spurs by its return to B, but it is with collateral evidence; and Berlioz did not find it necessary to end either the *Symphonie funèbre* or the *Te Deum* in the original key (both go F–B♭), although the latter, in the final 'Marche pour la présentation des drapeaux', actually returns to two themes from the first movement. Still, the lack of tonal unity may be the point at which *La damnation* departs from *Roméo*, dramatic legend from dramatic symphony; but it is worth recalling that its original subtitle was 'concert opera', although several contemporary critics referred to it as a symphony. Neither Gluck nor Beethoven (in the final form of *Fidelio*) insisted on tonal unity in opera.

If tonality plays any part, it is a dramatic one. Ex. 114 indicates striking correspondences between tonal and melodic returns, given the element of identity which in Berlioz obtains not only between a major key and its parallel and relative minors, but between it and its punned minor as well – witness Faust's personal attraction to F♯ minor and F major which flavours movements, particularly the 'Invocation', framed by some other key. It would probably be a mistake to try to translate such correspondences into verbal symbolism; they operate on a musical level. Thus my failure to encapsulate this huge score even into a tonal scheme like that of *Roméo* (which goodness knows is loose enough) is no reflection on the integrity of *La damnation* as a species of musical drama. The examination of tonalities and motives in relation to the unfolding of dramatic ideas does reveal, in *La damnation* as in *Les troyens*, a network of correspondences made audible by the composer to the experienced listener, to the enrichment of his understanding through the multiplicity of perspectives they provide.

15   In conclusion

'The language of Schumann, Berlioz, and Liszt is the classical language . . .
in the classical style chords are resolved . . . I hear in them all the same kind
of music. Berlioz is much further removed from Bach and Mozart than [is]
Wagner. He is less tonal than Wagner.'
Debussy (cited in E. Lockspeiser, *Debussy: his Life and Mind* 1, London,
1962, repr. 1979, p. 204)

In this study I have tried to maintain some kind of balance between the
singularity and the normality of Berlioz's art; and I have tried to do this by
applying to him as many methods of analysis as seemed useful. My selection
of these, and of works to be analysed, doubtless differs from what anybody
else's would be, but at least I have ranged widely over Berlioz's output. I
have gone from details of polyphonic practice, with a little consideration for
the historical framework, to larger forms, with rather less. I would like to
begin my conclusion, therefore, by discussing where Berlioz comes in the
history of musical forms, and what is his progeny.

The shortest answer is, nowhere, and none. Tovey, with some
embarrassment, found himself unable to include Berlioz in the main stream
of a history of instrumentation (of all things); and the entire 'History of
Rhythm in Western Music' in *The New Grove* is accomplished without
mention of Berlioz. Nor has Friedrich Blume much to say about Berlioz in
his generally masterly *Classic and Romantic Music*; and a study of the slow
introduction at this period leaves Berlioz out altogether.[114] These omissions
are, it must be said, partly the result of Berlioz not being German; Italians
and Russians fare hardly better in large parts of the literature. But it may
also be because of his isolation; because he never imitated even his
acknowledged heroes (the essential qualities of his apparent models may
seem conspicuously absent, even from the works most indebted to them);
and because, never repeating his own inventions, he produced no class of
works capable of serving as a general model for others.

To be more specific: the influence of Beethoven even on *Fantastique* and
Lear is sporadic, and Berlioz's symphonic forms (as I have tried to show in
Chapters 12 and 13) depend for their grand design and their coherence on
different factors from Beethoven's. The influence of Gluck may be felt in all

sorts of ways; but Gluck's single-minded dramatic approach is not the point even of Berlioz's most overt homage, in *Les troyens*. What is apparent in later composers is, correspondingly, less any general stylistic influence – of, say, Berlioz on Chaikovsky – than the specific influence of one work on another – of, say, *Harold* on *Manfred* or on Rimsky-Korsakov's *Antar*, or of *Roméo* on Franck's *Psyché*. And this influence is very specific within those works. It is not an influence of Berlioz's style but, with the Russian works, of the construction of a series of scenes linked by a hero with his 'idée fixe' and, with the Franck, of the representation of the deepest feelings by the orchestra within a choral symphony. Other such clear influences include *Roméo* on *Tannhäuser* and *Tristan*, and the *Fantastique* on the Lisztian apotheosis and distortion of themes; the opening of Liszt's 'Mephisto' almost quotes 'Songe d'une nuit de sabbat'.[115] But it would be hard to find a pair of mid-nineteenth-century works so un-Berliozian as *Tristan* and *Eine Faust-Symphonie*.

One could multiply such instances, no doubt. There is also a certain general influence on the French school of the next generation, such as Gounod, Saint-Saëns, Bizet, Chabrier; Chailley even detects a specific influence on Franckian chromaticism (ChaBH, 16). Yet no group of composers could be called Berliozian in the sense that quite a considerable constellation could be called Wagnerian. And the more we know of Alkan, the less appropriate seems the sobriquet 'the Berlioz of the piano'. In his work as in his life Berlioz was a lone wolf.

Is he, then, related to any traditions at all? Emphatically, yes; perhaps to more than one. But it is a strange relationship. He stands perpendicular to the line of their development and is not part of them. He is really no more than a footnote to the history of nineteenth-century opera, dominated by Rossini, Meyerbeer, Verdi, Wagner; yet he wrote three unique operas of abiding fascination. The symphonic tradition remained Germanic; even the thematic transference of the *Fantastique*, frequently adapted in later nineteenth-century symphonies, had other sources, among them Schubert; while the linking of slow and fast sections of a movement, so crucial to Berlioz's forms, goes back at least to Haydn. His sacred works belong to traditions already dead when he wrote them – if indeed Lesueur and the music of the French Revolution deserve the name of tradition. In the history of programme music Berlioz occupies a major place, albeit one widely misrepresented; but its future lay mainly with the symphonic poem, which he did not invent. Thanks to Schubert's 'Wanderer' fantasia, even the *Fantastique* is not the most important precursor as far as novel musical forms are concerned. Whatever hard things have been said of Berlioz, it is generally agreed that whatever he did is very much his own; nobody has ever accused him of being merely an Interesting Historical Figure.

But Berlioz does belong to one more loosely defined but very significant tradition which, despite Boulez's assertion that there is no such thing, one might call a French tradition. I refer to Berlioz's aspect as a decorative rather than architectural composer.[116] Berlioz's tonal 'flatness', his arcade-structure, his organization of dramatic works as far as possible into self-contained musical numbers with minimal connecting material, all suggest a composer of the decorative type – a type to which, it seems, Rameau, Debussy, Ravel, Messiaen, even Boulez himself (in *Pli selon pli*) belong, as do other, less significant French composers. It is a tradition which has little time for discursiveness or abstraction, in which Boulez's sonatas are exceptional. Even its symphonic works are constructed in broad tableaux, which stand perpendicular to a main idea: *Symphonie fantastique, La mer, Turangalîla, Pli selon pli*. In its dramatic works characters play out their fate in the foreground, but they are on a smaller scale, within a larger landscape, like a painting by Claude, than would be the case with Verdi or Wagner who epitomize other traditions. *Pelléas* is exceptional, and lies outside this tradition, which stemmed from Lully and Rameau and was corruptible by a Meyerbeer but still accessible to a Berlioz. The interest in *La damnation* and *Les troyens* is concentrated on three characters, but their background is developed to the point where it ceases to be a background at all and has equal stature, because of the musical riches lavished upon it. Hence the 'Marche hongroise', the 'Menuet des follets', the 'Marche nocturne' – even, although it is in a piece meant to be staged, the 'Chasse royale' – develop the descriptive, sometimes danced, symphony and ballet so important to Rameau and (despite the opening of *Iphigénie en Tauride*) relatively uninteresting to Gluck.

In Italian opera tone-painting tends to cease when the characters are in action. In Wagner it blends with the symphonic thread, but also seems to emerge from the dramatic situations (notably in *Parsifal*). In Berlioz it has intrinsic value – or is a colourful irrelevance, according to the point of view. The 'Chasse royale' is fully developed music which reflects obliquely on the love of Dido and Aeneas but is untouched by it (see above, p. 131). Similarly the 'Menuet des follets' is not seen to make any impact upon Faust and Margaret; but its intervention before the love-scene sheds a particular darkness on the latter (in 'fact' rather than performance, it would occur *during* 'Le roi de Thulé' and the E major duet – a simultaneity split into chronological succession, and permitted, like the instant scene-change it requires, in this ideal 'theatre of the mind'; see Warrack, 1964). In Part IV the scene of the pact is accompanied by hunting horns which are not only as evidently ironic as the screams of the satyrs in the 'Chasse royale', but are distanced, alienated, suggesting the indifference of humanity to tragedy; as in Auden's 'Musée des beaux arts':

> About suffering they were never wrong,
> The Old Masters . . .

In Breughel's Icarus, for instance: how everything turns away
Quite leisurely from the disaster; the ploughman may
Have heard the splash, the forsaken cry,
But for him it was not an important failure.

The analogy with narrative painting is one I have made already (p. 200). It sheds light not only on Berlioz's forms, but on his dramatic or programmatic intentions, which are, again, decorative. In *Lear*, for example, Berlioz chose to balance the demands of tonal and thematic resolution in a sonata form against a clear, but by no means narrative, relationship to Shakespeare's play. The play is not irrelevant to the music, as has been maintained, but nor is the music flawed by not being a replica of the play, or by its vigorous ending.[117] The spirit of the music is inspired by the spirit of the play, and our involvement with the former is deeper for recognizing this.

This is much more true of the *Fantastique*, Berlioz's only purely programmatic work besides *Roméo*, in which much of the programme, being sung as Prologue, is incorporated into performance of the music.[118] The programmes of these works are not optional, especially (since the literary source of *Roméo* is well known) that of the *Fantastique*. Of course the music can be discussed 'as music', but we no more appreciate all either symphony has to offer that way than we would fully appreciate *Les troyens* without understanding the words. The qualities which make the *Fantastique* worth examining as music are the results of its prodigiously original conception as musical biography; this, like *Die Winterreise*, can be interpreted internally, as an analysis of emotional states, or externally, as a tale.[119]

I do not wish to reopen the hoary question of the legitimacy of programme music. The standard objection, that the programme is external to the work, ought really to apply to other works of Berlioz as well. His works are narrative in quality; they do not contain narratives (for instance, we hear nothing of the ten years from the rape of Helen to the rise of the curtain). His whole aim was to fill the framework of a plot with musical and dramatic invention, while preserving as far as possible music's autonomy, its own forms. At the same time he had no interest in musical abstraction: a fugue was good, as opposed to ingenious, if it was proper for the sentiment. Recitative, and dialogue connecting musical numbers, are sub-music or not music. The programme (*Fantastique*) eliminates them, the sung programme (*Roméo*) sets them apart, while *La damnation* and *Les troyens* reduce recitative to a bare minimum. Should we not be grateful for the removal of musical desert from the landscape? For, distant from its origins in Italian, much nineteenth-century recitative (I do not speak of Wagner) is dusty stuff indeed. Unpredictable to the last, Berlioz produced in *Béatrice* a neo-classical comedy with spoken dialogue, but he still scaled down the drama in order to concentrate fully on the musical development of one dramatic idea.

Béatrice and *Benvenuto*, marvels as they are, are in some sense not Berliozian schemes; whereas *Les troyens*, for all that it is an opera, is his own from beginning to end. Everything is converted to song, dance, chorus, or dramatic *scena*; connective matter is reduced to a minimum, and by running sections into each other Berlioz gets, in Act V, very near to continuous opera, albeit on a Gluckian rather than Wagnerian (symphonic) model. Sometimes his approach leads to exaggerated treatment of inessentials; the delightful trio for flutes and harp in *L'enfance* is an obvious case of something the musical and dramatic exigencies of the subject scarcely warrant, and a bad let-down of tension near the end. Then there is the 'Marche hongroise', a blazing climax too near the beginning. Berlioz justified its inclusion in *La damnation* on what he called musical grounds: he wanted the piece to be heard, so the hero had to go to Hungary. It is a poor argument, and, despite the skilful integration of the march into the introduction, it is not in fact a musical argument at all, still less what it ought to be, a dramatic one; it is a purely mercantile argument. Few composers do not commit offences of this general nature in one or other dramatic work (consider *La forza del destino*!); unfortunately for Berlioz some of the obvious comparisons – in their mature operas, Gluck, Mozart, Wagner – are among those few.

This argument cannot, however, be pursued very far to Berlioz's detriment. To name these composers for comparison is to propose for Berlioz a very high place in musical and dramatic art. And one should not generalize from individual failures of judgment, however tempting it may be to do so. To ask why the background to Herod's dream requires a lengthy 'Marche nocturne' is to question a whole approach to dramatic music; for can we class that piece as a dramatic irrelevance without also asking why the shepherds assemble to an extended fugato with modal inflections? Yet is not that just as reasonable as to have them abiding in the field to a pastoral symphony of Sicilian character? I hope that a sense of perspective is gained by drawing Bach and Handel into the picture, for to question such things as the 'Marche nocturne' on principle – or for that matter the extended treatment of inaction in 'Le repos de la sainte famille', one of Berlioz's most haunting and exquisite pieces – is to question the right of music to involve itself with dramatic subjects in the decorative mode, or on any other principle than that which informs a symphonic music-drama or a sung play. The time should be past when we judge Berlioz by criteria derived from a Wagnerian aesthetic.

Berlioz's way is neither architectural nor developmental, but illustrative. His *Requiem* (contrary to a common opinion) is the least dramatic of the great settings; it nowhere concerns itself with the fate of the individual, but everywhere expresses the terrors and exaltation of mankind. Where Verdi's soprano in 'Libera me' is as much an individual as any operatic character with a local habitation and a name, Berlioz uses a solo tenor in 'Sanctus' as a musical contrast (he permitted performance by ten singers from the choir).

Despite its designation, 'Symphonie dramatique', *Roméo* is dramatic only in a limited sense; it *is* a sort of symphony and its avowed subject is the musical potential of chosen scenes, not of the play itself. A more literary or narrative approach, even in symphonic form, would have made a rondo-like recurrence of the street fighting, as in Chaikovsky's admirable fantasy-overture, and would have found no room for such a huge scherzo derived from a single speech by a secondary character. But in the miraculous 'Mab' Berlioz does what 'Shakespeare lui seul' could not do with his too-articulate medium of words – epitomize the midsummer madness which leads to violence and the pretended death of Juliet, his next musical number. *Roméo* notoriously ends as an operatic scene, completely stageworthy, after proceeding through such stages as the abstract musical form made dramatic (I, fugato for the fighting); a vocal form made instrumental (the Prince's recitative); narrative recitative (Prologue) and commentary which goes so far outside the drama as to mention Shakespeare himself ('Strophes'); the symphonic development of moods (II, 'tristesse') and scenes ('Concert et bal'; III, 'Nuit sereine') with touches of operatically compatible vocal music (in the latter and in V, 'Convoi'); richly developed symphonic music (III, IV, 'Mab'); and totally programmatic symphonic music (VI, 'Roméo au tombeau'). It seems necessary to reach pure opera for the sake of completeness, and, as well as including a small musical return, it is a return to specifics. Nevertheless at its instrumental heart – see Berlioz's preface – *Roméo* is an illustrative, not a dramatic, conception, a static exploration of the subject's essences.

Elsewhere I have tried to suggest that certain views of these most problematic works of the middle years, *Roméo* and *La damnation*, reveal some concern for coherence on musical levels.[120] It may be difficult to accept as adequate Chabrier's succinct response to their being accused of lack of unity (see epigraph to Chapter 14), but pronounced unity is certainly not among their virtues – or vices, for certainly they lack uniformity, conformity, tedium. To close the mind to them because of 'uncertainty' of genre, even of aim, is like fastidious dissociation (as by Mendelssohn and Chopin) from 'uncertainties' in Berlioz's technique; it is to reject an artistic manifestation on *a priori* grounds. But *merde* to such arguments; this music, these works, have so much to *give*.

The main matter of this study, however, is not Berlioz's large-scale organization but the elements and functioning of his musical language. It is here that he has probably had least influence; and it will probably always be a matter of dispute as to whether his language works. It seems palpably absurd to suggest that he had a poor ear; I doubt if the capacity to hear musically is so selective that one can be as marvellously acute as Berlioz in virtually everything connected with instrumentation, yet still have a poor ear for harmony. The singularity of Berlioz's polyphony may be taken in more than one way. Schenker's was outright rejection; Tovey's was more complex – rejection tempered by fascination, even love. Both he and Ernest Newman underwent a late conversion to *Les troyens* and magnanimously said so in public; what this reveals is that true appreciation of Berlioz depends on nothing so much as hearing. How could such a composer be weak in that department?

There has, I think, been some influence from Berlioz's polyphonic thought on significant developments since, but not where it might be expected (in France). I do not mean his use of space, which is theatrical rather than constructively stereophonic.[121] It is the anti-tonal nature of his music, which Debussy may have been the first to notice (see epigraph). Berlioz is, in a sense, and obviously, a tonal composer; I would not wish to discount appearances in this any more than in his use of sonata forms. But he is tonal on the surface, in his choice of a framework of triadic reference; he is not tonal profoundly, as Wagner was, or Brahms, in this the true successors to Beethoven. Berlioz is outside that tradition, and outside by inner conviction, not just because he was French. I cannot say what most contributed to this musical fact: his upbringing, his ear, the guitar, or a grain of perversity. The fact remains. Just as nobody in his time so consistently evades the cadence of rhyme in favour of the continual intensity of prose, so nobody orchestrates so anti-functionally; nobody so often progresses *à rebours* or employs so many non-tonal inflections without historical self-consciousness; nobody reharmonizes not for the sake of variation but because there *is* no fundamental harmonization; and so on. Elements from all the above chapters (and no doubt from some unwritten) could be called in to support Debussy's view.

On Debussy this recognition seems to have had comparatively little effect. Like many Wagnerians, he had an ambivalent attitude to Berlioz. David Drew, however, remarks that Berlioz's 'unwillingness to modulate tonally in circumstances where other kinds of modulation seem to him sufficient anticipates Debussy'.[122] It also anticipates Mahler, who often does not modulate structurally in his symphonies, preferring to juxtapose tonal areas; his longer movements are often more fruitfully approached from some angle other than sonata form and may (like *Fantastique* I) fall into a rondo-like pattern. Mahler's instrumentation is intrinsic, not applied, and he composes without feather-bedding, polyphonically, although with a far higher dissonance toleration. How much of Berlioz's music he knew intimately, besides the *Fantastique* (which he conducted), I do not know, but his use of an E♭ clarinet for purposes of parody is only the most trivial influence from that work.

Berlioz's influence in Russia is well known, and perhaps not very profound. However, I cannot but wonder if Stravinsky's vilification of Berlioz results from an early love–hate relationship. 'His basses are . . . uncertain'; but Stravinsky capitalizes on lack of direction in his own basses. Berlioz is often harmonically static, and thought in stratified terms to some extent; Stravinsky is notoriously static, and stratifies consistently. I do not suggest that he tried consciously to distance himself from an influence he felt ashamed of, although there are precedents enough for such behaviour in musical history. Quite clearly, the Russian and Debussian aspects have priority in any estimate of the formation of Stravinsky's style. Nevertheless Berlioz is an outstanding example of how to avoid falling into the pianistic and harmonic clichés of the German-dominated nineteenth century, as was another great original and admirer of Berlioz, Mussorgsky. And Stravinsky, in his own words, was 'brought up on Berlioz'.[123]

However, it must be accepted that Berlioz's influence is selective, and overall rather slight, just as he himself owed little to anyone else; such comments will distress only those blinkered by a particular form of historical determinism. It is hard to believe that the subsequent history of music would have been so very different if Berlioz had settled into general medical practice. Given that he cannot have affected the formation of Chopin, Schumann, or Mendelssohn, can we seriously suggest that Wagner's musical language would have been very different without him? or Liszt's, wedded as he was to the piano? or Debussy's?[124]

I began by remarking on the extraordinary extent of the vilification of Berlioz in the critical heritage. It is true that had he been less of an individualist, and had the development of other musicians been more affected by him, this hostility would have been far less. But as Drew remarks, 'in the historical context, the opponents were right to be wrong. It is the first recognition due to perfect idiosyncrasy . . . No twist in the history of music will ever legitimize something so proudly on the wrong side of the conventional blankets' (see note 122). What matters more are the doubts of the sympathetic, from Schumann's critical masterpiece of 1835 to the present day. This is, however, still the price of singularity. I would not say that many of the nineteenth-century works I most admire – even *Parsifal* – are free from spot; but Berlioz can be disconcerting to a quite unprecedented degree. It is not surprising that so personal a language should sometimes seem crude or inarticulate even to the most willing and intelligent hearer. Individuals will differ about what percentage of Berlioz sounds wrong to them; the amount is likely to be reduced by repeated hearings. But to undertake to listen again one must be intrigued; and one must believe in the possibility of being convinced. There is nothing the critic can do about the first condition, but the second is really the subject of this book. I can only hope to have convinced some of those willing people – and there are many – for whom passages in Berlioz do not sound right, that to feel that nearly all he wrote *does* sound right is reasonable and possible, and not evidence of what Stravinsky calls literary-mindedness or poor musicality. I do not wish to deny Berlioz's eccentricity, still less to turn him into an ordinary classic. To hear him so would be to hear him without the challenge to routine which he can still pose, and which even in his gentlest music – in *La belle voyageuse*, or the 'Air de Faust' – is so vital a part of his emotional and intellectual fascination.

Notes

INTRODUCTION

1. Leonard B. Meyer, *Explaining Music* (Chicago, 1973), p. ix.

1 BACKGROUND AND EDUCATION (1)

2. For an index to Tiersot's collections of folk material, see *The New Grove* 18, p. 818.
3. Research has not so far enabled me either to refute or substantiate Vallas' claim that numerous melodies of Berlioz are taken from folk and liturgical repertories of the Dauphiné (ValG5, 664). His references are generally imprecise, but one folksong he mentions, the Provençal 'O Magali', is indeed identical for ten notes with the melody in the 'Chasse royale' from bar 30. The original is in 6/8, however, and the most characteristic turn in Berlioz's melody (bars 34–40) forms no part of it. If this is 'the most characteristic case of [Berlioz's] unconscious borrowing' it is a slight matter; and even if such borrowing were proved to be widespread it would not, as Vallas implies, be to Berlioz's discredit. The use and new extension of folk material is not, after all, usually held against, say, Haydn, Mahler, or Stravinsky.
4. The principal source of this account is Berlioz, Mem, early chapters; see also Hiller (1880); Boschot (1906); Cairns's annotations in his edn of Mem; and MacNG.
5. E. J. Dent, *The Rise of Romantic Opera* (Cambridge, 1976), index entries under 'Berlioz'.
6. On the strict, classical modelling technique, see J. Kerman, *The Beethoven Quartets* (London, 1967), 57ff; C. Rosen, *The Classical Style* (London, 1971), 455ff; idem, 'Influence: Plagiarism and Inspiration', *19th-Century Music* 4 (1980–81), 87.

2 CONCERNING METHOD AND STYLE

7. Hiller (1880): 'Music for him was never entirely the mother tongue. He translated his poetic images . . . into notes, and often succeeded to an astonishing degree. The empire of colours, however . . . often fails to conceal the faults of his earliest education' (p. 106). Letter to Verdi, 26 January 1879, according to R. Sietz, 'Aus Ferdinand Hiller's Briefwechsel 4', *Beiträge zur rheinischen Musikgeschichte* 60 (1965), 106: he recalls Berlioz's 'relative schwere Schaffensart' and adds (text given in French) 'however, he did attain to some extraordinary effects. Did he ever attain to real music? That is a question.' See also J. W. Klein, 'Berlioz's Personality', *Music & Letters* 50 (1969), 23.
8. Bars 46–54 of 'Chanson de brigands' are cited by the Marxist music historian Knepler in a context indicating approval of their liberated and anti-bourgeois sentiment (1961, p. 296).

3 CONCERNING PITCH (1): CHORD AND PROGRESSION

9. The statement in MemPS deserves the closest study. It forms the basis of Cone's remarkable account of Berlioz in ConSH, for which reason I have not considered it so closely here.
10. P. Boulez, *Boulez on Music Today* (London, 1971), 37.

11. Other critics have approached Bockholdt's emphasis on spatial elements. Sandford (1964) is cited by Bockholdt in support of his claim that Berlioz must be analysed in terms of simultaneous operation on different planes, a view anticipated in Cone (1953). Sandford's work is, however, mostly traditional formal analysis, and his efforts to compel Berlioz's overtures into sonata patterns go beyond persuasion to Procrustean torture. See also Bass (1964, 1967, 1969); Weihrauch (1968, 1975); and Chapter 6.

12. Tiersot (1904), 310; Koechlin (1928), 177. Koechlin discusses Berlioz under 'licences' (87ff) and in a historical sequence which amounts to a catalogue of 'hardiesses' (175ff), often the results of linear collision rather than truly vertical thought.

13. *Cosima Wagner's Diaries* I (London, 1978), 332.

14. M. J. E. Brown, 'Schubert', *Grove's Dictionary*, 5th edn (1954), vol. 7, p. 560 (original italics).

15. Berlioz deleted the passage ending with a cadence in C♯ minor, but he could as easily have removed that ending in C major. He seems to have considered the inclusion of both to be a musical tautology whose removal mattered more than the preservation of the sense of the text. The bars appeared in the first edition but were deleted from the second; this revision is entered in the autograph score and several copies of the first edition, and in both OBE (7, p. xvii) and NBE (9, p. 170) the original reading is confined to the critical commentary. For some reason the cut bars in 'Quaerens me' (but not those in the 'Offertoire') are included in the vocal score by Schirmer, presumably the source for Friedheim (FriRH, 288) and Primmer (PriBS, 48), who discuss the movement as though the cut had not been made (see RusBL, 64; but I had not then seen the Schirmer score).

4 CONCERNING PITCH (2): CHROMATICISM, TONAL RELATIONS, AND MODALITY

16. H. Schenker, *Harmony* (English edn, Chicago, 1954), 112–13; ConFS, 233–4 (Schumann) and 269.

17. Tovey (1949), 142.

18. L. B. Meyer, *Emotion and Meaning in Music* (Chicago, 1956), 180–81.

19. Schoenberg, *Structural Functions of Harmony*, ed. H. Searle (London, 1954), 6ff.

20. Reicha (1818), 21.

21. C. Rosen, *Sonata Forms* (New York, 1981), 295–6.

22. Letter to Hans von Bülow, 28 July 1854, in *Correspondance inédite de Hector Berlioz*, ed. D. Bernard (2nd edn, Paris, 1879), 211–12.

23. Letter of 20 June 1859, in *Briefe von Hector Berlioz an die Fürstin Carolyne Sayn-Wittgenstein*, ed. La Mara (Leipzig, 1903), 95.

24. O. Messiaen, *Technique de mon langage musical* (Paris, 1944). The second mode is adumbrated in certain works of Berlioz's contemporaries, Chopin and Liszt; see L. J. H. Trevitt, *The Use of the Diminished 7th . . .* (unpubd diss., U. of East Anglia, 1976).

25. Berlioz's review, republished in MM, is translated in D. Brown, *Glinka, a Biographical and Critical Study* (London, 1974).

5 EDUCATION (2): CONCERNING CATEL, THE GUITAR, AND WORKS OF THE 1820s

26. Catel (1802); the English translation by Mary Cowden Clarke (London, 1854) is in the same series as her translation of Berlioz GT.

27. L. Cherubini, *Cours de contrepoint et de fugue* (Paris, 1835), which despite its late date exemplifies the Conservatoire's teaching of the 1820s; several examples are by pupils.

28. *Lohengrin*, Act III, bar 21; cf. 'Roméo seul . . .', bar 113, where however the root of the chord appears as a pedal below the middle-of-texture 9th, and *Waverley*, bar 78, where the root is confided to the timpanist alone, a tone below the 9th in the 'cellos.

29. Reicha (1818), 68; H. M. Berton, *Traité d'harmonie* (Paris, 1815), 53 (the piano is blamed for the abuse of enharmony; it is 'un prisme trompeur'). The notion that Berlioz objected to enharmony apparently stems from a remark of Saint-Saëns (*Portraits et souvenirs*, Paris, 1903,

pp. 21–2) and still survives (MacNG, 599; Barzun, 1950, vol. 1, p. 460). In fact, Berlioz explicitly defended enharmony. In the *Traité* he condemns a form of concertina because its keys provided for a difference of pitch between enharmonically equivalent notes, 'thus conforming to the *doctrine* of acousticians, which is quite at odds with the *practice* of musicians'. He cites examples of enharmony from Gluck, Weber, Meyerbeer, and himself (GT, 278–9/E, 235–7).

30. See Holoman (1976) for the results of research on Gerono and Berlioz's Conservatoire attendance, including rather poor reports on progress (which embody Cherubini's opinion, however, rather than Lesueur's). On the Conservatoire and its rules, see C. Pierre, *Le conservatoire national de musique* (Paris, 1900); see also Bloom (1981).

31. Hiller (1880), 67ff.

32. 'Strophes' (Cat. 25/IB) was originally scored for guitar, not harp. Berlioz is alleged to have contributed studies and variations (on 'Là ci darem') to a guitar tutor published in the 1820s, but no trace of this work has been found. As Berlioz never otherwise wrote either studies or variations, this work, if it existed (the evidence is thin enough to permit doubt) was probably uncharacteristic hackwork. See HolCP, 40.

33. Tiersot (1904–6), article of 14 February 1904. Unfortunately Tiersot does not locate any of the 'numerous places' where guitar influence is found. A similar view was expressed by W. Denis Browne ('Modern Harmonic Tendencies', *Proceedings of the Musical Association* 40, 1913–14, p. 141); he ascribed the view to Dent, but twenty years later Dent offered another explanation of Berlioz's peculiarities (see p. 144).

34. The publication date of *Le dépit* is only conjectured to be 1819, but it must be before c. 1823. It could be the piece referred to in CG 1, pp. 32–3. The only surviving copy is in the British Library. I am indebted to Barry Gibson for this reconstruction.

35. Nevertheless Hiller liked *La belle voyageuse* best of the whole *Irlande* collection; he thought the others lacked spontaneity (1880, p. 105). As late as 1851 a critic remarked that the modulations in this song 'should not be offered as a model to any maladroit student', but they are essential to the rustic colouring: 'a bouquet of pastoral originality which instantly transports us to the velvet hills of green Erin' (*Revue et gazette musicale*, 6 April 1851; see NBE 13, p. xvi). In the first edition Berlioz characterized the singer of *La belle voyageuse* as 'Jeune paysan'.

36. I am indebted to Eric Gräbner for the loan of material for NBE 4 (*Les francs-juges* and *La nonne sanglante*). On *Les francs-juges* see chiefly HolCP; and MacBS on uses of the music in later works.

6 CONCERNING INSTRUMENTATION

37. Eduard Hanslick, *Aus dem Concertsaal . . . Geschichte des Concertwesens in Wien* 2 (Vienna, 1870), 80, 416. See BocMS. Hanslick shows his usual percipience in discovering what is original, while characteristically rejecting the result on aesthetic grounds.

38. For arguments to the contrary, which I do not find convincing, see Nowalis (1975). See also above, note 11.

39. On 'stratification' in Stravinsky, see Cone, 'The Progress of a Method', in B. Boretz and E. T. Cone, eds.: *Perspectives on Schoenberg and Stravinsky* (Princeton, 1968), 156.

40. Berlioz urged upon the French the introduction of the true bass trombone and the alto trombone, without which

'We are reduced exclusively to the tenor trombone, and these three instruments, alike in timbre and range, have to perform parts for three different instruments [alto, tenor, bass]. In consequence Parisian orchestras cannot properly play Gluck's *Alceste*, or the prelude to *Les Huguenots*, which both demand low C; the players have to transpose it up an octave, and so annul the effect'. *Le journal des débats* (10 November 1837); see also GT, 199/E, 152.

41. It appears that since Berlioz's day the bore of the horns in normal use has widened by up to 12 per cent, and the fashion of increasing the bore may well continue. Horn-players no longer use the pure funnel mouthpiece. The modern 'all-purpose' trombone couples the tenor and bass ranges but adopts a bass or more-than-bass bore, which may exceed that of the instrument normally used in French nineteenth-century orchestras (admittedly very narrow,

at c. 10 mm) by as much as 30–35 per cent. The effect on the sound of Berlioz's music must be very considerable. See A. Baines, *Brass Instruments* (London, 1976), 221–5, 243–6.

42. Recordings of the *Fantastique* are so numerous that no detailed comparisons can be made here. In *La damnation* it may be noticed how much better the lighter tubas sound (as opposed to a mixture of a heavy tuba and a trombone as prescribed in OBE) in the Colin Davis recording (6703 042) ('Choeur de buveurs' and 'Amen', Cat. 32B/6A, 6B). Relatively lightweight tubas comparable in bore and tone to the ophicleide in deeper notes, remained the norm in France until quite recently.

43. Compare the London Symphony Orchestra under Davis (SAL 3441), a performance whose fire is damped by precise and gentlemanly bassoon tone, and the Orchestre de la Radiodiffusion Française under Cluytens (33CX 1439). Davis is generally the more concerned for authenticity; but the brittle *frisson* of the French bassoon, and the narrow-bored brass which seems to vomit flame (V, bar 6), are certainly closer to the sounds Berlioz wanted.

44. GBL 5633.

7 CONCERNING THE BASS

45. R. Craft and I. Stravinsky, *Conversations with Igor Stravinsky* (London, 1959), 29. See also Schumann in ConFS, 242; Tovey (TovEM 4, p. 76); and Ravel's contention that Berlioz could not harmonize a simple waltz (NewBR, 117).

46. The resolution of a dominant $\frac{6}{2}$ chord onto a root position is in fact a commonplace in eighteenth-century recitative, from Bach to Mozart. Wotton alleges that Berlioz was censured for its use in *Absence* but his appeal for justification to the orchestral form is disingenuous; the piano version is the first, and even in the orchestral setting he omits to note the movement of the second violas and horn (WotHB, 69–70; see also J. A. Westrup, 'Berlioz and Common Sense', *The Musical Times* 101 (1960), 755, and D. Cairns, 'Berlioz and Professor Westrup', *ibid.*, 102 (1961), 21). It remains a mystery why *Absence* in particular should attract this attention; why not, for example, bars 23–4 of 'Marche hongroise' – exactly the same progression, even better known, and far louder?

47. Bockholdt aligns five versions of the 'idée fixe' from the symphony without harmony (1973); he includes *Herminie* in his commentary. Cone analyses the harmony with the aid of the rejected version (Ex. 52, D), deducing that the ambiguous treatment of the C major end to the consequent is of structural importance; he also proposes an alternative consequent, of eight bars in lieu of Berlioz's seven: 'to do so is to understand how right Berlioz was' (ConFS, 254ff).

8 CONCERNING COUNTERPOINT, PEDAL, AND FUGUE

48. Nineteenth-century critics, including Hadow, might have been surprised to find Berlioz cited with approval in mid-twentieth-century textbooks of counterpoint. Rubbra approves as a 'living expression of the meaning of the words' fugal passages in 'Requiem aeternam' (Cat. 22/1, bars 55–65) and *L'enfance* (Cat. 38/15; *Counterpoint, a Survey*, London, 1960, pp. 74–6). Piston mentions a thematic combination in *Harold* (Cat. 19/II, bar 64ff; *Counterpoint*, London, 1949, p. 80). Tovey approves the 'round' in 'Scène aux champs' and the fugue in the 'Ronde du sabbat' (Cat. 13/III, V; TovEM 6, p. 50). Longyear considers the 'Te Deum laudamus' (Cat. 33/1), which Hadow deplored, to be 'as good fugally as any of Mendelssohn's essays in this genre' (1969, p. 98/2nd edn, p. 152).

49. See Weihrauch (1975). The 'neo-renaissance' Berlioz is however a chimaera, created from biographical error and analytical selectiveness. There is no reason to suppose Berlioz knew much early music, and sufficient evidence that he disliked what little he came across. Primmer proposes a baroque influence (PriBS, 12, 15), but again there is no supporting external evidence, and little support from the music if comparison is made with Mendelssohn or Schumann.

50. Gautier was reviewing *Roméo* and refers to the 'Convoi funèbre'. See Boschot (1908), 282 and 292, in which it is suggested that Gautier took his ideas from Berlioz himself. But Berlioz knew perfectly well that upper pedals were not new; he pointed one out himself in the essay on

Beethoven's Fifth Symphony which appeared during the period of work on the *Requiem*, well before *Roméo* (it is 'one of the most daring harmonic effects of this sublime elegy', the slow movement: AT, 34/G, 52).

51. For the original form of the passage see NBE 16, p. 198 (ConFS, 203–4); this version is used in Liszt's transcription. A sketch of the final version is studied in Holoman (1975a; with facsimile). Even the first impression of the printed score contains the original version.

52. Berlioz showed Lesueur a 'canon in three parts', H 12 (Mem6), when they met in 1823. This may, however, have been the *Canon libre à la quinte*, which is a three-part piece, the texture making sense only with the free bass (piano).

53. Berlioz writes on fugue in *Le correspondant*, 21 April 1829 (see Prod'homme, 1898, p. 287); 'Est-ce une ironie', GM (on the 'Amen' in *La damnation*); and Mem13, making clear his disapproval of routine attitudes adopted by Reicha and his admiration for expressive fugue in Lesueur.

54. 'Anthologies' include all collections of songs (such as Cat. 27, 35, 36), *Tristia*, and *Lélio*. Fugue or substantial fugato appears (at least) as follows: Cat. 13 (*Fantastique*), I, 311ff; V, 241ff. Cat. 19 (*Harold*), I, opening and 321ff; IV, 428ff. Cat. 22 (*Requiem*), 1, 5, 6, 7, 9 ('Hosanna' twice). Cat. 23C (*Benvenuto*), 1 (introduction), 4, 16A. Cat. 25 (*Roméo*), I; II, 278ff; IV, 430ff; V; VII (reprise of I). Cat. 23E (*Le carnaval romain*), 304ff, 356ff. Cat. 30C (*Hymne pour l'élévation*). Cat. 32B (*La damnation*), 1, 4, 6B ('Amen'). Cat. 33 (*Te Deum*), 1, 2bis, 6. Cat. 38 (*L'enfance*), 1B, 7, 10, 12 (choral and orchestral fugati), 15. Cat. 40A (*Les troyens*), 8; 29; 39, 83ff. Cat. 42 (*Béatrice*), 6, 6bis. The incidence of fugue is clearly highest in sacred works, although the amount in *Roméo* is remarkable. I have omitted ideas that are imitative but not really fugal, such as the 'round' in *Fantastique* III; canon; fugue arising from reunions (e.g. *Requiem*, 'Dies irae'). Fugue may have been excluded from the *Symphonie funèbre* (Cat. 26, the only really large work not represented above) because of its 'popular' style, and to make for better ensemble when played on the march; there is a sort of fugato (III, 147ff, taken from *Scène héroïque*), but it lacks real counterpoint. There are two articles on Berlioz's fugues: Georges Favre, 'Berlioz et la fugue', *La revue musicale*, special issue no. 233 (1956), 38; and Hirschberg (1974), which is more comprehensive but analytically fallible.

55. Paris's fugue and those of other candidates, together with some counterpoint exercises, are bound with Berlioz's (see Cat. 5).

56. This fugue is bound with *Cléopâtre* (see Cat. 10A, 10B). It appears to be a fair copy but includes two rejected continuations (OBE 6, p. 5; K 519, p. 162). The eight-part fugue which precedes it in OBE is not by Berlioz (see Favre, op. cit., 39–40).

57. *36 fugues pour piano*, Op. 36, No. 22 (published 1805). No. 20 answers at the tritone (it is also in 5/8). Nos. 21 and 23 reverse the order of No. 22, with entries by descending 3rds (C, A, F, D).

58. If I may anticipate the terms of Chapter 12, the proportions of the 'Offertoire' come out as follows (A is fugal material, B the 'Canto espressivo'): 154 bars. A: at bar 60, key III, B, then A: bar 78, key VI, B, then fragmentation of A: a low point, centred on A minor (v) but undefined, violins only, triple *piano*, 96–7, then A merging with part of B: key III, 112, A by sequence to V at 131, coda resolving in tonic major. 154 divides symmetrically as 77 + 77; the exact mid-point is the second, *sforzando*, occurrence of B, establishing VI. GM of 154 is 59:95; it falls at bar 60, the first occurrence of B, the first full *forte*, the establishment of III. As 95:59 it falls at bar 96, the low point, in the ambiance of the only key other than the tonic to have any importance (through the fugal exposition). Thus three points are defined, each in two ways. In the original version there were 171 bars; the symmetrical bar 86 and first GM (bar 66) fall near, rather than on, the ends of B, a weaker point than its (and its key's) arrival; the other GM falls nowhere in particular, during a statement of A which is in the cut bars. The cut brings the proportions perfectly into focus.

9 CONCERNING RHYTHM

59. Surprisingly, discussion of Berlioz's rhythm has not been widespread, although it includes serious work such as GraAR, FriBR, and parts of BocBS. Berlioz's most important discussion of rhythm is a feuilleton in *Le journal des débats* (10 November 1837), quoted in the epigraph to

this chapter and on pp. 127–8. It is part-reprinted in G. Condé, ed., *Cauchemars et passions* (Paris, 1981) and part-translated in Barzun (1969, 2nd edn only). See also Mem53, in which Berlioz argues that the Conservatoire should have a class in rhythm.

60. Reicha (1824–6), vol. 1, p. 26. He applies 5/4 metre to an exercise in Palestrina style. The stretched metres are in piano works of c. 1800–5 – *L'art de varier*, Op. 57 (Variation 5 consists of six statements of the sequence 4/4, 3/4, 2/4), and *36 fugues* (No. 20 in 5/8; other metrical experiments in Nos. 24, 28, 30).

61. Philidor (*Tom Jones*, No. 1) has one singer in 4/4 and another in 12/8, successively then combined: Grétry said this was the first example of the kind. See also Mozart, *Die Entführung*, the quartet, which anticipates the *Benvenuto* trio (No. 3) where the lovers' tender 3/4 is combined with Fieramosca's muttered 9/8. Grétry himself combined two choruses, having first given them separately, in *La double épreuve* (Act III, scs. 6–8), with a common metre but distinguished by scoring (cf. *La damnation*, No. 8). Cherubini combined two arias, both in 3/4, in *Lodoïska* (No. 6); one is sentimental, the other a polonaise and thus, although sung by the servant, predominant in the combination. This anticipates *Les troyens* (No. 31), where the combination of metres is more apparent than real; Anna's 'Cavatine' in 3/8 falls into three-bar phrases to conform with Narbal's 9/8. Unusually for Berlioz, this simultaneity generates no tension, and as Narbal sings his air twice entire, with Anna joining only half-way through the repeat, it is an unusual example of tautology.

62. Tovey (1944), 65–6; Cairns (1966), 227.

63. This analysis substantially agrees with that in BocBS, 174ff; Bockholdt's plan (176–7), however, has no line C.

64. Letter to Gustav Schmidt, 6 March 1853, quoted from S. Morgenstern, *Composers on Music* (London, 1958), 170.

65. By my count, and ignoring passages broken up by *fermate* and the effective 9/8 (3/4) of the trio, the hiccups in *Mab* are: 9/8 bars in 170–72, 278–80 (repeat), 536–8 (neutralized by a 15/8 bar, 539–43), 580–82, 587–9; one 6/8 bar, 360–61; inserted 3/8 bars – the real hiccups – 293, 430, 475. This is not a large total in 769 bars, but it noticeably increases after the trio and is thus an aspect of formal articulation.

66. C. Rosen, *The Classical Style* (New York, 1971), 179.

67. Gluck pursues these accents rigorously even in depictions of mental disturbances. The most famous instance is Orestes's 'Le calme rentre dans mon coeur' (*Iphigénie en Tauride*). Berlioz wrote eloquently of the end of *Armide*, Act III (Mem51, 8th letter). Less declamatory, but still dependent for full expressive force on a dynamically inventive accompanimental rhythm, are his favourite aria 'O malheureuse Iphigénie' and the trio from *Paride ed Elena*, which Berlioz will have known through its inclusion in *Orphée* ('Tendre amour').

68. Cairns describes Berlioz as 'Toscanini to Wagner's Furtwängler' (*The Memoirs of Hector Berlioz*, 568). Wagner wrote to his wife of Berlioz 'rattling off' Mozart's G minor Symphony, and even to Liszt, with whom he might have been more diplomatic, he wrote that the performance 'scarcely edified him'. Berlioz referred to Wagner's rubato style, 'like Klindworth on the piano'. See A. W. Ganz, *Berlioz in London* (London, 1950); and E. Newman, *The Life of Richard Wagner* 2 (London and New York, 1937: Cassell edn, 440; Knopf edn 477).

69. See CG 1, p. 196. Unfortunately the MS (not autograph) repeats the earlier ♩ = 80, instead of giving 𝅝 = 80. This makes no musical sense, since the melody at the reunion of themes (bar 168) would emerge at half its original speed (OBE 10, p. v, has a contorted argument about the contradiction, failing to spot the mistake). The opposite process, halving the speed, occurs in the *Requiem* at the 'Tuba mirum' (Cat. 22/2), the point where Habeneck is supposed to have taken a pinch of snuff (Mem46). The direction 'One bar is equivalent to two of the preceding movement', and the marking ♩ = 72, imply a precise interpretation of the preceding general direction *animato*, since the 'Dies irae' began at ♩ = 96.

10 MELODY

70. P. Boulez, *Conversations with Célestin Deliège* (London, 1976), 20.

71. Reicha (1814). Reicha's general insistence on regular periodicity is not absolute. He allows the fermata ('point d'orgue') as a legitimate stretching of phrase-length and for the

extension of final phrases; although he is puzzled as to why this is acceptable, calling it 'a remarkable thing in the theory of rhythm [*rhythme* here means 'phrase'] which is that the final rhythm (which one might understand as a companion of the one before) sometimes has one more bar . . . without wounding our sensibilities' (p. 29). He also accepts asymmetry through 'suppressed bars', citing Mozart's 'Non so più' (*Figaro*). On earlier believers in the dogma of the 'période', see J. Rushton, 'The Theory and Practice of Piccinnisme', *Proceedings of the Royal Musical Association* 98 (1971–2), 31. On the melody in the *Symphonie funèbre*, see RusBL, 54ff. For Wagner's comment, see R. Jacobs and G. Skelton, eds., *Wagner Writes from Paris* (London, 1973), 132.

72. I will not repeat my doubts concerning the melodic analyses in PriBS (see RusBL); they do not affect the statistical demonstration of phrase and contour variety. See Schenkman (1979) and Réti (1951). Cone (ConFS, 276–7) also notes the cross-reference between works that is occasioned by the melodic use of flat and natural 6ths within a single phrase (*Fantastique, Requiem, Roméo*, and *La damnation*).

73. The following have been consulted: *Chants des bergers suisses ou Ranz des vaches* (Lyon, c. 1825). *Recueil des Noëls composés en langue provençale par Nicolas Saboly* [1614–1675] (Avignon, 1856; see L. Guichard, 'Berlioz et Saboly', *La revue musicale*, special issue no. 233, 1956, p. 55. A derivation is suggested for the transformation of the fugal overture of *La fuite* at the start of *L'enfance* Part III: the use of Noël-like material was noted by d'Ortigue in 1854). D. Arbaud, *Chants populaires de la Provence* (Aix-en-Provence, 2 vols., 1862–4). H. L. Delloye, *Chants & chansons populaires de la France* (Paris, 3 vols., 1843–4). C. Didier, *Chants populaires de la campagne de Rome* (Paris, 1844). R. Marchessou, *Velay et Auvergne, contes et légendes, chansons et bourrées* (Le Puy en Velay, 1903). P. Pittion, *Dauphiné . . .* (Grenoble, 1945). Idem, *En pays dauphinois* (Grenoble, 1950). J. Tiersot, *Chansons populaires recueillies dans les Alpes françaises: Savoie et Dauphiné* (Grenoble, 1903). J. B. T. Weckerlin, *La chanson populaire* (Paris, 1886).

74. Berlioz, letter to Charles Hallé, 1860, in J. Barzun, *Nouvelles lettres de Berlioz* (New York, 1954), 206. Tovey (1949), 96; the analysis of 'O malheureuse Iphigénie' shows phrase-lengths of 4, 6 (to vocal entry), 4, 8, 3, 3, 3, 3, and 5 bars. Berlioz's knowledge of the Italian source is apparent from SO, 23.

75. Tovey (1949), 95–7. He adds: 'The study of Gluck's most serious melody is a useful method of shaking modern criticism out of its conventional values.' Perhaps one might add Berlioz's melody also.

11 VOCAL FORMS: 'SATZ' AND 'URSATZ'

76. All three remarks come from Berlioz's letter to Princess Wittgenstein of 12 August 1856, in *Briefe von Hector Berlioz an die Fürstin Carolyne Sayn-Wittgenstein*, ed. La Mara (Leipzig, 1903), 27. Translation in Searle, *Hector Berlioz, a Selection from his Letters* (London, 1966), 149.

77. L. B. Meyer, *Emotion and Meaning in Music* (Chicago, 1956), 272.

78. MS F–Pn 1.179.

79. The sketches are part of the group in F–Pmeyer. Facsimile, NBE 2c, p. 784.

80. HadSM; TovEM. Schenker's most readily available complete Chopin analyses are in *Five Graphic Analyses* (New York, 1969; orig. *Fünf Urlinie-Tafeln*, Vienna, 1932). As far as I am aware Schenker scarcely refers to Berlioz outside the *Harmonielehre* (Stuttgart, 1906; English edn as *Harmony*, Chicago, 1954).

81. Schenker's general principles and practices should by now be well known. For commentary and bibliography the reader is referred to *The New Grove* ('Analysis'; 'Schenker'); and to Jonathan Dunsby, 'Heinrich Schenker and the Free Counterpoint of Strict Composition', *Royal Musical Association Research Chronicle* 16 (1980), 140. See also Felix Salzer, *Structural Hearing* (New York, 1962), who, however, analyses Debussy (vol. 1, p. 222ff; vol. 2, Ex. 478) as well as mediaeval and other modern music. Arnold Whittall has also applied Schenkerian analysis to Debussy in lectures and seminars.

82. I am aware that Schenker's concept of organicism has been questioned. The remarks of Eugene Narmour on the relationship of parts to the whole could have some application to Berlioz (*Beyond Schenkerism*, Chicago, 1977, p. 33).

83. ConSH, part III. See ConFS for use of analysis of a Schenkerian kind for a short passage

(the 'idée fixe'). I am indebted to Eric Gräbner for showing me his analysis of *Au cimetière*.
84. Almost any of the cadences Newman names is easier to justify than the little portamento in
the *Symphonie funèbre* (Ex. 95A, bar 29). Newman names the following:

A, B: the oboe solo in *Roméo* II and the C major statement of the love theme in *Roméo* III (Cat.
25/II, 81ff; III, 172ff). C, D: 'Le roi de Thulé' and Margaret's 'Romance' (Cat. 32A/6, 7;
32B/11B, 15). E: *La captive* (Cat. 18). F: Choroebus's arioso 'Mais le ciel et la terre' (Cat.
40A/3, Andante).

I cannot see the objection to, or improve upon, A, C (the cadence effectively stretches the
metre to an implied 9/8), D, or E (an elegant sequence). B needs its context: the cadence
comes seven times, but almost invariably before a new idea or change of speed; its sixth
statement is interrupted, and on two other occasions it is actually omitted, an effect given
strength by the expectation that it will come. F ends with a restatement of the opening of the
aria, an effective and fitting procedure since these are the only two perfect cadences in the
piece.
85. F–Po MS A 521A. This original version is corrected, but visible, in the autograph, F–Pn
1.508.

12 FORMAL SCHEMES IN INSTRUMENTAL MUSIC

86. HadSM, 140. Yet in the preceding essay on 'Music and Musical Criticism' Hadow
castigates criticism which 'contents itself with picking out the fifths' (see epigraph to Chapter
12):
> 'Yet this is precisely the function which pedantry loves to perform. It pays no heed to the
> vigour or subtlety of a composer's thought, it has no gratitude for the gift of a new melody or
> a new cadence, it shrinks aghast from the boldness that has extended the range of harmony
> or the limits of form (HadSM, 56).

87. This denunciation requires support, but I have no space for detailed polemics, and I can
only ask the reader to discover these analyses and test them rigorously against the score and
the music in performance. The 'Rondo' interpretation of *Benvenuto* is in Sandford (1964, pp.
77–8), and presents the work as A: B: A¹ C D: A² C¹: D¹ C² A³: A⁴ B¹ (colons at changes of
tempo; end of exposition; end of development; coda; i.e. bars 23, 89, 199, 228, 318). But the
musical material of A⁴ is quite different from that of A; and B is the whole slow section with
two themes (see Chapter 13). On Primmer's tonal designs, and their alleged logic, see RusBL,
60. Ballif's analysis of *Le corsaire* runs:
> C: B: A¹, A², A³, A⁴, B, A⁵, Bx, By, Bz, Bx, C (amorce), C div. A, pont A, div. Bx, By, Incipit
> A, fantastique A, Reprise A.
> Reexposition A complète. Marche, coda, reprise C, cadence finale. (Ballif, 1968, p. 85)

'Fantastique' means syncopated (bar 346ff); what 'Marche' means eludes me. B is the Adagio
theme, A the main Allegro theme, so the piece opens with C, which is certainly confusing; we
are perhaps to understand the order of letters hierarchically. The author claims that his table
shows a 'malicious spiral structure [*en colimaçon*], like the Game of Goose', certainly an
intriguing analogy but one difficult to reconcile with a temporal art or to deduce from a plan
with no keys.
88. Newman is referring to the *Lohengrin* Prelude, which Berlioz declared was a masterpiece
(AT, 309/G, 326). In its 75 bars, 50 (i.e. two thirds) precede the brass entrance. The dynamic
climax, however, is at bar 55. Newman observes reasonably enough that 'a bar or two one way
or the other makes no perceptible difference'; precise figures, in any case, may be expected
only when the composer calculates them in advance. Moreover, a diminuendo in slow tempo
may create an impression of greater length (cf. *Hamlet*, see p. 186; or the ends of *Harold* II and
Roméo VI). E. Newman, *The Wagner Operas* (New York, 1949), 129.
89. On the other hand, to me, the diminuendo to the tonic which ends the 'Chasse royale'
(Cat. 40A/29) always seems to be too short. Newman called this piece 'one of the most perfect
creations of form that the art can show' (NewBR, 230; see also 114); but the climactic period
(bars 246–76) is way beyond two thirds, whether or not the opening Larghetto is included in
the count.

90. The outer movements of the *Symphonie funèbre*, both marches, contain 280 and 240 bars, although neither proceeds in regular four-bar phrases. In I, GM falls when the recapitulation ceases simply to repeat the exposition (bar 175: a dynamic drop but a structural turning-point). In III, the first 90 bars are rooted in the tonic; the first tonal departure, from bar 93, defines the smaller proportion of a GM.

91. The term 'peroration' is used by Tovey for Haydn's bolder recapitulations (1949, pp. 55ff). It enables us to avoid unintentionally insulting references to 'a series of codas', a concept surely incompatible with good form (MacBO, 35, of *Fantastique* I, the codas 'occupy nearly half the movement'; *ibid.*, 49, of *Roméo* II, 'most of the movement is devoted to an extended coda'. The true codas begin respectively at bar 491 (where the movement originally ended: see NBE 16, p. 204) and at bar 375).

92. It is worth noting that the *later* of these pieces, *Le carnaval*, has a vocal origin; its double exposition consists of a transcription of part of the Carnival scene (Cat. 23C/8). Part of the *Harold* movement originated in sketches for *Le retour de l'armée d'Italie* (HolCP, 132–3); whether or not this was to be a vocal piece, there is no evidence of a vocal source for the *form*.

93. Reicha's 'Grande coupe binaire' (1814) is reproduced in William S. Newman, *The Sonata since Beethoven* (Chapel Hill, 1969), 32. Newman remarks that Reicha 'does not quite recognize the ternary implications of the design', but historically it is obviously correct to regard a form with two repeated sections (as a contemporary of Beethoven would think of it) as binary.

94. Whether *Fantastique* I should be considered as actually in, only related to, or not in, sonata form is a matter on which critics diverge strikingly. Those who consider that it is a sonata form include Einstein: 'The strictly musical sonata form to which he still clung' (*A Short History of Music*, London, 1936, p. 173); Tiersot: 'The first movement is constructed in the most regular form . . . an allegro on two themes, the second modulating [*sic*] to the dominant' ('The Berlioz of the Fantastic Symphony', *The Musical Quarterly* 19, 1933, p. 303); Dika Newlin, for whom this is ammunition: 'talented musicians could still imitate the classic gestures of their great forbears, but the gestures had lost their meaning, as we see plainly in the stereotyped padding of the first movement of Berlioz's *Symphonie fantastique*' (*Bruckner, Mahler, Schoenberg*, New York, 1947, p. 37).

Assessment of what the form is bears no direct relationship to an assessment of its value. A common definition is sonata with modifications. Nicholas Temperley, editor of NBE 16: 'Berlioz preserved the outlines of conventional forms . . . [he] does not attempt to tie his narrative to the details of sonata form' (1971, pp. 603–4); J. H. Elliot: 'Identifiable with the classical symphonic practice, if not with the traditional outline in all its details' (in R. Hill, ed., *The Symphony*, London, 1949, p. 156); Bernard Shore, using sonata terminology while stressing unconventionality (*Sixteen Symphonies*, London, 1947, pp. 176ff); Antony Hopkins, using conventional terminology with the rider 'in so far as it is not fairly futile to force this work into the corset of normal symphonic form' – which seems reasonable until one tries to equate, say, Beethoven's symphonic forms with a corset (*Talking about Symphonies*, London, 1961, p. 96); and indeed Schumann and after him Cone: 'Schumann is on the right track when he describes the allegro as what might be called an arched sonata form' (ConFS, 251). On the other hand Macdonald declares roundly that 'the form of the movement has little in common with classical sonata form' (MacBO, 34), and Cairns refers to its 'fundamental dissimilarity from sonata form' (1966, p. 220). Only Einstein's interpretation – that it is identifiable with (or, as for Hadow, a vain attempt to write; see p. 182) a classical form – seems unequivocally wrong.

95. The MS of *Le corsaire*, F–Pn MS 1159, entitled *La tour de Nice* (deleted) and *Ouverture du Corsaire rouge* ('rouge' deleted), contains the final version but with a residue of the first layer of 1844 (the MS contains Berlioz's hand of c. 1844 and c. 1852, as well as that of his copyist Rocquemont). Assuming – and I do not think it is certain – that the surviving pages of the 1844 layer are still in their original order, it seems possible that *La tour de Nice* was recast as *Le corsaire* [*rouge*] by deleting a slow section and two statements of the 'adagio' theme both in the fast tempo, in A minor (exposition) and C minor (reprise); but it cannot be ascertained whether this melody ever appeared as an Adagio. A redundant restatement (C minor being no more a resolution than A minor) becomes in the final version a true resolution (in C, of A♭), in

lieu of development. The original form appears surprisingly loose and tautological for 1844; the final form is a remarkable blend of freedom and compactness.

96. The belated modulation to V in certain movements is the more effective because the dominant is normally the first modulation. This can work well in vocal movements also, for example *Le spectre de la rose* (cadence at bar 49) and two duets in *Les troyens* (No. 3, the strophes are all in B major with no more than touches of V, but F♯ major appears when Cassandra yields her 'chaste baiser d'épouse', bar 782ff. No. 37, bar 95, the last statement of the refrain, now '*forte avec exultation*', is in V; the sketches show that an earlier dominant statement was intended, around bar 49, but rejected in favour of iii, B♭ minor).

97. To my knowledge Richard Pohl (1884, pp. 149ff) is the only commentator to have noticed this connection, which is obvious only from the original Prologue (OBE 3, pp. xxviii–xxix; K 519, pp. 96–7).

98. Stravinsky, 'Foreword' to E. E. Lowinsky, *Tonality and Atonality in Sixteenth-Century Music* (2nd edn, Berkeley, 1962), p. vii.

99. I find it impossible to relate the admittedly arched (but certainly not sonata) form of Chopin's G minor Ballade to *Fantastique* I, as is suggested by Gerald Abraham (*Chopin's Musical Style*, London, 1939, p. 55). *Pace* Abraham, Berlioz's 'second-subject theme' returns, truncated, in the tonic, not the contrasting key; Chopin's central apotheosis is on theme B (in A major), not really like Berlioz's central dominant 'idée fixe'; Chopin has no repeated exposition, but his keys – g, E♭, A, E♭, g – really arch where Berlioz's two alternate. The analogy is not, however, so far-fetched as Hadow's attempt to relate *Le corsaire* to Beethoven's Sonata Op. 109, first movement (HadSM, 101n.; reproduced by Dannreuther, *Oxford History of Music* 6, London, 1905, p. 136). These two authors appear to take the patronizing attitude that a form of Berlioz's that works must be legitimized by a classical parallel.

100. The term 'synoptic comprehension' I gratefully accept from Cone, *Musical Form and Musical Performance* (New York, 1968). Cone does not, however, discuss Berlioz in this book, and the attempt to reconcile the apparently desirable quality of synoptic comprehensibility with the wave-like motion to a series of proximate goals (Cone on Berlioz: see p. 173), which is one of my goals in Chapters 12 and 13, is my own responsibility.

13 THE OVERTURE 'BENVENUTO CELLINI': AN ANALYSIS

101. The original bridge on B³ was four bars longer, and included lame anticipations of the beginning of D (motive 'Y'). 23 bars of neutral activity, related to B¹, were cut between bars 178 and 179; they were an unnecessary mingling of tonic and dominant material and spoiled the pleasant coincidence of the cadence at bar 179 with the varied upbeat for the repeat of D. Bars 296–8 of the final version replace fifteen bars including a reunion of motive 'Y' in its chromatic form (as in melody D) with B¹ – ingenious, but excessively delaying the full tonic returns that follow. The cadence at bar 318 was originally a completed V–I; six bars on B¹, further anticipating (and spoiling) its reprise at the reunion, intervened before the present bar 318. These changes may have been made before the first performance of the opera (at which the overture was one of the few successes); they are not in the copyist's MS score at the Opéra (F–Po A 521a). My source is OBE 5 (pp. xxii, xxiii, xxv, ix; K 519, pp. 148–55, 137); there is no autograph of the overture.

102. See GraAR, passim; much of the article is devoted to this overture. He suggests various interpretations for the accentuation of the opening bars (p. 20); they include the 'unlikely' 5/4 + two bars of 3/4. They are quickly subsumed into the four-bar periodicity, however, when the second group ends (bar 8) on a strong beat. Friedheim notes that the first syncopation (bar 2) is characteristic of other melodies in the opera, and that the opening is the only music of Berlioz cited by Sachs in *Rhythm and Tempo* (FriBR, 26).

103. H. Eimert, 'Jeux', *Die Reihe* 5 (English edn, 1961), 3 (Reports, Analyses). On stratification, see note 39.

14 THE FIGURE AND THE BACKGROUND: FAUST IN 'LA DAMNATION'

104. Wolf thought this movement almost the only one unworthy of Berlioz (H. Pleasants, ed., *The Music Criticism of Hugo Wolf*, New York, 1978, p. 200). It would seem more appropriate to single out the 6/8 finale, in which Cairns has suggested that Berlioz is using banality to a dramatic end ('Berlioz and Criticism: Some Surviving Dodos', *The Musical Times* 104, 1963, p. 548).

105. A similar effect of timeless, isolated notes draws us across time as well as space for the epilogue of *L'enfance*. Berlioz was perfectly capable of writing bridge-passages between movements of totally different mood, as is shown in Part II of *La damnation* – the transitions to Auerbach's cellar and from it to the banks of the Elbe. Primmer writes of the double meaning of the G♯ before Faust's 'Invocation' that 'in this ability to suggest the complex character and function of even a single note, Berlioz reveals something of the inner processes of Romanticism itself' (PriBS, 97); while David Drew, certainly not less sympathetic to Berlioz's aims, uses it as an example of one of those 'things, frankly, which one just has to lump . . . when Berlioz proceeds from F major to C♯ minor by suspending a solitary G♯ in mid air, and then diving straight down to his new tonic key like a seagull which has suddenly sighted a fish, it is no use complaining about the absence of Beethovenian transition. He was not that kind of composer . . . and if you say "more's the pity", the loss is yours' (Drew, 1963).

106. Friedheim uses this air to illustrate reharmonization (introduction and line 1); 'weak' progressions (e.g. down a tone, bars 5–6 and 9–10, although line 1 is also called 'conventional'); modulation by a tritone through non-functional diminished 7ths; and the use of ♭III (FriRH, 283–4, 286, 288). Cone refers to two 'reversed resolutions' (see above, p. 38), in bars 51 and 64 (ConSH, part IV).

107. The text of 'Air de Faust' is by Berlioz's collaborator Gandonnière. In the 1846 libretto the lines 'O seigneur [*sic*], après ce long martyre / Que de bonheur' appear between 'comme je respire un air pur' and 'O jeune fille', as well as at the end. There is no indication that Berlioz ever thought of setting them in this way to produce a refrain structure.

108. The coda has its own proportional scheme. Before and after the wind phrases (bars 80–85) there are 15 bars, those preceding divided 9:6 by the 'modulation' to E minor, those following 6:9 by the viola entry. The woodwind phrase inserts an extra bar during what was (bars 44–7) a four-bar phrase; the coda is thus a palindrome – 9:6:2:1:2:6:9.

109. Even in his 'romantic' youth Berlioz adhered to classical values in verse (reflecting, no doubt, his even earlier upbringing on Virgil). For him Hugo's *Hernani* contained things sublime and ridiculous: 'how I detest, in the theatre, these *enjambements* from one line to the next – these broken hemistiches which send all the classics to the devil are a matter of complete indifference to me because, when spoken, they are just like prose; perhaps I should like them for that reason; all the same, I consider that since *Hernani* is written in verse, and Hugo knows very well how to make his lines do what he wants, it would have been easier to follow both the rules and public taste . . . it is an innovation which leads nowhere' (letter to Nanci Berlioz, 20 April 1830, CG 1, p. 321). He also complains that the librettist of Gluck's *Iphigénie en Aulide* has 'needlessly spoiled Racine's verses which could perfectly well have been used in their pure beauty for the recitatives' ('Avant-Propos' to *La damnation*, 1854).

110. The sketches are found on the backs of leaves used to make corrections in the autograph of *Harold* III (F–Pn MS 1.189). See Rushton (1975) and HolCP, 146–7, which include facsimiles. The sketches show that the atmosphere of the piece, which so pressed upon Berlioz that he decided to write the text and go ahead without waiting for his librettist (Mem54), did not dictate its tonality. One sketch suggests a bass-figure in B minor with tremolo (not used); the vocal sketch begins in F minor.

111. A stimulating, but not unchallengeable, case for interlocking tonal structures is made in G. George, *Tonality and Musical Structure* (New York, 1970).

112. Tovey's denial of meaning to tonal links without collateral (usually thematic) evidence is a *Leitmotiv* of his criticism, of which the main exposition is perhaps EM 1 (*Symphonies*) (London, 1935), 9.

113. A. Lorenz, *Das Geheimnis der Form bei Richard Wagner* 2: *Die musikalische Aufbau von Richard Wagners 'Tristan und Isolde'* (Berlin, 1926, repr. 1966).

114. Tovey, *The Forms of Music: Musical Articles from the Encyclopaedia Britannica* (London, 1944), 82; see also Tovey (1949), 390ff. *The New Grove*, 'Rhythm', §II, (1980), vol. 15, pp. 810ff: even the mention of 5/4 metre in the nineteenth century refers only to folk or nationalistic influence, inapplicable to Berlioz; all the composers named are German, which I mention not even more in sorrow than anger, but to underline how atypical Berlioz is even in domains in which his inventiveness is unrivalled. F. Blume, *Classic and Romantic Music* (London, 1972), see index. R. Klinkhammer, *Die langsame Einleitung in der Instrumentalmusik der Klassik und Romantik*, Kölner Beiträge zur Musikforschung 65 (Regensburg, 1971).

115. See above, p. 191; G. Abraham, 'The Influence of Berlioz on Richard Wagner', *Music & Letters* 5 (1924), 239; J. Warrack, 'The Musical Background', in P. Burbidge and R. Sutton, eds., *The Wagner Companion* (London, 1979), 112.

116. Boulez even claims to value Berlioz not for his music but because it proves that there is no such thing as a French tradition (*Conversations with Célestin Deliège*, London, 1976, p. 18). Even if true, it is a bizarre reason for valuing anything, especially a composer whose competence is being called into question. The term 'decorative' has been correctly applied to Berlioz by F. Goldbeck (1958; also at a colloquium, 'Berlioz our Contemporary', held at the Institut Français, London, in 1969, where it appeared to arouse some opposition through being misunderstood as in some way diminishing the composer's stature). See also note 121.

117. *Lear* provides a rare agreement between Hanslick and Wolf, both of whom, like Tovey, admired the music but not its programmatic aspect. However, Hanslick declared that association between music and a play or programme cannot by definition have any significance; Tovey felt that as the music does not follow the scenes in the manner of a symphonic poem, association of the two was a waste of time; and Wolf that such association was perfectly proper, but that the music was not adequate to the purpose, for all its qualities. Hanslick, *The Beautiful in Music* (Vienna, 1854: trans. New York, 1891; see p. 114). Tovey, EM 4, p. 83ff. Wolf, op. cit. (note 104), p. 31.

118. It may still be necessary to point out that the programme-note attached to *Rêverie et caprice* in OBE 6 is not authentic. Only *Fantastique* and *Roméo* really require attention to a literary programme for full understanding; where *Lear* is a single piece, and thus musically self-sufficient, the symphonies use a programme to explain the sequence of movements (see note 77 and p. 170). Tovey insisted that *Le corsaire* and *Harold* require no attention to Byron, but Berlioz never said they should. On the former, see note 95. Byron's prefatory remark to *Childe Harold's Pilgrimage* is applicable to the symphony: 'A fictitious character is introduced for the sake of giving some connexion to the piece.' This is Berlioz's intention in the *Fantastique* programme; as for *Harold*, it is just as much a fiction to pretend that Byron is *not* Harold, as to pretend that the symphony is not based on Berlioz's own impressions, and that Berlioz, too, 'is' his own Harold. Berlioz copied into the autograph score of *Waverley* (F–Pn MS 1.507) a lengthy extract from the novel, then dismissed it by writing 'fatiguant', three times. The lines published in the score are a motto, not a programme. The other overtures are all related in some way to operas; *Hamlet* is sublimated incidental music; and so on.

119. Temperley (1971) demonstrates how mistaken is the idea that Berlioz devised the programme merely as advertisement and would have preferred it dispensed with; in fact he wanted it distributed if possible (had he been ashamed of it he would scarcely have revised it so often; see NBE 16). Guiomar, in an opaque but at least musical study of the composer (1970), rejects the conception of programme music altogether. He proposes instead this 'analyse catégorielle' of the *Fantastique*:

   I Prédisposition *crépusculaire*, à tendances mortuaires;
   II Tentation et Refus du *Divertissement*;
   III Une Cosmo-analyse personnelle fondée sur le *Funèbre* et le *Lugubre*;
   IV Une demarche vers l'*Insolite*;
   V Un Seuil de l'Au-delà, s'ouvrant sur une lumière *infernale*.

I cannot but wonder if this could have been arrived at purely through the music, without considering the programme; it seems particularly inadequate as a response to the complexities of the first movement. And is the last, with its satirical brilliance, *inherently* infernal? There is, of course, the 'Dies irae'; but to understand that one must know what it is – in fact, recognize the chant and thus take into consideration something outside the symphony itself. And is not Guiomar's interpretation merely the substitution of a new programme for the authentic one? *Cui bono*?

120. See Chapter 14; RusBL; Rushton, 1975. David Cairns has, however, very properly reproved me for describing in the latter article the composition of *La damnation* as 'higgledy-piggledy'; it was, indeed, no more so than a host of works which strike most hearers as well organized.

121. Boulez observes that the ancestry always cited for modern spatial effects had quite other aims: 'Berlioz and the Venetians are the most exterior, the most decorative of composers' (*Boulez on Music Today*, London, 1971, p. 66).

122. Drew (1963), still possibly the best short summary of Berlioz's singularity. He considers that Berlioz is outside the nineteenth-century French tradition (whatever that may be), as well as incompatible with the German: 'Berlioz's debt to other composers (including Beethoven) is not comparable to Beethoven's debt to *his* forbears'.

123. I. Stravinsky and R. Craft, *Conversations with Igor Stravinsky* (London, 1959), 29.

124. While not forgetting Varèse, another original who admired Berlioz (see L. Varèse, *Varèse: a Looking-Glass Diary*, London, 1973, pp. 128ff and 270), one should not press the search for Berlioz's influence on the twentieth century to unreasonable lengths. In particular, the developments associated with Schoenberg – atonality, serialism – are as unaffected by the Viennese composers' probably partial knowledge of Berlioz as they must be by Liszt's 'Bagatelle without tonality', which was published only in 1956. Berlioz's influence on Mahler is most apparent in aspects of Mahler's work which are least prophetic of Schoenberg, Berg, and Webern. Yet Chailley finds it worth while to remark that 'before Schoenberg [Berlioz] seems to take up the atonal procedure of avoiding, in a chromatic phrase, any return notes already heard, a procedure systematized by dodecaphony' (ChaBH, 24). Citing this, Sandford rightly observes that 'it might be impossible to trace a direct musical connection between Berlioz and Schoenberg'; yet he continues 'Berlioz was an important part of the tradition, along with Chopin and Wagner, without which there could have been no 20th-century music as we know it' (Sandford, 1964, p. 250). But Berlioz is precisely *not* 'along with Chopin and Wagner'; his chromaticism is radically different.

Additional note (see p. 13): The rediscovery of the sketchbook (reported by D. Kern Holoman in *19th-Century Music* 6, 1982–3, pp. 93–4; see also HolCP, 54–6) came too late for me to study its contents, which may well be of interest for the analysis of 'Je crois en vous' (pp. 104–7 above). The reported complexity of these sketches qualifies what Berlioz himself said about the 'improvisation' of romances (see p. 13).

Selective catalogue of Berlioz's works

The following catalogue is intended to help the reader orient himself within this study. It is not a complete work-list, for which the reader is referred to MacNG; Holoman's catalogue, from which 'H' numbers are included here, is forthcoming as NBE 25 (see also HolCP for works to 1840). These and Macdonald, 1982, are the principal sources for the catalogue, but the responsibility for its organization, and for any inaccuracies, is mine.

The basis is chronological, but certain works are grouped out of order; they include works completely assimilated into a larger work (e.g. Cat. 32A, *Huit scènes de Faust*) and works later published as a set by Berlioz (e.g. Cat. 34, *Tristia*). Certain works rejected by him but not absorbed elsewhere as a whole (e.g. Cat. 16, *Rob Roy*) are listed separately. A number of pieces, mostly very small, which are not mentioned in this study, are silently omitted.

The catalogue is intended to convey the following information: abbreviations of title used within the text of this book; uses of a work's ideas in a later work and, conversely, uses of earlier works in the present work; volume numbers for NBE (asterisked if published by 1982); volume numbers for OBE, which remains (with its reprint by Kalmus) the most comprehensive collection of Berlioz's works, editorial defects notwithstanding; other recommended sources in miniature score.

The breakdown of each work into sections follows, in general, some scheme of the composer's. I have tried to adhere to divisions in NBE as far as possible but in some cases (e.g. Cat. 38, *L'enfance*) have had to guess. Roman numerals are used for large parts of symphonic works; letters for independent pieces in anthological collections; numbers for other divisions (which in *La damnation* are scenes).

Each entry is on the following pattern:
1st line: **Catalogue number Abbreviated title** Holoman number
2nd line: Full title or completion of it (author of text) (date(s) of composition and other information)
3rd line: Cross-references to earlier use of this music (in the form 'Source N/N') or later use (in the form 'See N/N')
4th line: NBE volume; OBE volume (reprint as miniature score, K is Kalmus edition); other useful score or source, including MS if unpublished
5th and subsequent lines: Breakdown into component parts, with bar numbers if possible

The information is occasionally compressed (e.g. Cat. 1, where each song has its own H number).

279

1 Romances   H 7, 9, 10, 13–16
    ——[early songs, 1–3 voices with piano] (pub. c. 1819–23)
      NBE 15; OBE 16, 17 (K 1233, 1234)
    1A *Le dépit de la bergère* H 7 See 42/2bis
    1B *Pleure, pauvre Colette* (Bourgerie) H 11
    1C *Le maure jaloux* (Florian) H 9
    1D *Canon libre à la quinte* (Bourgerie) H 14
    1E *Le montagnard exilé* (Duboys) H 15
    1F *Amitié, reprends ton empire* (Florian) H 10
    1G *Toi qui l'aimas, verse des pleurs* (Duboys) H 16

2 Guitar songs   H 8, 31
    ——[unpublished, date uncertain, mostly arrangements]
    2A *Recueil de romances* H 8
      (arrangements, various authors and composers, ? c. 1820; source post-1822)
      NBE 22; DalIU; MS, F–CSA
    2B *Nocturne à deux voix* 'Je veux dans l'inconstance' H 31
      (presumed original, ? c. 1820; source post-1825)
      NBE 15; DalIU; MS, US–NYcu
    2C *Nocturne à deux voix* 'Restons ici'
      (doubtful attribution; see *19th-Century Music* 2/1, 1978, p. 89)
      MS, F–G Rés.R. 10759

3 Resurrexit   H 20
    'Resurrexit – Et iterum' from *Messe solennelle en grande symphonie* (1824, otherwise
      lost; *Resurrexit* survives in MSS of c. 1828, entitled *Le jugement dernier*, and 1831)
      See 22/2, 23C/8, 23F/8, 33/4
      NBE 12a; OBE 7 (K 1225)
    Resurrexit; Et iterum (Andante, 76); Allegro (106); 421 bars

4 Scène héroïque   H 21
    La révolution grecque, scène héroïque à grands choeurs et à grand orchestre (1825–6; survives
      in MS of c. 1828; new version of 3 and 4, H 21B, 1833)
      See 26/III (No. 2), 6E (No. 4)
      NBE 12a; OBE 10 (K 506)
      1 Recit.; air (34); 76 bars
      2 Choeur de guerriers; 365 bars
      3 Prière; 85 bars
      4 Final; 275 bars

5 Fugue   H 22
    ——à quatre parties (for Prix de Rome, 1826)
      NBE 6; MS, F–Pn W.33 (10)

6 Les francs-juges   H 23
    ——Opera (Ferrand) (1826; overture and 5 movements out of fourteen survive)
      See 23C/8, 23F/8, 26/II (fragments, not numbered below)
      NBE 4; MS, F–Pn Rés Vm² 177; libretto HolCP

6A Movements in full score H 23A
  1 Choeur de soldats et de peuple No. 1
  2 Duet No. 2
  3 Choeur de bergers No. 6
  4 Invocation; hymne des francs-juges No. 11
6B *Nocturne à trois voix* (piano reduction, c. 1828) H 23B
6C Francs-juges overture   H 23D
  Grande ouverture des francs-juges Op. 3 (1826; pub. 1836)
  NBE 4; OBE 4; Eulenburg 618
    Adagio; Allegro (60); 646 bars
6D *Marche des gardes* (?1829 or earlier); see 13/IV
6E *Le cri de guerre de Brisgaw*   H 23C
  ——intermezzo (Ferrand, Gounet); unrealized project (1833–4); sources 4/4,
  6A, 6B, 37D
    Libretto HolCP

7 Orphée   H 25
  La mort d'Orphée, monologue et bacchanale (Berton), Prix de Rome cantata (1827)
    (MS of c. 1828)
    See 17/IV, V (Nos. 1, 2, 4)
    NBE 6; Facsimile of MS pub. 1930
    1 Introduction, recit.; 54 bars
    2 [Air], Larghetto; 68 bars
    3 Recit.; Bacchanale (31); 241 bars
    4 Tableau musical; 30 bars

8 Waverley   H 26
  Grande ouverture de Waverley Op. 1 (by 1828; pub. 1839)
    NBE 20; OBE 4; Eulenburg 617
      Larghetto; Allegro (82); 441 bars

9 Herminie   H 29
  ——*scène lyrique* (Vieillard), Prix de Rome cantata (1828)
    See 12F (from 4, Prière), 13 (idée fixe, from 1, 3)
    NBE 6; OBE 15 (K 511)
    1 [Introduction]; Recit. (55); 91 bars
    2 No. 1 Air; Recit. (82); 100 bars
    3 No. 2 Air; Recit. (180); 208 bars
    4 No. 3 Air; Prière (117); Tempo 1 (161); 327 bars

10A Fugue   H 35
  ——à 3 sujets (for Prix de Rome, 1829)
    NBE 6; OBE 6 (K 1224)

10B Cléopâtre   H 36
  La mort de Cléopâtre, scène lyrique (Vieillard), Prix de Rome cantata (1829)
    See 23C/3, 23F/3, 23E (No. 2); 17/II, VI (Nos. 3 and 4)
    NBE 6; OBE 15 (K 512)
    1 [Introduction]; Recit. (53); 77 bars

2 [Air]; Recit. (102); 116 bars

3 Méditation; 52 bars

4 [Air]; 192 bars

11 Le ballet des ombres   H 37

——*ronde nocturne* (Duboys) Op. 2 (cancelled) (1828–9)

See 25/IV

NBE 14; OBE 16 (K 1231)

12 Irlande   H 38

Neuf mélodies [irlandaises], later *Irlande* (Gounet, from Moore, except J) Op. 2 (1829, pub. 1830, rev. 1849–50)

Orchestrated: B, F NBE 12a; OBE 14 (K 1227); D NBE 13; OBE 15 (K 1229)

With piano: choral, solo NBE 14, 15; OBE 16, 17 (K 1231, 1233, 1234)

12A   *Le coucher du soleil* H 39

12B   *Hélène* H 40

12C   *Chant guerrier* H 41

12D   *La belle voyageuse* H 42

12E   *Chanson à boire* H 43

12F   *Chant sacré* H 44 source 9/4 (Prière)

12G   *L'origine de la harpe* H 45

12H   *Adieu, Bessy* H 46

12J   *Elégie en prose* H 47

13 Symphonie fantastique [Fantastique]   H 48

Episode de la vie d'un artiste: Symphonie fantastique en cinq parties Op. 14 (1830; rev. 1832 and till pub., 1845)

Sources 9/1, 3 (idée fixe); IV is 6D

NBE 16* (Eulenburg 422); OBE 1; Eulenburg 422 (older edn); Norton, ConFS

I   Rêveries, passions

Largo; Allegro (64); 1st/2nd-time bars (166); 525 bars (ConFS has 2nd-time bar 168; 527 bars)

II   Un bal (Valse); 368 bars

III   Scène aux champs Adagio; 199 bars

IV   Marche au supplice 178 bars

V   Songe d'une nuit de sabbat

Dies irae (127); Ronde du sabbat (241); Dies irae et ronde du sabbat ensemble (414); 524 bars

14 Sardanapale   H 50

La mort de Sardanapale (Gail), Prix de Rome cantata (1830)

See 25/II; 39; 40A/10

Fragmentary. NBE 6; MS, F–Pn Rés Vm² 178; libretto, Bloom 1981

15 Lear   H 53

Grande ouverture du roi Lear, Op. 4 (1831; pub. 1839)

NBE 20; OBE 4; Eulenburg 619

Andante; Allegro (86); 637 bars

16 Rob Roy H 54

Intrata di Rob Roy Macgregor (1831)

See 19 (idée fixe from Larghetto; I from Allegro)

NBE 20; OBE 4 (K 1219)

Allegro; Larghetto (260 and 275); Tempo 1 (264 and 322); 618 bars

17 Lélio H 55

Le retour à la vie, mélologue en six parties (Berlioz), Op. 14bis, the second part of *Episode de la vie d'un artiste* (see 13) (1831; pub. 1855 as *Lélio, ou Le retour à la vie, monodrame lyrique*)

Sources: 13 (idée fixe) and as listed

NBE 7; OBE 13 (K 509); I and IV as song with piano, NBE 15, OBE 17 (K 1234)

I Le pêcheur (ballad, Duboys from Goethe), 3 (originally 4) verses; ?comp. c. 1828

II Choeur d'ombres (source 10B/3); 57 bars

III Chanson de brigands (source *Chanson de pirates* (Hugo), lost, H 34); 190 bars

IV Chant de bonheur (source 7/2); 68 bars

V La harpe éolienne (source 7/4); 29 bars

VI La tempête H 52

Fantaisie dramatique sur la tempête, drame de Shakespeare (1830)

Source: 10B/4

Prologue (Andante); Storm (Allegro, 51); Action (Un poco meno mosso, 198); Dénouement (Tempo 1, più animato, 595); 744 bars

18 La captive H 60

——*orientale* (Hugo), Op. 12 (1832)

Version A/C (piano/'cello obbligato), NBE 15, OBE 17 (K 1235). Version B (guitar), MS, F–G Rés.R.10759. Version D, recomposed, with orchestra (H 60F), NBE 13*, OBE 15 (K 1229)

19 Harold H 68

Harold en Italie, symphonie en quatre parties (with solo viola), Op. 16 (1834; pub. 1848)

Sources: 16; *Le retour de l'armée d'Italie* H 62 (sketch, c. 1832)

NBE 17; OBE 2; Eulenburg 423

I Harold aux montagnes

Adagio; Allegro (upbeat within 94); 1st/2nd-time bars (198); poco animando (323); 493 bars

II Marche des pèlerins

Allegretto; Canto religioso (169); 334 bars

III Sérénade

Allegro assai; Allegretto (32); Allegro assai (136); Allegretto (166); 208 bars

IV Orgie de brigands

Allegro frenetico; Adagio (12); Tempo 1 (18); Tempo 1 (end of introduction, 118); 583 bars

20 Sara la baigneuse H 69

——*ballade* (Hugo), Op. 11 (1834; orchestral version with 3 choirs, 1850)

NBE 12a; OBE 14 (K 1228)

21 Le cinq mai　H 74

———*Chant sur la mort de l'Empereur Napoléon* (Béranger), Op. 6 (by 1835)

NBE 12a; OBE 13 (K 510)

22 Requiem　H 75

Grande messe des morts, Op. 5 (1837; pub. 1838, superseded by 2nd edn, 1852, and later edns)

Source: 3 (Tuba mirum)

NBE 9*; OBE 7 (Eulenburg 1091; K 503)

1　Requiem et Kyrie; 209 bars

2　Dies irae; Tuba mirum (140); 251 bars

3　Quid sum miser; 49 bars

4　Rex tremendae; 110 bars

5　Quaerens me; 74 bars

6　Lacrimosa; 201 bars

7　Offertoire; 154 bars

8　Hostias; 47 bars

9　Sanctus; Hosanna (46); Sanctus (92); Hosanna (139); 203 bars

10　Agnus: Te decet (79); Quia pies (179); 200 bars

23 Benvenuto　H 76

Benvenuto Cellini, opera semiseria in 2 (later 3) acts (de Wailly and Barbier) (1834–8; rev. version 1852)

Sources: 3, 6 in No. 8; 10B in No. 3; 23A, 23B

See 28

23A *Je crois en vous*　H 70

———*romance* (Guérin) (1834)

See 23C/8, 23D

NBE 15; OBE 17 (K 1235)

23B *Chansonnette*　H 73

———*de M. de Wailly* (1835)

See 23C/1 (Serenade)

NBE 15; HolCP

23C Benvenuto Cellini, 1838 version　H 76A

NBE 1; not so far published (excerpts, 1838)

I　Act I, 1st tableau (Monday before Lent)

1　Introduction; Serenade (73) (sc. 1)

2　Recit. and air (Teresa); Cavatine (24), Allegro (94) (sc. 2)

3　Trio (scs. 3–4); 3A Recit. (sc. 5)

4　Finale (sc. 6)

Act I, 2nd tableau (Shrove Tuesday)

5　Recit. and romance (Andantino, 27) (Cellini) (sc. 8)

6　Scene and chorus (scs. 9–11); 6A Air (Ascanio); 6B Chant des ciseleurs

7　Recit. and air (Fieramosca) (sc. 12)

8　Finale (the carnival) (sc. 13)

II　Act II, 3rd tableau (Ash Wednesday)

9　Entr'acte

10   Scene: chorus of monks, prayer (scs. 1–2)

11   Scene: Cellini's narration; 11A Duet (in 2 movements) (sc. 3)

12   Recit. and sextet (scs. 4–5)

Act II, 4th tableau (Evening of Ash Wednesday)

13   Air (Ascanio) (sc. 7)

14   Air (Cellini) (sc. 8)

15   Chorus (workmen: popular song) (sc. 9)

16   Scenes 10–19: dialogue, some music lost; 16A Chorus of workmen

17   Finale (sc. 20); casting of the statue; ending with reprise of 6B

23D Benvenuto overture   H 76B

Grande ouverture de Benvenuto Cellini

Sources: 23A, 23C/8, 12 (Larghetto), 3, 12 (Allegro)

NBE 1; OBE 5; Eulenburg 622; 1838 publication in K 513

Allegro deciso con impeto; Larghetto (23); Allegro (89); 420 bars

23E Le carnaval romain   H 95

——*ouverture caractéristique*, Op. 9 (1843)

Sources: 23C/3 and 8

NBE 20; OBE 5; Eulenburg 620

Allegro assai con fuoco; Andante sostenuto (19); Allegro vivace (78); 446 bars
(Eulenburg miscounts on p. 49, ends at 440 bars)

23F Benvenuto Cellini, 1852 version

K 513; various vocal scores

I   Act I: 23C, 1st tableau (cuts in No. 1)

II   Act II: 23C, 2nd tableau (new entr'acte before No. 5, using 23E)

III   Act III: 23C Act II rearranged as follows: 9 (Entr'acte and chorus, formerly 9, 16A); 10 (formerly 15); 11 (13); 12 (10); 13 (11, 11A, but without first movement of duet); 14 (12, considerably cut); 15 (14); 16 (17, cuts in casting music, alteration of detail, ends as before with 6B)

24 Erigone   H 77

——*intermède antique* (after Ballanche) (1835–9)

Fragmentary; to incorporate 27/D

NBE 23; MS, F–Pc 1186 (fragmentary score, incomplete libretto)

25 Roméo   H 79

Roméo et Juliette, Symphonie dramatique (Deschamps, after Shakespeare), Op. 17 (1839; pub. 1847)

Sources: 11 (in IV); 14 (in II)

NBE 18; OBE 3; Eulenburg 424 (Peters E424)

I **A** **Introduction** (Combats, tumulte; intervention du Prince, 78); 199 bars

     B **Prologue** cites II (36); cites III (91); Strophes (99); Scherzetto (157); cites V (273); 289 bars

II **Roméo seul–Bal**

    Roméo seul (Andante); bruits lointains (Allegro, 63); Larghetto (81); Grande fête chez Capulet (Allegro, 107); Réunion des deux thèmes (226); 414 bars

III   Scène d'amour

Nuit sereine (Allegretto); Chorus of Capulets (45, uses II); Adagio (124); Allegro agitato (181); Adagio (243); 389 bars

IV   Mab

La reine Mab ou la fée des songes. Scherzo (prestissimo); 1st/2nd-time bars (93); Allegretto (354); Tempo 1 (418); 769 bars

V   Convoi funèbre

——de Juliette. Andante; E major signature (68); 142 bars

VI   Roméo au tombeau

——des Capulets. Allegro agitato; Invocation (Largo, 48); réveil de Juliette, joie délirante (using III) Allegro (90); 227 bars

VII   Finale Allegro; molto più lento (37); Recit. and air (Laurence) Larghetto (136); Allegro non troppo (190); Allegro (uses IA, 238); Serment de réconciliation, Andante (370); 457 bars

26 Symphonie funèbre   H 80

Grande symphonie funèbre et triomphale, Op. 15 (1840)

Sources: 4/2 (in III); 6A fragments (in II)

NBE 19* (Eulenburg 599); OBE 1

I   Marche funèbre; 280 bars

II   Oraison funèbre; Andantino (39); Andante (58); 108 bars

III   Apothéose; 240 bars

27 Les nuits d'été   H 81

Les nuits d'été (Gautier), Op. 7 (c. 1840, piano version pub. 1841; orchestral version 1843 (D), c. 1855 (the rest), pub. 1856)

Piano: NBE 15; OBE 17; various edns, some following 1841 text, some the orchestral version

Orchestra: NBE 13*; OBE 15; Eulenburg 1093

A Villanelle   H 82

B Le spectre de la rose   H 83 (introduction added for orchestral version)

C Sur les lagunes (Lamento)   H 84

D Absence   H 85 (see 24)

E Au cimetière (Clair de lune)   H 86

F L'île inconnue (Barcarolle)   H 87

28 Rêverie et caprice   H 88

——*romance* (solo violin, orchestra), Op. 8 (1841)

Source: rejected material from 23C

NBE 21; OBE 6 (K 1224)

Adagio; Allegro (42); Adagio (86); Allegro (124); 200 bars

29 La nonne sanglante   H 91

——Opera (Scribe), fragmentary (1841–7)

NBE 4; MS, F–Pn Rés. Vm² 178

30 Harmonium pieces   H 98–100

Trois morceaux pour orgue-mélodium (1844)

NBE 21; OBE 6 (K 1224)

A   Sérénade agreste à la Madone H 98
B   Toccata H 99
C   Hymne pour l'élévation H 100

31 Le corsaire H 101

Ouverture du corsaire, Op. 21 (first version, *La tour de Nice*, 1844; final version, first
called *Le corsaire rouge*, 1852)
NBE 20; OBE 5; Eulenburg 621
Allegro assai; Adagio sostenuto (31); Tempo 1 (54); 463 bars

32   Faust
32A Huit scènes H 33

——*de Faust* (Nerval, after Goethe), Op. 1 (cancelled˙) (1829)
All used in 32B
NBE 5*; OBE 10 (K 507)
  1 Chants de la fête de Pâques (see 32B/4B): 96 bars
  2 Paysans sous les tilleuls (see 32B/2); 37 bars (4 verses)
  3 Concert de sylphes (see 32B/7B); 150 bars
  4 Histoire d'un rat (see 32B/6B); 59 bars (3 verses)
  5 Histoire d'une puce (see 32B/6C); 81 bars
  6 Le roi de Thulé (see 32B/11B); 36 bars (3 verses)
  7 Romance de Marguerite; Choeur de soldats (126) (see 32B/15, 8); 238 bars
  8 Sérénade de Méphistophélès (see 32B/12C); 106 bars

32B La damnation H 111

——*de Faust, légende dramatique en quatre parties* (Nerval, Gandonnière, Berlioz),
Op. 24 (1846; pub. 1854)
Sources: 32A; Marche hongroise (32B/3)
NBE 8*; OBE 11–12 (Eulenburg 994; K 508); Costallat (reprint of 1854 score)
  I   Plaines de Hongrie
      1 [Introduction pastorale]; 150 bars
      2 Ronde de paysans (32A/2); Allegro (1, 93); Presto (38, 62, 169);
      Andantino (56, 80); Recit. (187); 206 bars
      3 Marche hongroise; 156 bars
  II North Germany; Faust's study
      4 A: [introduction]; 55 bars. **4B:** Chant de la fête de Pâques (32A/1); Recit.
      (94); 115 bars
      5 Recit. (entry of Mephistopheles); 59 bars
      Auerbach's cellar at Leipzig
      6 A: Recit.; Choeur de buveurs (18); 111 bars. **6B**: Chanson de Brander
      (32A/4); Amen (184); Recit. (216); 243 bars. **6C**: Chanson de Méphis-
      tophélès (32A/5); Andantino (125); 145 bars
      Banks of the Elbe
      7 A: Air de Méphistophélès; 36 bars. **7B:** Songe de Faust (Choeur de
      gnomes et de sylphes, 32A/3); 111 bars. **7C:** Ballet de sylphes; 108 bars. **7D:**
      Recit. 24 bars
      8 Finale: Choeur de soldats (32A/7); Chanson d'étudiants (77); Choeur et
      chanson ensemble (132); 240 bars

III   Margaret's room
    9 A: Retreat; 55 bars. **9B:** Air de Faust; 100 bars
    10 Recit.; 26 bars
    11 A: Entry of Margaret (27); 82 bars. **11B:** Le roi de Thulé (32A/6); 108 bars
    Street before Margaret's house
    12 A: Evocation (55 bars). **12B:** Menuet des follets; Presto (125); Recit. (174); 181 bars. **12C:** Sérénade de Méphistophélès (32A/8); 121 bars
    Margaret's room
    13 [Finale] Duet; Andante (19); 122 bars
    14 Trio and chorus; 6/8 time (157); 288 bars
IV   **15** Romance de Marguerite (32A/7); Allegro (122); 203 bars
    16 Invocation à la nature; 55 bars
    17 Recit. et chasse; 89 bars
    18 La course à l'abîme; 128 bars
    19 A: Pandaemonium; Epilogue (116); 132 bars. **19B:** Dans le ciel; 74 bars

33 Te Deum   H 118
Te Deum laudamus, Op. 22 (1849, planned earlier; pub. 1855)
    Sources: 3 (No. 4)
    NBE 10* (Eulenburg 1065); OBE 8
1   Te Deum laudamus (Hymne); 156 bars
2   Tibi omnes (Hymne); 194 bars [2bis Prélude, omitted; 58 bars]
3   Dignare Domine (Prière); 111 bars
4   Christe, Rex gloriae (Hymne); 196 bars
5   Te ergo quaesumus (Prière); 128 bars
6   Judex crederis (Hymne et prière); 231 bars
7   Marche pour la présentation des drapeaux; 117 bars

34 Tristia   H 119
Tristia, Op. 18 (various dates; pub. 1852)
    NBE 12b; OBE as below
A Méditation religieuse (after Moore) H 56B
    (1831 version H 56A, lost); 55 bars
    OBE 14 (K 1227)
B La mort d'Ophélie (Legouvé) H 92
    (1842; also for 1, 2 voices and piano); 160 bars
    OBE 14 (K 1228)
C Hamlet march H 103
    Marche funèbre pour la dernière scène d'Hamlet
    (?1844); 118 bars
    OBE 6 (K 1224)

35 Vox populi   H 120
——Op. 20 (pub. 1849)
    NBE 12b; OBE 14 (K 1228)
A La menace des Francs (1848) H 117
B Hymne à la France (1844) H 97

36 Feuillets d'album   H 121

——[miscellany, various dates], Op. 19 (pub. 1850 as a group with piano, Nos. 1
and 6 are orchestrated, No. 3 was originally a cantata with orchestra)
A, F: NBE 13*; OBE 15 (K 1229). C: NBE 12b; OBE 14 (K 1227). D: NBE 14;
OBE 16 (K 1232). A, B, E, F: NBE 15; OBE 17 (K 1235–6)
A *Zaïde* (de Beauvoir) (1845) H 107
B *Les champs* (Béranger) (1834) H 67
C *Le chant des chemins de fer* (Janin) (1846) H 110
D *Prière du matin* (Lamartine) (by 1846) H 112
E *La belle Isabeau* (Dumas) (1843) H 94
F *Le chasseur danois* (de Leuven) (1844) H 104

37 Fleurs des landes   H 124

——[miscellany, various dates], Op. 13 (pub. as a group, 1850)
Orchestral versions, D: NBE 13*; OBE 15 (K 1229). E: NBE 14; OBE 16 (K
1231). All with piano: NBE 15; OBE 17 (K 1233, 1236)
A *Le matin* (Bouclon) (by 1850) H 125
B *Petit oiseau* (same text as A) (by 1850) H 126
C *Le trébuchet* (Bertin and Deschamps) (by 1849) H 113
D *Le jeune pâtre breton* (Brizeux) (1833; see 6E) H 65
E *Le chant des bretons* (Brizeux) (1835) H 71

38 L'enfance   H 130

L'enfance du Christ, trilogie sacrée (Berlioz), Op. 25 (II, 1850–52; III, 1853; I, 1854;
pub. 1855)
NBE 11; OBE 9; Eulenburg 1092
 I Le songe d'Hérode
    Jerusalem
       1 A: Narrative; 30 bars. 1B: Marche nocturne; Recit. (148); 258 bars
       2 Air d'Hérode; Andante (27); 126 bars
       3 Recit.; 12 bars
       4 A: Recit. (13); 4B: Dance (62); 4C: Finale (142); 281 bars
    Bethlehem
       5 Duet; 107 bars
       6 Chorus of angels; 80 bars

 II **La fuite**
    ——*en Egypte* H 128
       7 Ouverture; 164 bars
       8 L'adieu des bergers; 126 bars
       9 Le repos de la sainte famille; 157 bars
 III L'arrivée à Saïs
      10 Narrative; 125 bars
      11 Duet; Tempo 1 (81, 160, 212); Un peu moins vite (270); 293 bars
      12 Le père, chorus, Allegro; Recit. (183); 247 bars
      13 Trio (2 flutes and harp); 159 bars
      14 Recit.; Andantino (4); 114 bars (the last silent)
      15 Lento; Récit. mesuré (17); Andante mistico (46); 123 bars

39 L'impériale H 129
——[cantata] (Lafont), Op. 26 (1855)
  Source: 14
  NBE 12b; OBE 13 (K 1226)

40 Les troyens H 133
——*Grand opéra en cinq actes* (Berlioz) (1856–8, 1860) (I, II, also *La prise de Troie*;
  III–V also *Les troyens à Carthage*; division made unwillingly, 1863)

40A Les troyens
  Source: 14 (in No. 10)
  NBE 2* (Eulenburg 925)
  I Plain before Troy
     1 Chorus; Allegro vivace (139); 165 bars
     2 Recit.; Air (43) (Cassandra); 134 bars
     3 Duet (Cassandra, Choroebus); Recit.; Cavatine (50, 187); Andante
       (237); Duet (305); 527 bars
     4 Marche et hymne; 124 + 6 bars
     5 Combat de ceste (ballet); 51 bars
     6 Pantomime (Andromache); 93 bars
     7 Recit. (Aeneas); 82 bars
     8 Octet and chorus; 85 bars
     9 Recit. and chorus; 40 bars
    10 Air (Cassandra); 99 bars
    11 Finale (Marche troyenne); 244 bars
  II Aeneas's palace
    12 Scene and recit.; Andante (Hector) (75); 142 bars
    13 Recit., chorus; 159 bars
    Priam's palace; temple
    14 Chorus (prayer of Trojan women); 56 bars
    15 Recit. (Cassandra), chorus; 82 bars
    16 Finale; 'Complices de sa gloire' (1, 114); 293 bars
  III Carthage: Dido's palace
    17 Chorus; 39 bars
    18 'Chant national'; 35 bars
    19 Recit. (Dido); Air (31, 111); reprise of No. 18 (77); 154 bars
    20 Ballet 1: Entrée des constructeurs; 31 bars
    21   2: Entrée des matelots; 45 bars
    22   3: Entrée des laboureurs; 39 bars
    23 Recit. and chorus (reprise of No. 18); 69 bars
    24 Duet (Dido, Anna); Andantino (109); 184 bars
    25 Recit.; Air (14); 55 bars
    26 Marche troyenne (mode mineur); 64 bars
    27 Recit.; 68 bars
    28 Finale; E major (84); B major (162); Recit. (222); Allegro (279); 415
       bars
  IV 29 Pantomime: Chasse royale et orage; Allegretto (44); 351 bars
    Gardens of Dido's palace

30 Recit.; 78 bars
31 Air (Narbal); Cavatine (Anna) (31); Air et cavatine ensemble (58); 90 bars
32 Marche (on No. 18); 27 bars
33 Ballets: A: Pas des almées; 56 bars. B: Danse des esclaves; 124 bars. C: Pas d'esclaves nubiennes; 104 bars
34 Scene; Chant d'Iopas (41); 109 bars
35 Recit.; Quintet (27); 128 bars
36 Recit.; Septet (9); 66 bars
37 Duet (Dido, Aeneas); Mercury (136); 147 bars

V Carthage, the port: night
38 Chanson d'Hylas; 186 bars
39 Recit., chorus (Trojans); 114 bars
40 Duet (sentries); 70 bars
41 Recit. (Aeneas); Air (98); Allegro agitato (132); 255 bars
42 Scene (ghosts); 33 bars
43 Scene and chorus (cites No. 11); 118 bars
44 Duet (Dido, Aeneas); cites No. 11 (143, 169); 202 bars
Interior of Dido's palace; dawn
45 Scene (Dido, Anna); 68 bars
46 Scene; 125 bars
47 Monologue (Dido); 55 bars
48 Air (Dido); 42 bars
Gardens of Dido's palace; funeral pyre
49 Cérémonie funèbre; 75 bars
50 Scene; cites No. 49 (17); 62 bars
51 Chorus; 42 bars
52 Imprécation (on No. 11); 38 bars

40B *Prologue* to *Les troyens à Carthage* (1863) H 133A
Uses 40A/3 in Prelude; 40A/11
NBE 2c; K 516

40C *Marche troyenne* (concert version, on 40A/11 and 43) (1864) H 133B
NBE 21; OBE 6 (K 1224)

41 Two choruses
A *Hymne pour la consécration du nouveau tabernacle* (de Vries) (1859) H 135
B *Le temple universel* (Vaudin), Op. 28 (1861) H 137
NBE 14; OBE 16 (K 1232)

42 Béatrice   H 138
Béatrice et Bénédict, opera in two acts (Berlioz, after Shakespeare) (1860–62)
Source: 1A in No. 2bis
NBE 3*; OBE 19–20 (K 517)

Overture. Allegro (on No. 15); Andante (on Nos. 10, 8) (39); Allegro (on Nos. 15, 14, 3) (79); 318 bars
I i Chorus; 112 bars
2 Chorus (reprise of No. 1); 2bis Sicilienne (58); 143 bars

    3   Air (Hero); Allegro (75); 219 bars
    4   Duet (Beatrice, Benedick); Allegro (132, 200); 283 bars
    5   Trio (of men); 2/4 time (183); Allegro ¢ (284); 339 bars
    6   Epithalme grotesque; 6bis, reprise (ornamented); 66 bars
    7   Rondo (Benedick); 178 bars
    8   Duo-nocturne; Andantino (12, 68); 160 bars

II   Entr'acte (Sicilienne); 89 bars
    9   Improvisation and drinking chorus; 206 bars
   10 Air (Beatrice); Recit.; Andante (49); Allegro (152); 277 bars
   11 Trio (of women); 204 bars
   12 Distant chorus (with guitars); 46 bars
   13 Marche nuptiale; 74 bars
   14 Enseigne (cites No. 5); 13 bars
   15 Scherzo-duettino; 118 bars

Arrangements:

43 Recitatives to Weber's *Der Freischütz* (1841)
     NBE 22; vocal score (K 514)

44 Instrumentation of Weber's *Aufforderung zum Tanze* (1841)
     NBE 22; OBE 18 (K 1238); Eulenburg

45 Instrumentation of Schubert's *Erlkönig* (1860)
     NBE 22; OBE 18 (K 1237)

Bibliography

Abbreviations used for reference within the text are indicated; an asterisk is a recommendation, for works particularly relevant to this study.

Abraham, G. *A Hundred Years of Music*. London, 1938; 3rd edn, 1964

Ballif, C. *Berlioz (Solfèges)*. Paris, 1968

Barraud, H. *Hector Berlioz (Musiciens d'hier et aujourd'hui)*. Paris, 1955; 2nd edn, 1966

Bartenstein, H. *Hector Berlioz' Instrumentationskunst und ihre geschichtlichen Grundlagen*. 2nd edn, rev. Baden-Baden, 1974

Barzun, J. *Berlioz and the Romantic Century*. Boston, 1950; 2nd edn, 1969

Bass, E. C. *Thematic Procedures in the Symphonies of Berlioz* (unpubd diss.) U. of N. Carolina, 1964

    'Thematic Unification of Scenes in Multi-movement Works of Berlioz', *The Music Review* 28 (1967), 45–51

    'Musical Time and Space in Berlioz', *The Music Review* 30 (1969), 211–24

GT   *Berlioz, H. *Grand traité d'instrumentation et d'orchestration modernes*. Paris, 1843. 2nd edn, 1855; English trans., London, 1855. Reference is made to 2nd edn/English edn

SO   *Les soirées de l'orchestre*. Paris, 1852; ed. L. Guichard, Paris, 1968. Reference is made to chapter (i.e. the evening)

GM   *Les grotesques de la musique*. Paris, 1859; ed. L. Guichard, Paris, 1969. Reference is made to 1859 edn/G[uichard] edn

AT   *A travers chants. Paris, 1862. 2nd edn, 1872; ed. L. Guichard, Paris, 1971. Reference is made to 2nd edn/G[uichard] edn

Mem   **Mémoires d'Hector Berlioz*. Paris, 1870; ed. P. Citron, Paris, 1969; English trans., ed. D. Cairns, London, 1969. Reference is made to chapter (not page), Postscript (PS), and Postface (PF)

MM   **Les musiciens et la musique* (selected articles), ed. A. Halloys. Paris, 1903

CG   *Correspondance générale d'Hector Berlioz*, ed. P. Citron. Paris, 1972- (for other letters, see list of published correspondence in MacNG, 607)

Bloom, P. A. 'Berlioz and the *Prix de Rome* of 1830', *Journal of the American Musicological Society* 34 (1981), 279–304

Bockholdt, R. 'Eigenschafter des Rhythmus im instrumentalen Satz bei Beethoven und Berlioz', *Bericht über den Internationalen Musikwissenschaftlichen Kongress, Bonn, 1970*. Kassel, 1972, pp. 29–32

293

'Die idée fixe der Phantastischen Symphonie', *Archiv für Musikwissenschaft* 30 (1973), 190–207

BocBS   **Berlioz-Studien.* Tutzing, 1979

BocMS   *'Musikalischer Satz und Orchesterklang im Werk von Hector Berlioz', *Die Musikforschung* 32 (1979), 122–35

Boschot, A. *L'histoire d'un romantique: 1 La jeunesse d'un romantique*, Paris, 1906; *2 Un romantique sous Louis-Philippe*, 1908; *3 La crépuscule d'un romantique*, 1913. Definitive edn, *Hector Berlioz: une vie romantique*, 1951

Cairns, D. 'Hector Berlioz', in R. Simpson, ed., *The Symphony*. London, 1966

The Memoirs of Hector Berlioz (ed. and trans.), see Berlioz, Mem

'Spontini's Influence on Berlioz', in *From Parnassus: Essays in Honor of Jacques Barzun.* New York, 1976

Catel, C. S. *Traité d'harmonie.* Paris, 1802; English trans., London, 1854

ChaBH   *Chailley, J. 'Berlioz harmoniste', in *Hector Berlioz 1803–1869 (La revue musicale*, special issue no. 233) (1956), 15–30

*Collet, R. 'Berlioz: Various Angles of Approach to his Work', *The Score and I.M.A. Magazine* (December 1954), no. 10, pp. 6–19

*Cone, E. T. Record reviews, *Les troyens à Carthage* and *Roméo* (extracts). *The Musical Quarterly* 39 (1953), 138–41, 475–8

ConFS   **Berlioz. Fantastic Symphony* (Norton Critical Score) (ed. and contrib.). New York, 1971

ConSH   *'Inside the Saint's Head', *Musical Newsletter* 1 (1971), 3 (parts I–III), 16 (IV–VI); 2 (1972), 19 (VII–XI); and *Berlioz Society Bulletin* (1975), no. 86, pp. 8–14 (parts I–III); no. 87, pp. 8–16 (IV–VI); no. 88, pp. 17–25 (VII–XI). Reference is made to part, not page

'Berlioz's Divine Comedy', *19th-Century Music* 4 (1980–81), 1–16

Crabbe, J. *Hector Berlioz, Rational Romantic.* London, 1980

DalIU   Dallman, P. J. *Influences and Use of the Guitar in the Music of Hector Berlioz* (unpubd diss.) U. of Maryland, 1972

Dent, E. J. 'The Romantic Spirit in Music', *Proceedings of the Musical Association* 59 (1932–3), 86–95

Dickinson, A. E. F. *The Music of Berlioz.* London, 1972

*Drew, D. Review of 1963 Edinburgh Festival. *New Statesman and Nation* 66 (1963) no. 1694, p. 264

Ernst, A. *L'oeuvre dramatique de Berlioz.* Paris, 1884

FriRH   *Friedheim, P. 'Radical Harmonic Procedures in Berlioz', *The Music Review* 21 (1960), 282–96

FriBR   *'Berlioz and Rhythm', *The Music Review* 37 (1976), 5–44

Gautier, T. 'Notice sur Berlioz', *Journal Officiel* (Paris, 16 March 1870), in *Histoire du romantisme.* Paris, 1874

Goldbeck, F. 'Berlioz', in *Encyclopédie de la musique.* Paris (Fasquelle), 1958, vol. 1, pp. 398–403

GraAR   *Gräbner, E. H. 'Some Aspects of Rhythm in Berlioz', *Soundings* 2 (1971–2), 18–28

Guiomar, M. *Le masque et le fantasme.* Paris, 1970

HadSM   Hadow, W. H. *Studies in Modern Music* 1: *Berlioz, Schumann, Wagner.*
                 London, 1893; 11th impression, 1926

             Hiller, F. *Künstlerleben.* Cologne, 1880, pp. 63–143

             Hirschberg, J. 'Berlioz and the Fugue', *Journal of Music Theory* 18 (1974),
                 152–88

             Holoman, D. K. (1975a). 'Reconstructing a Berlioz Sketch', *Journal of
                 the American Musicological Society* 28 (1975), 125–30

                 (1975b). 'The Present State of Berlioz Research', *Acta Musicologica* 47
                 (1975), 31–67

                 'Berlioz au Conservatoire: notes biographiques', *Revue de musicologie*
                 62 (1976), 289–92

HolCP   *The Creative Process in the Autograph Documents of Hector Berlioz, c.
                 1818–1840.* Ann Arbor, 1979

             Hopkinson, C. *A Bibliography of the Musical and Literary Works of Hector
                 Berlioz.* Edinburgh, 1951. 2nd edn (rev. R. Macnutt), Tunbridge
                 Wells, 1981.

             Knepler, Georg. *Musikgeschichte des 19tes Jahrhunderts* 1, [East] Berlin,
                 1961, pp. 290–315

             Koechlin, C. *Traité de l'harmonie* 2. Paris, 1928, pp. 175ff; 3. Paris, 1930,
                 pp. 87ff

             Longyear, R. M. *Nineteenth-Century Romanticism in Music.* Englewood
                 Cliffs, N.J., 1969, 2nd rev. edn, 1973

MacBS   *Macdonald, H. 'Berlioz's Self-borrowings', *Proceedings of the Royal
                 Musical Association* 92 (1965–6), 27–44

             A Critical Edition of Berlioz's Les Troyens (unpubd diss.) U. of
                 Cambridge, 1968 (see also NBE 2)

MacBO   *Berlioz Orchestral Music.* London, 1969

             'Berlioz's Orchestration: Human or Divine?', *The Musical Times* 110
                 (1969), 255–8

             'Hector Berlioz 1969: a Centenary Assessment', *Adam International
                 Review* 34 (1969), 35–47

             'Two Peculiarities of Berlioz's Notation', *Music & Letters* 50 (1969), 25

MacNG   *'Berlioz', in *The New Grove Dictionary of Music and Musicians.* London,
                 1980, vol. 2, pp. 579–610

             Berlioz (The Master Musicians). London, 1982

             Mellers, W. 'A Prophetic Romantic', *Scrutiny* 7 (1938), 119–28

             The Sonata Principle (Man and his Music). London, 1957, pp. 183–97

NBE   *[New Berlioz Edition] *Hector Berlioz: New Edition of the Complete Works,*
                 general ed. H. J. Macdonald. Kassel, 1967–

             Newman, E. 'Berlioz, Romantic and Classic', in *Musical Studies.* London,
                 1905

NewBR   *Berlioz, Romantic and Classic* (selected articles), ed. P. Heyworth.
                 London, 1972

NosFS   Noske, F. *French Song from Berlioz to Duparc.* New York, 1970

             Nowalis, S. M. *Timbre as a Structural Device in Berlioz's Symphonies* (unpubd
                 diss.). Case Western Reserve U., 1975

OBE   [Old Berlioz Edition] *H. Berlioz: Werke.* Leipzig, 1900–07
          Pohl, R. *Hektor Berlioz: Studien und Erinnerungen.* Leipzig, 1884; repr. 1974
PriBS   Primmer, B. *The Berlioz Style.* London, 1973
          Prod'homme, J. G. *La damnation de Faust.* Paris, 1896
          L'enfance du Christ. Paris, 1898
          Hector Berlioz. Paris, 1904; 3rd edn, 1927
          'Bibliographie berliozienne', in *Hector Berlioz 1803–1869 (La revue musicale,* special issue no. 233) (1956), 97–147
          Reicha, A. *Traité de mélodie.* Paris, 1814
          Cours complet d'harmonie. Paris, 1818
          Traité de haute composition musicale. 2 vols. Paris, 1824–6
          Réti, R. *The Thematic Process in Music.* New York, 1951, pp. 285–94
          Riemann, H. *Geschichte der Musik seit Beethoven* 3. Berlin and Stuttgart, 1901, pp. 359–77
          Rushton, J. 'The Genesis of Berlioz's *La Damnation de Faust*', *Music & Letters* 56 (1975), 129–46
RusBL   *'Berlioz through the Looking-Glass', *Soundings* 6 (1977), 51–66
          Sandford, G. T. *The Overtures of Hector Berlioz* (unpubd diss.). U. of S. California, 1964
          Schenkman, W. 'Fixed Ideas and Recurring Patterns in Berlioz's Melody', *The Music Review* 40 (1979), 25–48
          Schumann, R. *Gesammelte Schriften über Musik und Musiker.* 2 vols. Leipzig, 1914. See also ConFS
          Temperley, N. 'Berlioz and the Slur', *Music & Letters* 50 (1969), 388–92
          'The Symphonie Fantastique and its Program', *The Musical Quarterly* 57 (1971), 593–608
          Tiersot, J. 'Berlioziana', *Le ménestrel* 70–72 (1904–6), 75–7 (1909–11); detailed index in HolCP, 365–7
          Hector Berlioz et la société de son temps. Paris, 1904
TovEM   *Tovey, D. F. *Essays in Musical Analysis* 4 (*Illustrative Music*). London, 1936; 6 (*Miscellaneous Notes*). London, 1939; both repr. 1972
          Beethoven. London, 1944; repr. 1965
          Essays and Lectures on Music. London, 1949
ValG5   Vallas, L. 'Berlioz', in *Grove's Dictionary of Music and Musicians.* 5th edn, London, 1954, vol. 1, pp. 653–73
          Wagner, R. 'Über Franz Liszt's Symphonische Dichtungen', in *Gesammelte Schriften.* Leipzig, 1872, vol. 5, pp. 235–55
          Wagner Writes from Paris, ed. R. Jacobs and G. Skelton. London, 1973
          Warrack, J. 'Berlioz and the Theatre of the Mind', *The Listener* 72 (1964), 738; in F. Aprahamian, ed., *Essays on Music.* London, 1967, pp. 49–52
          Weihrauch, R. F. *The Orchestrational Style of Hector Berlioz* (unpubd diss.). U. of Cincinnati, 1968
          'The Neo-Renaissance Berlioz', *The Music Review* 36 (1975), 245–52
          Wotton, T. S. *Berlioz: Four Works.* London, 1929
WotHB   *Hector Berlioz.* London, 1935; repr. 1970

Index

Bold figures indicate the more important references and all those with musical examples; a parenthesized reference to a music example means that the music is mentioned by a cross-reference to that example and not by name.